THE MA'LŪF IN CONTEMPORARY LIBYA

To
Tania, Claire and Mark

The Ma'lūf in Contemporary Libya

An Arab Andalusian Musical Tradition

PHILIP CIANTAR
University of Malta

Routledge
Taylor & Francis Group
LONDON AND NEW YORK

First Published 2012 by Ashgate Publisher

Published 2016 by Routledge
2 Park Square, Milton Park, Abingdon, Oxon OX14 4RN
711 Third Avenue, New York, NY 10017, USA

Routledge is an imprint of the Taylor & Francis Group, an informa business

British Library Cataloguing in Publication Data
Ciantar, Philip.
The Ma'lūf in contemporary Libya : an Arab Andalusian musical tradition. – (SOAS musicology series)
1. Music – Libya – History and criticism. 2. Arabs – Music – History and criticism.
3. Songs, Arabic – Libya – History and criticism.
I. Title II. Series III. University of London. School of Oriental and African Studies.
781.6'29270612–dc23

Library of Congress Cataloging-in-Publication Data
Ciantar, Philip.
The Ma'lūf in Contemporary Libya – An Arab Andalusian Musical Tradition / Philip Ciantar.
pages cm – (SOAS musicology series)
Includes bibliographical references and index.
ISBN 978–1–4094–4472–5 (hardcover : alk. paper)
1. Music – Libya – History and criticism. 2. Songs, Arabic – Libya – History and criticism. 3. Arabs – Music – History and criticism.
I. Title.
ML355.L75C53 2012
781.62'9270612–dc23

ISBN 9781409444725 (hbk)

Contents

List of Figures *vii*
List of Musical Examples *ix*
Technical Notes *xi*
Preface *xiii*

1 Libya: Society, Culture and Music 1

2 The *Nawba* in North Africa and in Libya 29

3 The *Ma'lūf al-Idhā'a*: Change, Continuity and Contemporary Practices 65

4 The Musical Making of *Ma'lūf* 107

5 The Libyan *Ma'lūf* in the Realm of Arab Music Aesthetics 137

Epilogue 163

Glossary 167
Bibliography 169
Index 177

List of Figures

1.1	Libya in North Africa	4
1.2	1962 advertisement announcing an oriental cabaret in Tripoli	10
1.3	Jamāl in his workshop	15
1.4	A 2002 production of a *zamzamāt* audio cassette	17
1.5	Cheb Jilāni's album *Oyouni Sahara* [5285] EMI 2003	21
1.6	Professionally trained musicians in rehearsal	23
1.7	Young bandsmen playing informally at the Islamic Arts and Crafts School in downtown Tripoli	25
1.8	A Tripolitan wind band composed of male and female musicians	26
2.1	Modes of musical discourse	30
2.2	*Dhikr* at the *zāwiya l-kabīra*	39
2.3	Sufi members playing hand-drums and cymbals in *zāwiya*	40
2.4	The *ghayṭa* player, *sheikh ma'lūf* (centre) and *kinjī*	41
2.5	The *naqqārāt* player	41
2.6	*Nawba* and *bandīr* players	42
2.7	A *bandīr* being heated on a *kānūn*	43
2.8	Outline of a *ma'lūf* parade	43
2.9	The *ma'lūf* parade greeted with incense and orange blossom water	44
2.10	An *Ārusīyya* ensemble	44
2.11	The set-up of a *ma' lūf* ensemble in *zāwiya*	46
3.1	At Qatar al-Fajr al-Jadīd recording studio	67
3.2	A wall-to-wall picture showing Hassan Araibi leading his ensemble	74
3.3	Hassan Araibi showing a manuscript of *ma'lūf* text written by his grandfather	85
3.4	The violin section in rehearsal	86
3.5	The choir section in rehearsal	88
3.6	Hassan Araibi rehearsing his ensemble	89
3.7	Hassan Araibi leading his ensemble in Testour (July 2002)	95
3.8	The set-up of a modern *ma'lūf* ensemble	96
3.9	Araibi's ensemble in Testour (July 2002)	97
4.1	Professor Abdalla El Sibaei	110
4.2	*Ma'lūf* songs classified according to their *maqām* and *īqā'*	110

5.1	Hand movements in a *ma'lūf az-zāwiya* parade (Mawlid, 1 May 2004)	141
5.2	The jury panel of the 2004 festival	146
5.3	Poster announcing the 2004 festival in honour of sheikh Khaliyfa 'r-Rammāsh	148
5.4	Framed picture of a sheikh in front of a *zāwiya* ensemble	149
5.5	Sheikh Albahlul (standing) rehearsing the singers	150

List of Musical Examples

2.1	*Īqā' maṣmūdī kabīr*	35
2.2	The *īqā'āt* of the Libyan *ma'lūf*	56
2.3	*Maqām muhayyar*	56
2.4	The *istikhbār* to *nawba nāḥ al-ḥamām*	57
2.5	The *istiftāḥ*	58
2.6	The first hemistich of the *muṣaddar* section	60
2.7	The initial hemistich of the first song in *barwal*	60
3.1a	Extract from the instrumental prelude	99
3.1b	Antecedent and consequent phrases	99
3.1c	Cadential delay	100
3.2	The first part of the choral passage	100
3.3	The first song in *muṣaddar*	101
3.4	The second song in *muṣaddar*	102
3.5	*Murakkaz*	103
3.6	The first song in *barwal*	103
3.7a	The first set of calls and responses	105
3.7b	The second set of calls and responses	105
3.7c	Responsorial verse	105
4.1	*Maqām rāst*	112
4.2	The total range of *maqām rāst*	112
4.3a	Low register beginnings	114
4.3b	Middle register beginnings	115
4.3c	High register beginnings	115
4.4	*Ma'lūf* song *yā muḥammad* as transcribed by El Sibaei	116
4.5	The reworking of a phrase in *yā muḥammad*	117
4.6	An alignment of a cadential unit	118
4.7	Common melodic material occurring in two songs belonging to the group beginning in the middle register	119
4.8	Truncation techniques employed in melodic criss-crossing	120
4.9	Monotonic movements	120
4.10	The employment of tetrachord *bayyāti*	120
4.11	Implied pentachord *nikriz*	121
4.12a	Low register beginnings in *rāst* songs (*barwal*)	122
4.12b	Middle register beginnings in *rāst* songs (*barwal*)	122
4.12c	High register beginnings in *rāst* songs (*barwal*)	122
4.13	The reiteration of cadential units	123

4.14 Similar cadential units showing rhythmic variety 123
4.15 A cadential unit common in both *barwal* and *muṣaddar* songs 123
4.16 Insertion and omission techniques in the reworking of a cadential unit 124
4.17 Cadential units in *rāst* songs common in both *īqā' muṣaddar* and *barwal* 124
4.18 Low, middle and high beginnings in *murabba'* and *'allājī* songs 125
4.19 A persistently present cadential movement common to all *rāst* songs 126
4.20 Similar beginnings in two different *maqāmāt* 126
4.21 Monotonic passages revolving around the same note 127
4.22 Melodic criss-crossing in performance 130
4.23 Small-scale interpretative alterations 131
4.24 Stable and variant phases in a phrase 132
4.25 Three interpretations of a phrase from YM 132
4.26 Two renditions of the same verse 134

5.1 A short *lāzima* 154
5.2 Ornamental *lawāzim* 154
5.3 A *lāzima* as a fully-fledged interlude 154
5.4 A *lāzima* as an episodic marker 155
5.5 A *lāzima* placing musical emphasis on the main beat of the bar 155
5.6 A *taqsīm* on the *'ūd* with a *lāzima* on the violins 156
5.7 A *lāzima* (framed) played in unison by *qānūn* and *nāy* with the violins playing the rest of the example 157
5.8 The *nāy* winding up an instrumental prelude 157

Technical Notes

Transliteration of the Arabic Alphabet

Arabic letter	Name	Transliteration
أ	’alif	ā
ب	bā’	b
ت	tā’	t
ث	thā’	th
ج	jīm	j
ح	ḥā’	ḥ
خ	khā’	kh
د	dāl	d
ذ	dhāl	dh
ر	rā’	r
ز	zāy	z
س	sīn	s
ش	shīn	sh
ص	ṣād	ṣ

Arabic letter	Name	Transliteration
ض	ḍād	ḍ
ط	ṭā’	ṭ
ظ	ẓā’	ẓ
ع	‘ayn	‘
غ	ghain	gh
ف	fā’	f
ق	qāf	q
ك	kāf	k
ل	lām	l
م	mīm	m
ن	nūn	n
ه	hā’	h
و	waw	w or ū
ي	yā’	y or ī
ء	hamzah	’

Diacritical signs for short vowels

◌َ	fatḥa	a
◌ِ	kasra	i
◌ُ	damma	u

Pitch Specifications

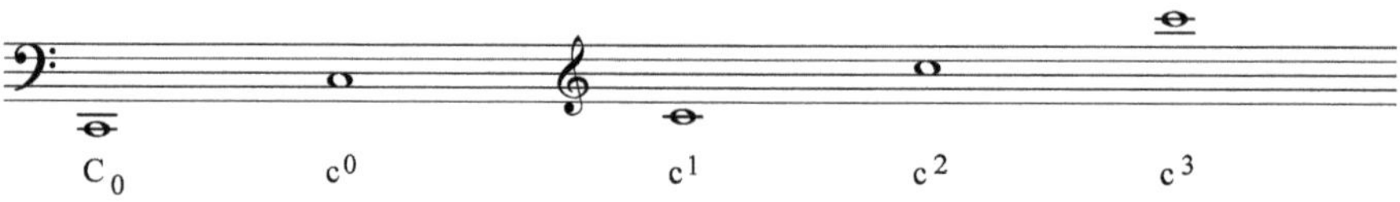

The musical examples do not necessarily correspond to the actual pitch performed; instead they adopt the pitches that conventionally belong to the *maqām* in question.

Preface

At the time this work is being finalized, news agencies report the killing of Libya's ex-leader Colonel Muammar Gaddafi following crossfire in Sirte, the Colonel's hometown, between ex-leader loyalists and fighters from the transitional authorities. Months before this, bloody insurgencies were reported between pro-Gaddafi forces and anti-Gaddafi rebels led by the National Transitional Council based in Benghazi. The fall of former Presidents Zine El Abidine Ben Ali of Tunisia and Hosni Mubarak of Egypt led the Libyans to follow suit and, on 15 February 2011, many took to the streets of Benghazi protesting peacefully for democracy, freedom and human rights. Within a week, this escalated to an uprising that spread across the country, with Colonel Gaddafi struggling to remain in control of a country that he had ruled with an iron fist for 42 years. Meanwhile, military force and other measures, such as censorship and the blocking of communications, were imposed with all this transforming the country into an inferno of civil war that came to a halt on 20 October 2011 with the announcement that the Colonel had been killed. There were more than eight months of bloodshed, during which contacts with Libyan friends and informants, who since June 2002 have helped me and supported me so much during my research, have become impossible either by telephone or Internet. In such a turmoil one wonders where all the music that I experienced in their company has gone, how it can return and fit into a new social and political order. In this context, the present work transforms itself into a compilation of flashbacks of people whom I had met in Libya raising an eyebrow at the expression of my interest in the music tradition of *ma'lūf*, not expecting such interest from a Westerner, followed by extensive discussions about the 'sweetness' of *ma'lūf*, its place in today's Libya, and its bond with both the remote and more recent past.

Ma'lūf, which literally means 'familiar' or 'customary', bears the auditory traces of music brought to North Africa by Muslim and Jewish refugees escaping the Christian *reconquista* of Spain between the tenth and seventeenth centuries. In Morocco this musical genre is known as *āla* (instrumental music), in Western Algeria it is known as *gharnāṭī* (from Granada), in Algiers *ṣan'a* (work of art), while in Libya and Tunisia it is called *ma'lūf*. An important distinction made in Libya, and worth pointing out at this stage, is that between the *ma'lūf az-zāwiya*, sometimes also called *ma'lūf at-taqlīdī* (*taqlīdī* means 'traditional'), and the *ma'lūf al-idhā'a*. Whilst the former refers to performances of *ma'lūf* in the traditional context of Sufi ceremonies, the latter is associated with performances as evolving in the domain of the recording industry or broadcasting (*idhā'a* means 'broadcasting'). The present study scrutinizes both forms and enters into the worlds from which each arises.

Studies have been made of this Arab–Andalusian music tradition in other parts of the region but, so far, the Libyan version has not received Western scholarly attention. Meanwhile, Libyan scholars have been mainly concerned with either the text of the *ma'lūf* or the collection, classification and documentation of its melodies. The work of Abdalla El Sibaei (2001), *Turāth an-Nawba al-Andalusiyya fīy Lībyā* (The Andalusian *Nawba* Heritage in Libya), represents a milestone in the research of the musical aspect of this music tradition, especially through his collection and classification of an extensive repertoire of *ma'lūf* songs, which when brought together would make up a *nawba*, that is the form through which *ma'lūf* songs are entwined. Nevertheless, there remains much scope for an English language study informed by the theory and method of ethnomusicology: the present work attempts to fill that lacuna.

This book investigates the place of this orally transmitted music tradition in contemporary Libyan life and culture. It scrutinizes the people who make it and the institutions that nurture it as much as the tradition itself. Patronage, music making, discourse about life and music, history and ideology all unite in a music tradition that looks unpretentious from the outside but becomes quite intriguing and intricate the more one explores it. Throughout the present work the *ma'lūf* becomes a means by which particular social processes within Libyan society are brought to light and analysed, even if a verbal explanation perhaps remains remote, as it might step over the boundary of local politics and, therefore, discussion is best avoided.

A cardinal aspect that stands out in this work rests on a hypothesis underlying much ethnomusicology: that is, musical signification is not something 'static' in the music but rather something that people construct, such that its meaning may vary from time to time, place to place and person to person. In this sense, an exploration of the Libyan *ma'lūf* and the meanings attributed to it as occurring in contemporary Libyan life emerges as a complex task requiring a multidimensional approach that involves, amongst other things, the interpretation and understanding of behaviours that are quite demanding for the researcher to decode and comprehend, though essential in the understanding of meanings and experiences. As most ethnomusicology shows, the meanings that people attribute to music are strongly linked to other aspects of their culture, including the processes by which values and meanings are assimilated and/or conceived by members of the same society. All this impacts on the way people eventually form ideas about their own music (both individually and collectively), with this determining not just the meaning/s they attribute to it but also the way they make it and the various 'events' they go through to preserve it in some way.

My interest in Arab music and the *ma'lūf* in particular was sparked in the 1990s when as a postgraduate ethnomusicology student at Durham University (UK) I encountered the writings of Ruth Davis on the Tunisian *ma'lūf*. Trips to Tunisia further enhanced my interest in this musical genre, with eventual awareness of the existence of the Libyan *ma'lūf* occurring during a casual chat I had with a Libyan resident in Malta during a reception held by the Libyan Embassy in Malta (my native country and place of residence) to commemorate the 1969 Gaddafi Revolution.

A few months after that encounter I embarked on the present research project for my doctoral thesis at the University of Sheffield, with eventual research trips to Libya that, to some extent, were facilitated by the geographical approximation of Malta and Libya as well as the strong historical links and diplomatic relationships between the two countries.

Fieldwork in Libya included interviews with music scholars, performers, *ma'lūf* aficionados, *shuyūkh al-ma'lūf* (that is, masters of the *ma'lūf* tradition) and informal chats with a wide range of people. The participant–observer approach I employed throughout assisted me in writing ethnographic accounts that in themselves bring to life this music tradition and the world from which it arises. Since the *ma'lūf* tradition is mostly present in Libya's capital Tripoli, most of the present research took place there, with occasional visits to the neighbouring cities of Misurata and Tajura when this was necessary. Other fieldwork activities included my attendance at rehearsals and performances of Libya's leading ensemble, Firqat al-Ma'lūf wa al-Muwashshaḥāt wa al-Alḥān al-ʿArabiyya (The Ensemble of *Ma'lūf*, *Muwashshaḥāt* and Arab Melodies) and two trips with the same ensemble, in 2002 and 2003, to the Tunisian town of Testour for the Ensemble's participation in the *ma'lūf* festival that is held there annually. Aware of the fact that fieldwork, whilst vitally important and in itself a core activity, 'is not likely on its own to provide a particularly balanced representation of a culture without being supplemented by diverse readings, broadened reflection' (Van Maanen 1988: 139) and other research approaches, my work comprised substantial library work at the SOAS Library and the British Library. Similar work was carried out at the Institute for the Research of Arab Music and several public libraries in Tripoli, as well as at the University of Sheffield and the University of Malta.

In order to inform the present work and my own observations and experiences with supplementary ethnographic data, I availed myself of the ethnographic literature about Libya that was available, though most of this was primarily concerned with Libyan rural and tribal life (see, for instance, Albergoni and Vignet-Zunz 1982, Fathaly and Palmer 1980, and Mason 1975). Ethnographic writings on contemporary Libyan urban life are meagre, and when available they mainly treat on economic issues and related topics (see, for example, Collins 1974, Peters 1982, and Vandewalle 1986). A book that I considered as maintaining an intelligible balance between rural and urban ethnography, and which proved to be very useful for the present work, is Paula Hardy's *Libya* (2002). Hardy's ethnography brings forth the dominant dialectic of modernism and traditionalism and the blend of both in Libya's contemporary society—a theme quite central to the present work. Other available ethnographic writings are those produced by Italian travellers and writers visiting Libya at the time the country was under Italian occupation (see Panetta 1963 for a comprehensive annotated bibliography by Italian writers on the ethnography and folklore of Libya).

The first chapter of this book introduces Libya's socio-cultural and musical context. The aim here is to put together a socio-cultural and musical background for the *ma'lūf* that in itself will serve as a frame of reference for the discussion that takes place in the subsequent chapters. Apart from discussing aspects related to Libya's history and culture, I present ethnographic vignettes that highlight aspects of Tripoli's everyday musical soundscapes and music-related activities. Through these vignettes and observations, the existence of 'old' and 'modern' Libyan musical tastes and practices coalesces, providing a background for further understanding when the *ma'lūf* is set against such a background. The same chapter discusses issues related to developments in the music industry and music education in the years following the Gaddafi revolution on 1 September 1969 and the impact such developments had on the dissemination and growth of the *ma'lūf*.

The second chapter unfolds in the same way that most of my interviews in Libya were shaped, that is discussions with quite extensive preambles about Arab music in general, narrowing down to an explanation of the Andalusian *nawba* and, finally, a focused discussion of the Libyan *nawba* in particular. Apart from devoting most of its content to the Libyan *nawba* as traditionally performed in the context of Libyan *'Īsāwiyya* Sufism, this chapter also provides an essential understanding of the main musical and poetical elements that make up the North African *nawba*, with reference to the four *nawba* traditions of the Maghreb, that is the Moroccan, Algerian, Tunisian and Libyan traditions. The same chapter will also highlight and discuss important episodes in the history of the *ma'lūf* in Libya, with most of these accentuating the role of past prominent *ma'lūf* and their role in safeguarding the tradition from becoming extinct as well as from abandoning its 'authenticity'.

Chapter 3 treats on the issue of modernization in the Libyan *ma'lūf*—a transformation process officially launched in 1964 through the initiatives of Sheikh Hassan Araibi (one of Libya's leading artists in the art of *ma'lūf* who passed away in April 2009). The modernization of the *ma'lūf* in Libya followed the path taken up by several neighbouring countries years before, with Egypt mainly at the forefront through the proliferation in Cairo of the recording industry and the music business it generated in the region. The same chapter explains the impact of these developments on the Libyan *ma'lūf* and how all this blended with the revolutionaries' reforms in the domain of music education, which in turn resulted in the setting up of music schools and university music programmes that were aimed at preparing professionally trained musicians in Arab music for jobs in the recording industry and the education sector. Inevitably, such developments had a strong bearing on the professionalization mechanisms of the *ma'lūf* and, consequently, on its transmission and consumption.

Chapter 4 examines the composition of *ma'lūf* songs, with particular attention paid to the much-employed technique of melodic criss-crossing (that is, the borrowing or reusing of melodic material from other songs within the same repertoire) and how this has over the years nurtured and sustained the melodic identity and, consequently, significant stylistic characteristics of this repertoire. The employment of this technique and other related ones, such as those of augmentation and truncation, occur in conjunction with characteristic moves particular to a number of Arab melodic modes to which each *ma'lūf* song belongs. Moreover, in this chapter I also point out the fact that, apart from this internal mechanism of song making, the stylistic identity of the *ma'lūf* relies on other aspects, such as interpretation and body movement, that further support its stability.

In Chapter 5 I evaluate the aesthetic potential of the modernized *ma'lūf* and the level of affect that it is capable of generating. The same chapter also scrutinizes the transferability of certain aesthetic values and parameters from the traditional *ma'lūf* as performed in the Sufi context on to the modernized *ma'lūf* as performed by Firqat al-Ma'lūf wa al-Muwashshaḥāt wa al-Alḥān al-ʿArabiyya and other modern *ma'lūf* ensembles. This evaluation is set against visible affective experiences that I witnessed both in Sufi lodges and on audio-visual material available to me, as well as during public concerts. This chapter will also bring to light and discuss performance practices in the Libyan *ma'lūf* related to affect and the way these are visibly or sonically transformed in the course of performance. Ethnographic depictions and Arab music aesthetics as well as technical musical considerations serve as the basis for the discussion that unfolds in this chapter.

The present work has depended primarily on knowledge, ideas, information and experiences provided by others. First and foremost, I would like to thank Jonathan P. J. Stock and Andrew Killick for their useful suggestions and support throughout the preparation of the initial draft of this work. I would like to thank all my friends and informants in Libya who were always ready to share with me their knowledge of the art of *ma'lūf*. They were many and, therefore, it would be impossible to acknowledge them all by name. Yet there are some whose contributions have been pivotal and who must be identified directly. The late Hassan Araibi was instrumental in introducing me to this art; he was always able to spare me some of his time for interviews from which I benefited greatly. I would like to thank Abdalla El Sibaei, at the time of research Professor of Arab Musicology at the music division of the Faculty of Arts and Communications at Al-Fātiḥ University, for being ever patient with my endless questions. I am particularly indebted to all the members of Firqat al-Ma'lūf wa al-Muwashshaḥāt wa al-Alḥān al-ʿArabiyya, in particular Muhammad Gebril al-Elasshab, Habīb al-Tourablsi and Yusuf Araibi, for always being willing to share with me their knowledge of *ma'lūf* and offering me their constant friendship and support during fieldwork. I also benefited greatly from the feedback I received from participants attending my Olwen Brogan Memorial Lecture on this topic organized by the Society for Libyan Studies, which was held at the British Academy in May 2003. Other conferences from which I benefited immensely were the three-day conference on the *Muwashshaḥ*: History, Origins and Present Practices, held in London at the School of Oriental and African Studies (October 2004), the European String Teachers Association International Conference on Cross Strings held in Malta in March 2005 and the ICTM Mediterranean Music Studies Study Group conference on Musical Translations Across the Mediterranean held in Malta in July 2010. I am also grateful to members of the academic staff at the Mediterranean Institute (University of Malta), in particular to Ranier Fsadni, who helped me in establishing fruitful contacts with the World Islamic Call Society. The consistent encouragement and support of the late Peter Serracino-Inglott, the then Chairperson of the same Institute, were invaluable to pursue with my research and the writing up of this work. Thanks are due to Martin Zammit, Senior Lecturer in the Department of Oriental Studies at the University of Malta, for his advice and assistance in matters related to transliteration. During the period of planning and writing, I have benefited from the advice and assistance of Martin Stokes, Rich Jankowsky, Henry Stobart, Marcello Sorce Keller and Ruth Davis.

The study could not have been made without financial assistance. For this I am deeply obliged to three research grants awarded to me by the Society for Libyan Studies (London). My grateful thanks also goes to the World Islamic Call Society (Malta Branch), the Libyan Embassy in Malta and the Maltese Embassy in Tripoli for their multifarious support in all aspects of the fieldwork phase.

A special acknowledgement is due to my wife, Tania, and our two children, Claire and Mark, for their patience and understanding in the making of this study. To them, with love, I dedicate this work.

Chapter 1
Libya: Society, Culture and Music

> How fine, dignified and intriguing is this Libyan race! Who would have the heart to interfere with this simple people in their tranquil, pastoral ways? How many reflections on the vanity of modern civilization cross one's mind on entering one of these tents ....
>
> (Camperio 1912, *Pioneri Italiani in Libia* [trans. Wright 2005: 191])[1]

My Libya diary begins from home, Malta—an island country only an hour flight away from Libya. The first fieldwork note is dated 2 April 2002, the day when I was to leave for my first trip to Libya as guest of the Islamic Call Society (Jamaʿiyyat ad-Daʿwa al-Islamiyya).[2] During that trip I was supposed to meet Hassan Araibi, Libya's main exponent of the *ma'lūf*. However, the previous day, at around 9 p.m., I had received a phone call from the Society's representative in Malta informing me that the trip was being postponed to a later date. Consequently, the tone of my first note was sombre, full of disappointment, although inquisitive at the same time:

> Today I was supposed to leave for Libya; however, I was informed yesterday by the Islamic Call Society in Malta that my trip is being postponed to a later date which will be communicated to me later on. A really big disappointment when I had everything prepared. The reason that I was given was that Hassan Araibi was in Dubai and, therefore, it wasn't possible for me to meet him. However, in a telephone conversation that I had afterwards with a Libyan friend of mine residing in Malta and a person close to the Society, he indicated to me that the Society was very preoccupied over my security due to massive demonstrations

1 Camperio was an Italian traveller who travelled to the Far East, Ceylon and India. He was also the founder of *L'Esploratore*, the official journal of the Società di Esplorazione Commerciale e Scientifica di Milano. In the 1880s he travelled to Libya to evaluate the commercial, agricultural and economic potential of Tripolitania and Cyrenaica. His book *Pioneri Italiani in Libia* was published 13 years after his death and a year after the invasion of Libya by the Italians (Wright 2005: 190).

2 Martinez (2007: 68) puts in a nutshell the activity of the Islamic Call Society as follows: '[The Islamic Call Society] established the infrastructure appropriate for the propagation of [Islam], taking its model from the zawiya tradition of the Brotherhoods. It built mosques, cultural centres, and radio stations broadcasting Islamic programmes, as well as undertaking the provision of health care, the distribution of free copies of the Quran and other measures.' [*sic*]

> being held in Tripoli in support of the Palestinians and against the besiegement of Yasser Arafat in his West Bank quarters.

Apart from the Palestinian incident, my first planned trip coincided with a time when Libya had just started to recover from the international sanctions imposed on it by the United Nations Security Council in 1992, which sanctions included an embargo on air travel. The sanctions came into effect after Libya had refused to extradite two Libyan nationals considered by the United States and the United Kingdom to be the culprits of the US Pan American Airways airliner bombing of 21 December 1988 over the Scottish village of Lockerbie. The French government had also requested the extradition of six Libyans suspected of involvement in the UTA flight 772 bombing on 19 September 1989 when an aircraft with 170 passengers blew up en route from Brazzaville to Paris. As in the case of the former request, this request was rejected by the Libyan government. Following the lifting in 2001 of the imposed air embargo, which had put Libya in absolute isolation, the country's airports gradually started to return to normality, with European airway companies such as British Airways, Alitalia and Air Malta fixing weekly flight schedules to Tripoli, Libya's capital.

My first trip took place on 6 June 2002, two months later than planned. Most of the passengers on board were Maltese working in Libya's petroleum industry and related jobs. The two Maltese gentlemen sitting next to me on the flight seemed to know each other very well as they chatted all the way through. As the plane touched down at Tripoli Airport at 2.00 p.m. we were informed that the temperature outside the aircraft had reached 41°C! The two gentlemen sitting next to me commented that in 1922 the temperature had reached almost 58°C. 'I hope it won't go up that much whilst I'm here', I intervened jokingly in an attempt to start some last-minute conversation. 'Everything is possible to happen here ... it's better for you to get prepared for any eventuality', one of them replied smilingly. 'Are you working here?', asked the other one. 'I'm here to carry out research on Libyan music', I replied hastily. 'Libyan music ...?!', exclaimed the first. 'Will you be working on music in the desert?', he asked again with a somewhat shrill voice of surprise. 'We work on an oil rig in the desert and occasionally we hear music coming to us in the evening. You're most welcome to visit us if you want to do research there', he added whimsically whilst standing to line up in the queue moving out of the aircraft, hardly giving me the chance to thank him. His descriptive snippet reminded me of the accounts I had read a few days before of Western travellers' expeditions in the Sahara, riding on camelback and struggling with the hard conditions of the most arid place on earth, the largest area of dry desert in the world. My thinking could not be prolonged, though, as I too had to join the queue on its way out of the aircraft to begin my first onsite experience of and encounter with Libyan society, life and music.

Based on those onsite experiences, this chapter aims to put together a socio-cultural and musical backdrop for the Libyan musical tradition we are concerned with in this book. It aims to bring forth some of the dichotomies, if not also paradoxes, that coexist in Libya's culture and, by extension, musical domain. Such ideas and debates concern aspects related to issues such as 'modernism' versus 'traditionalism', the 'old' and 'new' and the blending of both, as well as the identification of what is considered as 'local' or 'imported'. The jumbled sounds and aspects of Libya's musical life highlighted in this chapter—with which the *ma'lūf* not only coexists but sometimes merges intrinsically—can be partially explained, if initially placed within a conventional order, commencing with a description of the land and the people inhabiting it, together with a short historical survey of Libya that locates Gaddafi's 1969 revolution in a historical chronology. This is then followed by a discussion concerning music and related cultural and educational policies in the post-1969 revolutionary years that in some way or another had an impact on Libyan music in general and the *ma'lūf* in particular. Following that, a discussion will unfold concerning the different aspects of Libya's contemporary musical life as Tripoli's emerging diverse soundscape. Other musical domains treated in this chapter include Libya's folk music and its role in contemporary musical life and the official culture more widely, the recording industry and its proliferation in the post-1969 revolutionary era and, finally, formal music education in Tripoli and the making of the professional musician. All this aims to contribute towards the construction of the context that will assist us in retrieving 'what lies behind' the Libyan *ma'lūf* tradition and its role in today's Libya.

The Land and the People

Libya is a vast North African country with land covering an area of 1.8 million square kilometres, 90 per cent of which is desert. This makes its area the fourth largest in Africa and the seventeenth largest in the world.[3] At the time of the present research, Libya's population was 5.7 million, 1.7 million of whom resided in the capital, Tripoli. Its 1,900 km coastline borders the Mediterranean Sea to the north whilst inland it borders Egypt to the east, Sudan to the south-east, Niger and Chad to the south, Algeria to the west, and Tunisia to the north-west (see Figure 1.1). Due to its strategic geographical position between Africa and Europe, Libya has always served as a natural trading route between the two continents. In addition, its position between the Maghreb (West) and Mashriq (East) countries of the Arab world has over the years facilitated transit missions between the two areas.

Most of Libya's population is composed of Arabic-speaking Muslims of mixed Arab and Berber ancestry. Libya's population also comprises Greeks, Maltese, Italians, Egyptians, Afghanis, Turks, Indians and sub-Saharan Africans.[4] Considering

---

[3] For further reading about Libya see Habib (1979), Fergiani (1983), Ashiurakis (1993) and Hardy (2002).

[4] Libya has become the preferred country of transit for illegal immigrants from sub-Saharan Africa, from where they embark on the more suicidal journey of crossing the Mediterranean Sea into Italy and Malta.

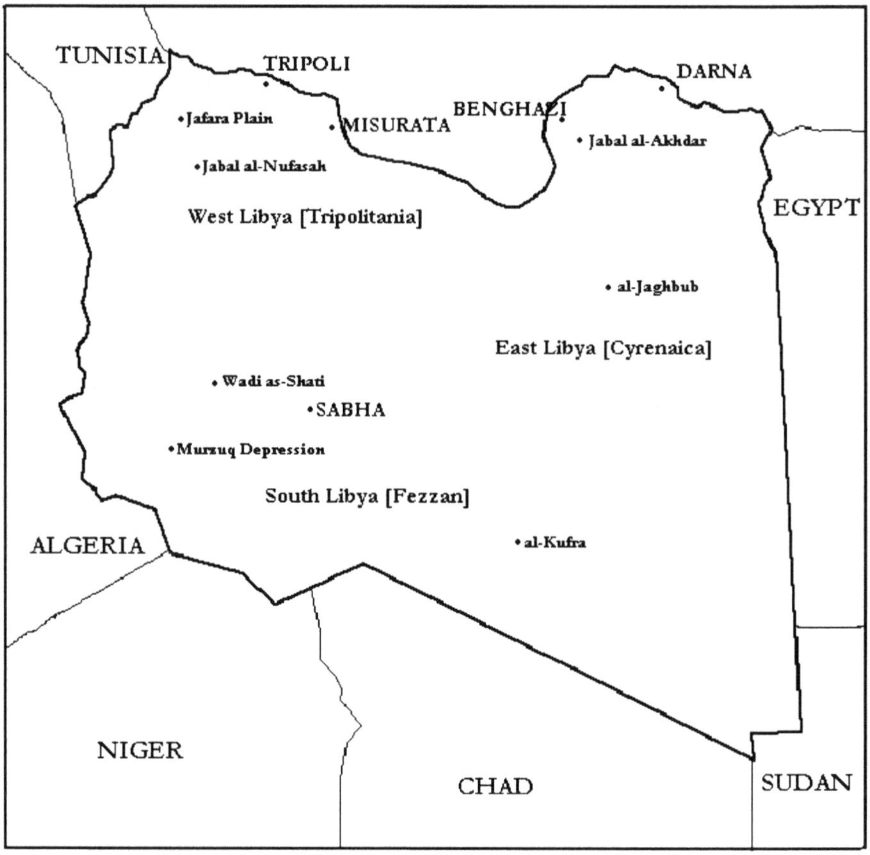

Figure 1.1 Libya in North Africa

its large territory, Libya is one of the least densely populated nations in the world. In fact, 90 per cent of its population lives in less than 10 per cent of its territory, mostly along the Mediterranean coast. More than half of the population is urbanized and mostly concentrated in the two largest cities of Tripoli and Benghazi. Since the 1960s 'the benefits of modernization have tempted most tribal people to swap tough conditions for a more comfortable and stable life in the towns—government schemes have provided new housing in the larger oases' (Hardy 2002: 66).

Historically, Libya was divided into three regions: Tripolitania in the north-west, Cyrenaica in the east and the Fezzan in the south-west. Nowadays, these three regions are known as West, East and South Libya. The Tripolitanian region embodies a fertile north-western peninsula known as Jafara that extends towards a hilly area known as Jabal al-Nufasah. The capital Tripoli, took its name from the region in which it is situated. The Cyrenaica region in East Libya comprises a narrow fertile coastal strip with a high plateau covered by trees known as Jabal al-Akhdar (the Green Mountains), as well as the city of Benghazi, considered to be the second largest city in Libya. With the exception of some scattered oases like those of al-Jaghbub and al-Kufra, the lowlands south of Jabal al-Akhdar are mostly deserted. This part of the desert is one of the most arid places on earth and is considered to be the largest area of dry desert in the world. To the south, the region of the Fezzan comprises a number of scattered oases like those of Murzuq and Wādī ash-Shāṭī. The Fezzan also contains the town of Sabha situated 800 kilometres south of Tripoli. Considering Libya's vast land area and the large stretches of desert that for years have separated urban areas such as Benghazi and Sabha from Tripoli (this being the cradle of the *ma'lūf* tradition in Libya), one can understand why, in those circumstances, it was difficult for the *ma'lūf* to reach with strong diffusion remote urban areas like those mentioned above. Until present times, although one might find *ma'lūf* performed in Benghazi and Sabha, its popularity there is incomparable to that in Tripoli. Several Libyans I spoke to insisted that the *ma'lūf* remained concentrated in Tripoli even after the unification of the three regions in 1963, when the mobility of *ma'lūf* musicians could have been facilitated by the newly constructed network of highways and air routes.

Libya Until the 1969 Revolution

In ancient times the area that is now known as Libya was colonized by both the Phoenicians and the Greeks.[5] The latter used to refer to the entire North African region—excluding Egypt—as Libya. The Greeks thought that all the people living in North Africa looked alike, and therefore they attributed to them the name Lebu; the Lebu people are nowadays known as Berbers. At this time the country was divided into two major provinces, Tripolitania and Cyrenaica, with the Phoenicians occupying the former and the Greeks the latter. Punic settlements on the Libyan coast included Oea (Tripoli), Labdah (later Leptis Magna) and Sabratah, in an area that came to be known collectively as Tripolis, or the 'Three Cities'. Moreover, the Phoenicians had built up an efficient agricultural infrastructure and a sophisticated system of trade, leaving desert trade in the hands of the desert people themselves. In the fifth century BC Tripolitania was incorporated into the Carthaginian Empire, while in around 500 BC Cyrenaica was annexed to the Persian Empire. All of Libya was then ruled in turn by the Egyptians (323 BC), Romans (74 BC), Vandals (AD 455) and Arabs (AD 643).

The Arab conquest is considered to be the one that has had the most profound and lasting influence on the country. Both the religion (Islam) and the language (Arabic) of Libya came from the Arabs, and have lasted over the centuries. The Arabs were diffused all over the country and eventually integrated with the

[5] The Phoenicians seem to be the first people known to have settled in Libya. There is disagreement, though, amongst historians on the exact date of this settlement.

local inhabitants. In 1500 the Spanish landed in Tripoli and ruled it until 1530 when Emperor Charles V, the Holy Roman Emperor, bestowed it on the Order of the Knights of St John. Fifty-one years after the Spanish conquest, in 1551, the Turks captured Tripoli from the Knights and integrated it into the growing Ottoman Empire, which at that time already included Cyrenaica, Egypt, Algeria and Tunisia. Under the Ottomans, Tripoli became the headquarters of the Barbary pirates. In all, the Ottomans ruled Libya for more than 300 years (1551–1912) during which period Libyan prosperity degenerated.

In the meantime, a Sufi Order was founded in Mecca in 1837 by Sayid Muhammad bin Ali al-Sanusi al-Idris al-Hasani, an Algerian and grandfather of Idris, Libya's first king. The Sunni movement was established with the aim of restoring the purity of Islam and assisting its members. The founder chose Cyrenaica as a centre for his movement and settled there in 1843. Later on the movement spread all over Cyrenaica and Fezzan through the establishment of several Sufi lodges (or *zawāyā*). These lodges gained importance not only as centres of learning and religion but also as a source of political influence for the Sanusis (as the followers of the founder were known). Evans-Pritchard (1949: 80) describes the role of the *zāwiya* (singular of *zawāyā*) as follows:

> Sanusiya lodges served many purposes besides catering for religious needs. They were schools, caravanserai, commercial centres, social centres, forts, courts of law, banks, besides being channels through which ran a generous stream of God's blessing. They were centres of culture and security in a wild country and amid a fierce people and they were stable points in a country where all else was constantly on the move ... But the chief benefits these lodges conferred on the Bedouin were ... that they and their children might learn from scholarly and pious men the faith and precepts of Islam, that they might have the opportunity to worship in a mosque, and that by charity to their lodges they might earn recompense hereafter.

Whilst the roles described above are still applicable, the modernization experienced by Libyan society since the 1960s, as well as political manoeuvring on part of the state to suppress the importance of these lodges, had restrained the above-mentioned roles. Nevertheless, the political influence of the Sanusi order in the past was so dominant that it claimed 'natural leadership of the Libyan resistance against the Italian occupation after 1911' (Joffe 1988: 618).

Early in the twentieth century Italy took possession of Libya from the Ottomans after sending a force of 35,000 troops to occupy the main coastal cities of Tripoli, Darna and Tubruq. The Italians confiscated and seized the best land in an ambitious plan involving the mass settlement of 500,000 Italian families in Libya. The first mass emigration began in 1938 with 20,000 Italian peasants attaining new farms in Tripolitania and Cyrenaica. The Fascists initiated a 10-year programme of development that included irrigation projects, the building of new roads, the importation of farm machinery and the enhancement of ports. Nevertheless, the Fascists were deeply resented by the Libyans, who eventually set up a resistance movement to gain independence. This led the colonial administration to commence a mass deportation of the people of Jabal al-Akhdar to concentration camps in order to obstruct the resistance movement from gaining further popular support. A prominent figure in this movement was Omar Mukhtar, who was captured and publicly hanged by the Italians in 1931.

During the Second World War the Italians and their German allies were banished from the country. Libya was then temporarily placed under British and French rule. After the war the victorious Allied Powers could not agree on Libya's future and, therefore, it was left up to the United Nations to decide Libya's destiny. In fact, in 1949 the United Nations decided that Libya should become an independent constitutional monarchy, a decision that was officially confirmed in 1951. Muhammad Idris Al-Sanussi, who had been the leader of the resistance movement, became the first ruler of the new United Kingdom of Libya.

With independence the Libyans had to face several challenges. For instance, due to the country having few well-educated workers Libya had to rely on foreigners to run much of the government. In addition, with few resources of its own, the nation had to depend for years on foreign aid. However, with Libya's discovery of oil in the 1960s the king embarked on projects to expand the educational system and improve public construction. The benefits of such initiatives were not felt by the public, with the consequence that most of the population continued to suffer from the poverty, illiteracy and poor health services that had characterized the 1950s. King Idris' reign lasted until 1969, when he was dethroned and forced into exile in Egypt by a group of Libyan army officers led by Colonel Muammar Gaddafi. When referring to the bad social conditions in which most of the Libyans were living and their relation to Gaddafi's seizing of power, Martinez (2007: 18) notes the following:

> In the 1950s, 94 per cent of the population had been illiterate, Libya had no doctors, and infant mortality stood at 40 per cent. In the period from 1951 to 1959, with an annual income of 35 dollars per head, Libya was regarded as one of the poorest countries. By terminating the reign of King Idris ... and installing in its place a distributive State, Gaddafi established himself as a genuine benefactor of the people.

The post-revolutionary years were mainly characterized by huge changes in all of Libya's social, political and cultural spheres. Inevitably, this had an impact on Libya's music and whatever is related to it, such as the recording industry and the setting up of educational music institutions, as well as music consumption and transmission.

Music in Post-1969 Revolution Policies and Ideology

Following the revolution of 1 September 1969, the 1951 Constitution was abolished. Twelve days later, on 13 September 1969, Gaddafi was appointed President of the Revolutionary Command Council (hereafter referred to as the RCC) at the age of

27. The RCC aimed at a more egalitarian society in which the old divisions of class and tribe would have very little importance. Moreover, the division of Libya into three provinces was abolished and replaced by a new political structure of Popular Committees. These committees had to promulgate the revolutionary political ideology of the Jamahiriya (the State of the Masses) as entrenched in Libya's official names during the Gaddafi era, that is Socialist People's Libyan Arab Jamahiriya from 1977 to 1986, and Great Socialist People's Libyan Arab Jamahiriya from 1986 to 2011.[6] Political parties were banned, as according to Gaddafi's *The Green Book*, written in the early 1980s, a political party was another form of 'contemporary dictatorship' (Al Qathafi 1999: 11). According to the same source, a political party or the party system was nothing more than 'the modern tribal and sectarian system' as it only represented part of the people (Al Qathafi 1999: 15). Instead, citizens were encouraged to participate in the decision-making that was taking place in the newly established Basic Popular Congress. In addition, *The Green Book* proposed a new social structure free from conflicts between modernism and traditionalism, tribes and states, and the city and the desert.

In the 1970s and 1980s several committees sprang up in universities, in municipalities and in state and business bureaucracies. All these had representation in the People's Committees, thereby fulfilling the concept of direct democracy as propounded in *The Green Book*.[7] During its first years in power, the RCC evacuated the remaining British and American military bases and nationalized all foreign banks, while bars and nightclubs were closed down. All alcoholic beverages were banned in accordance with the teachings of the Qur'ān. Martinez (2007: 75) notes that such banning 'had been a reaction to the supposed debauchery during the monarchy of King Idris'. This social rigidity was mainly intended to purge Libyan society of immoral social tendencies and loose attitudes that had accumulated under the monarchy.

The cultural values of the West in their various forms were considered by the RCC, especially in the early years following Gaddafi's revolution, as a threat to the Arab and Islamic identity of Libya. Road signs in the Latin alphabet, for instance, were banned and replaced by signs written in Arabic. Antipathy to the West and whatever symbolizes it was sometimes expressed not only through mass demonstrations organized by the revolutionary squads but also through the public destruction of Western symbols, such as Western instruments. For instance, according to informants, towards the end of the 1970s hundreds of items of musical equipment and instruments were looted from various social clubs and art organizations. This equipment was then brought together and burned in the central square in downtown Tripoli, known as the Sāha 'l-Hadra (the Green

[6] The term 'Jamahiriya' differs from 'Jumhuriyya' as employed in the official name of other North African countries in the sense that whilst the former means 'State of the Masses' the latter signifies 'Republic'.

[7] For a detailed discussion of *The Green Book* see Bleuchot (1982).

Square).[8] Some Libyans still remember this event being broadcast live on Libyan TV and later announced in the evening news. Music shops closed their doors for months after that, fearing the same fate. Another incident that had occurred as part of the RCC's Arabization campaign and its attempt to eliminate Western influence took place in March 1986 when students of the faculties of English and French at Al-Fātiḥ University successfully thwarted Gaddafi's intention to close their departments and to obliterate their libraries. Eventually, a compromise was reached by which the departmental libraries were saved from destruction as long as both foreign languages were gradually phased out of university curricula, as actually happened. The purpose behind all this was to rid Libyan society of foreign and 'polluting' influences, especially those coming from the West, whilst preserving the cultural values of Islam. In principle, this should have led to the strengthening and promotion of Libyan and Islamic culture more widely. Instead, as some remarked to me, the revolutionary squads 'neither knew nor cared for what was Libyan and what was not'.

The closure of entertainment venues in the early years of the 1969 revolution had a considerable impact on the musical life of the country. Advertisements such as the one in Figure 1.2 (below) give evidence of the thriving musical activity in these venues before the revolution, with cabaret nights hosting orchestras from Libya's neighbouring countries. In a 1967 article, for instance, Harrison (1967: 404) depicts a vivacious picture of Tripoli before the revolution:

> The hundreds of cafés in Tripoli are the centers of much of male social and business life; they are meeting places, amusement halls, employment exchanges, and offices all in one. There are the shops, the cinemas, nightclubs, restaurants, hotels, brothels. As the Libyans say, there is 'life' in Tripoli, and there is no counterpart anywhere else in western Libya.

Due to the closing down of the above-mentioned entertainment venues one may assume that the movement of foreign musicians in and out Libya for show business purposes reduced considerably. Some of these musicians also had posts teaching music in Libya's schools. To some extent this situation was counterbalanced by the new administration's commitment to reorganize the teaching of music in schools, and initiatives such as the creation of the General Organisation for the Theatre, Music and Folk Arts by an Act of 15 December 1973 that had as one of its objectives the teaching of the different areas falling within its remit (Brandily 1982: 210). Such educational initiatives in music led to the employment of more music teachers in preparatory schools, initially in Tripoli and then in Benghazi. In addition, these early projects were supported by Libyan TV, mainly through the public exposure of talented musicians and the broadcasting of music festivals held throughout Libya (El Sibaei 1981: 159).

---

[8] This square is now known as the Martyrs' Square.

Figure 1.2 1962 advertisement announcing an oriental cabaret in Tripoli

The first 20 years of the 1969 revolution were characterized by large-scale social and infrastructural projects. New educational laws were promulgated and replaced the ones passed by the previous government. The new policy for education had as its main objective the right of every citizen to knowledge (*al-'ilmu ḥaqqun li-kulli al-muwāṭinīn*: 'knowledge is the right of every citizen'). In the period 1970–86 the government claimed the construction of nearly 32,000 primary, secondary and vocational classrooms, while the number of teachers rose from nearly 19,000 to 79,000.[9] At the same time, 'the training of teachers was pushed in an effort to replace the Egyptian and other expatriate personnel who made up the majority of the teaching corps. Prefabricated school buildings were erected, and mobile classrooms and classes held in tents became features of the desert oases' (Anon: 2010a). Such educational development also included a widespread programme in musical education. Indeed, towards the end of the 1970s and the beginning of the 1980s the educational authorities embarked on a plan aimed at preparing and training an adequate number of Libyan music teachers who gradually had to replace the remaining foreign ones. This plan led the Libyan authorities to send students abroad to be trained in music education at highly renowned universities in the United States and Europe. Other initiatives in this sector included the setting up of music programmes within existing teacher training institutes in Tripoli and Benghazi specializing in elementary education, and the establishment of two evening music schools in the same two cities to provide instrumental tuition.

Tripoli: The City and its Soundscape

Since most of the present research was carried out in Tripoli, which according to a 2006 census had a population of 1,065,405, it is worth commencing this section by saying something about this city that in some tourist brochures is referred to as Tarābulus al-Gharb (Tripoli of the West), to distinguish it from Tripoli in Lebanon. Apart from being Libya's largest city, Tripoli attains importance as Libya's principal seaport, handling much of the country's foreign trade. Indeed, the city is the largest commercial and manufacturing centre in the country, and shares most of the government's important offices with Sirt (Muammar Gaddafi's birthplace).

As soon as one reaches the city, one is struck by the minarets of the numerous mosques that rise above the other buildings. Overlooking the port, one notes the As-Saray al-Hamra Castle (the Red Castle), a former palace and citadel that was originally built to protect the city against invasion by both land and sea, and which currently houses the National Department of Antiquities and a number of museums.[10]

---

[9] In the 1970s the presence of foreign teachers in Libya still remained very high. For instance, it is estimated that in 1977 out of 40,480 teachers, 17,545 were non-Libyan.

[10] The original design of the Castle was freely altered, and added to, to suit the tastes and wishes of successive rulers. The Castle covers a total area of approximately 13,000 square metres.

Throughout its history, as this castle attests, Tripoli served as a base for various conquerors and this added to its importance. In the Ottoman and Qaramanli periods (1551–1911) Tripoli, as a major trading centre, was embellished by large *fanādiq* (inns) and markets, and secular and religious buildings that served caravan routes. Apart from that, certain building structures in the Old City (or al-Madīna al-Qadīma) of Tripoli attest stylistic evidence of Andalusian architecture. This contrasts sharply with the architecture in the modern part of the city, which gives evidence of the grandiose Fascist 1930s architectonic style.

Andalusian refugees, comprising Muslims and Jews, spread all over the Maghreb after the Christian reconquest of Spain from the tenth to the seventeenth centuries. It is claimed that some of these refugees had entered Libya from Tunisia by the seventeenth century. Their presence is sometimes attested by references to architecture with Andalusian imprints. The Qaramanli Mosque, for instance, situated at the entrance of the Old City, is highly recognized among the Tripolitanians for its elegant arches and stucco work of Andalusian style.[11] Moreover, some families in Tripoli claim that they are descendents of Andalusians who had established residency in Tripoli. Such a historical bond, and in particular the artistic heritage inherited from it, is a source of pride for some Tripolitanians as it endows their city with prestige that in turn distinguishes it from other Libyan cities. In this context, the *ma'lūf* sometimes emerges as a reaffirmation of the historical connections that Tripoli had with this glorious period in the history of Islam.

Informants describe Tripoli as a city of 'art and culture' and the place from where most of Libya's professionals and intellectuals hailed. An old Tripolitanian, an aficionado of the *ma'lūf*, described the Tripolitanians as very proud of what they have achieved socially and culturally over the years. He described the Tripolitanians as 'people of culture', and the city itself as the place where 'art and culture flourish': 'That's why in Tripoli you find a strong tradition of *ma'lūf*', he told me. 'The tradition has fertile grounds here.' The man's comments make a lot of sense especially if understood in the context of Tripoli's thriving cultural and artistic life. Posters announcing art exhibitions held in Tripoli's main libraries and art galleries, such as *dār al-funūn* (The Artists' House), can be seen everywhere. Apart from an art gallery for contemporary art, *dār al-funūn* is occasionally used as a rehearsal venue for Libyan ensembles of Arab classical music. Musicians rehearsing at *dār al-funūn* explained to me how the elegance of that place matches the elegance of Arab classical music and, therefore, the place sets the right environment for rehearsal of this musical genre. Apart from these artistic venues and the events they host, one may also add that the setting up of music schools in Tripoli in the post-1969 revolutionary years helped considerably in the enhancement of musical activity in the city. Moreover, in the years following that

---

[11] Houses of Andalusian character can also be found in Darna—a city in East Libya (Fergiani 1983: 244). Moreover, when referring to the history of Darna, Ahmida (1994: 75) notes that 'Darna was revived by Andalusian refugees in the sixteenth century after the exodus of the Muslims and Jews'.

political change Tripoli saw the proliferation of several recording studios, as well as wider organization of music festivals, especially in summer. Putting all this together, the old man's comment becomes significantly genuine and meaningful.

Libya presents a world of musical diversity and Tripoli avers that. Walking through the streets of downtown Tripoli one would definitely be struck by the sound of the *adhān*, that is, the call to prayer from atop minarets or roofs of mosques. This calls the believers to the Friday holy service, as well as to the five prayers prescribed for the day—in the morning, at noon, in the afternoon, at sunset and in the evening. Like the recitation of the Qur'ān (known as *qirā'a*), the *adhān* is performed in Arabic, the language in which the Qur'ān was revealed to the Prophet Muhammad. In Islam, the *adhān* is not considered to be music, even though it may sound so to the Western ear. The traditional practice of the *mu'adhdhin*, the one who recites the *adhān*, using his voice to reach the surrounding community is still in practice. However, nowadays this is facilitated by the use of loudspeakers, local radio and television broadcasts. In this regard, Lee (1999: 86) observes that 'in almost every Islamic community today, the loudspeaker, radio, and television have become essential in the traditional call to prayer', and in itself this shows 'a remarkable juxtaposition of high media technology and conservative religious practices'. When these calls are made, shops are sometimes left unattended and if you happen to be shopping, you might be promised assistance after prayer time when everything returns to normal. The echoing calls to prayer transform Tripoli's soundscape into a cacophony of calls from minarets, which sounds blend with the loud music coming from car stereos, music ranging from *raï* (Algerian pop music widely diffused in North Africa) to Western rock music. Media technology in Libya gains prominence not only for its role in facilitating the reaffirmation of Libya's religious and cultural identity but, moreover, in mediating the dynamics of Islamic culture and, in a wider perspective, expediting Western and Arab cultural fusions.[12]

Musical transmissions from Libya's national radio include hours of Arab music varying from folk music to a type that is termed as 'classical'. Radio transmissions from neighbouring countries are also available and taken up. A journey in a taxi might evolve into an interesting trip through an array of musical styles and genres, an interesting musical journey that may begin with Whitney Houston's *All At Once* (thought by the driver to be appealing to a Western passenger), changing later on, and at the expression of interest in Libyan music, to a song by the Libyan singer Ahmed Fakrūn, internationally recognized as a leading figure in modern Arab pop music. In contrast, elder drivers might start the day with recorded recitations of the

[12] This is evident every Friday (the Day of Rest for the Muslims) when national Libyan TV transmits live religious services held in Tripoli's mosques. The service includes chanting from the Qur'ān by a sheikh Qur'ān (that is, a master knowledgeable in the art of Qur'ān recitation) aided by a microphone so as to fill the entire space of the mosque with his voice and making the words comprehensible for those present. The reciter 'attempts to raise and lower pitches, emphasize inherent durational patterns, and punctuate stopping places in his recitation ....' (Al Faruqi 1974: 266).

Qur'ān, shifting later on in the day to an *ughniya* (literally 'song', a term that refers to songs usually in colloquial text, shaped in a variety of musical forms) by the Syrian singer Sabāh Fakhrī, and welcoming sunset with the thrilling voice of the then diva of Egyptian music, Umm Kulthūm.[13] In this musical journey, one element remains central, and that is a strong preference towards vocal music. When referring to the importance of the voice in Middle Eastern music Blum (2002: 6) notes that 'the voice has remained central to the musics of the Middle East because it is the primary instrument of human communication. Voices can be effectively supported, extended, contradicted, or transcended by the other musical instruments.'

Crossing Tripoli's Sāha 'l-Hadra one may enter through one of the gates that lead to Tripoli's Madīna al-Qadīma. The sound of cars fades away the more one moves into the city. Passing through the alleys of the Madīna one is struck by the sound of recorded *qirā'a* coming out of workshops and shops, blending with the loud banging of blacksmiths and the sounds of carriages loaded with wheat sacks being pulled by Sudanese migrant workers. The narrow streets of the Madīna are a unique place where the hardships of everyday life are supported by the chanted divine words of the Qur'ān, and modern technology, even here, marks its socio-religious significance. The still glance, somewhat fatalistic too, of shop owners waiting for clients on their shops' doorsteps contrasts sharply with the ongoing activity of the elderly Jamāl. Jamāl is a drum maker with his own small workshop in the Madīna. Whenever you pass by his workshop you find him stretching and fastening wet membrane onto round drum frames (see Figure 1.3). His workshop is full of ready-made drums waiting to be sold. Jamāl's workshop conveys a strong impression of continuous activity that leaves him very little time to clear up. The drums piled behind his back bring to mind the diverse activities in which the same instruments are employed—activities that range from wedding music to celebrations held in the nearby Sufi lodges situated in the same Madīna, as well as the strong ongoing musical activity in the several recording studios scattered throughout the country.

Leaving Jamāl's workshop on a hot summer's day in mid-July and exiting the Madīna to find a pleasant air-conditioned cafeteria and a cold beverage to shelter and recover from the scorching mid-morning sun becomes an exigency. The nearest area to the Madīna where one finds a selection of cafeterias is 1 September Avenue (the principal avenue in downtown Tripoli). As you enter the cafeteria, the gentle cool air inside blends smoothly with the soft background music of the *nāy* (a vertical end-blown flute) provided on CD. The music includes fabulous arrangements of sound track themes for solo *nāy* accompanied by an orchestra in a Western set-up, themes from *Titanic* and *Schindler's List* amongst others. At that moment the only thing that reminds one of one's presence in a North African country is the idiosyncratic sound of the *nāy* itself that, together with the backing accompaniment of the orchestra, transforms the cafeteria into a place that interfaces the 'Arabic' with the 'non-Arabic' and the 'conventional' with the 'unconventional'. Libyan life is strongly characterized by an evident continuous

---

[13] For further reading on Umm Kulthūm see Danielson (1997).

Figure 1.3 Jamāl in his workshop

mediation between what is 'typically' Arab (and by extension Muslim) and 'non-Arab' (and, therefore, possibly not Muslim).

The shops in Tripoli remain open until late especially during the month of Ramadan, when most people traditionally break their fast after sunset and rush to grocery stores for bread, meat, sweets and dried fruits. In the evening the city's cafés are full of men socializing in groups while most women remain at home looking after their children. Whilst gender segregation in Libya still exists, this is less strong than it was in the past. Nowadays, men and women work together in the same workplace. Students attending universities and technical schools in Tripoli are taught in mixed classes. Gaddafi's policy encouraged equal job opportunities, even in traditionally male-dominated jobs such as the army, and women's participation in Libya's social life. Nevertheless, gender segregation is still observed in both public and private events. For instance, men and women still celebrate a wedding festivity in different halls of the same hotel. In addition, gender segregation is observed during festivals, when women sit behind the front rows occupied by men. Notwithstanding the initiatives by the state to involve women in Libya's social life, male presence is still very dominant in almost all strata of society, starting from the family and continuing up to social, administrative and political positions.

The Folk Music Domain

An important domain in Libya's musical spectrum where women still have an important role is Libya's folk music. When referring to the diffusion of folk music in Libya, El Sibaei (1981: 48) notes that this music is found in urban, rural and mountainous areas as well as amongst desert communities. Several informants remarked to me that Libyan folk music is still alive due to its functionality in Libyan life in all the above three contexts. In Tripoli, for instance, the inclusion of folk music in wedding festivities through the participation of *zamzamāt* singers is still a very strong diffused practice. The *zamzamāt* are black singing women who provide music services for women's wedding festivities held in Tripoli (El Sibaei 1981: 49–52).[14] During these festivities the *zamzamāt* sing wedding folk songs while a female guest dances within a circle of female guests clapping, singing, ululating and repeating melodies sung by the same *zamzamāt*.[15] Wedding festivities in Libya are very much marked by the active participation of guests in all the stages of a wedding that in Tripoli may be spread over a week.

Traditionally, the only two musical instruments employed by the *zamzamāt* in wedding performances are the *darabukka* (a goblet drum) and *bandīr* (a single-

---

[14] The term 'professional' as used here refers to the fact that these women get paid for the service they provide.

[15] The wedding context for the making and enjoyment of Libyan folk music is sometimes replaced by the stillness of the night and evening relaxation scenes. For instance Ostler (1912: 94–5), who was a Western traveller, presents folk music from the Fezzan in the following way: 'One night, when a company of Fezzanis had just come in, I rode into their encampment, drawn irresistibly by the rapid monotone of pulsing drums and the shrilling of the pipes. The men squatted, many deep, in a great half-circle before a fire of thorns that threw a flickering light upon their white teeth and rolling eyes. Two Negro lads beat with thumbs and fingertips on little egg-shaped drums that hung from their necks. As they thrummed they sang in high, whining voices, throwing back their heads like howling dogs, and sending forth the long-drawn notes quaveringly. Between them sat the player of the pipes. … He blew lustily, frowning, with fixed eyes and distended cheeks, and his fingers flew over the stops of the pipe. … Ceaselessly, rapidly he played, now loud, now soft, now with slightly changed accentuation, but ever the same odd, jerky trill, with unfamiliar intervals and unexpected breaks. He leaned his shoulder against the wall of a wattle cabin, and his face, as the fire-light waxed and waned, shone and grew dim like an incandescent.' A somewhat similar description is that of Tuareg musician inhabitants of Ghadames Oasis included in a 1993 tourist publication. In the following description, Tuareg music of Ghadames is 'romatically' presented in contrast with the quiet evening of the night. The string instrument that breaks the stillness of the night is called *imzad*, a monochord bowed instrument with a hemispherical gourd covered with skin and only played by Tuareg women: 'People loved to hear the stillness of the night being broken by the music of a simple cane flute; or to attend the scene of a curtain of silence being lifted by the artistic fingers of a Bedouin woman playing a beautiful tune on strings attached to a small leather-coated drum' (Ashiurakis 1993: 89).

Figure 1.4 A 2002 production of a *zamzamāt* audio cassette

headed frame drum).[16] However, today's live performances of this music may also include a synthesizer and a drum kit. The demands of the recording industry and the aesthetics proposed led these *zamzamāt* to expand their traditional instrumentation so that it approaches the sound produced on audio cassettes and CDs under studio conditions. In addition, live performances of *zamzamāt* music are also supported nowadays by technological facilities, such as in the employment of echo and reverb effects that enable the sound quality of live performances to approach that produced in recording studios. Moreover, the easy availability of recorded *zamzamāt* music (see Figure 1.4) means that the music that traditionally was encapsulated in gender segregation is now available to everybody and is reproduced at any time as often as desired. This dovetails with Racy's observation when referring to the impact of the phonograph on post-1904 Egyptian music (1978: 51–2). In this regard, Racy remarks that in pre-1904 Egypt, female professional musicians known as *'awālim* customarily performed only for female audiences while the *ālātiyya* (male musicians) only performed before male audiences. This traditional practice was phased out after 1904 when the phonograph dismantled these socio-musical

16 In an Italian tourist guidebook about Libya, the *zamzamāt* are described as follows: 'These *zamzamāt* are frequently paid lavishly in order to get from them the most pleasing and praising songs. One cannot argue with them over service charge, otherwise they would gossip terribly against you. Therefore, Arab families, who have pride so much at heart, would suffer the blackmail and let them extort high charges' [Trans.] (Bertarelli 1937: 99).

boundaries. In this sense, whilst *zamzamāt* performances continue to be held in the context of gender segregation, recordings of this music transcend borders determined by place, gender and occasion.

Desert communities living in remote areas also have their own musical traditions that are still alive and functional. El-Giernazi (1984: 23), for instance, explains how these people 'sing of the hardships of their lives, the desert, their courage in the battle, their camels and herds, and the beauties of those whom they love'. Such musical traditions are adorned with dances and typical instruments, the most prominent of which is the single-string fiddle *amzad*, mostly played by women to accompany songs sung around a fire in the evening, which sound might even reach the ears of nearby workers in Libya's prosperous petroleum industry, as in the case of the two Maltese workers encountered on my first flight to Libya. Along the number of oases scattered over large stretches of desert in the Fezzan one finds songs accompanied by the *ṭabal* (a double-headed cylindrical drum), *magrūna* (a single-reed double pipe instrument) and *bandīr* (a single-headed frame drum). All this has become a strong tourist attraction in more recent times, especially now that Libya is putting more emphasis on tourism as another potential source of income for the country's economy.

Online advertisement of tours in the Sahara includes visits and attendance at music festivals held in oases towns like Ghadames, Ghat, Nalut and Darj. Such adverts promise the direct experience of, for instance, Tuareg and Berber music, dancing, traditions and arts.[17] Annual festivals such as that of the town of Ghadames (an oasis town in the west of Libya whose population of 7,000 consists mainly of Tuareg Berbers) are promoted as international events that attract a strong influx of tourists every year. Tourists are promised a taste of 'the local people's life, how it was in the past, shows of how they cook, how they made things (hand crafts) live' (Anon: 2010b)—all this occurring over a strong musical activity that includes both formal performances on stage as well as less formal ones such as during street parades. Such festivals are normally organized by the respective municipalities and receive strong coverage by the Libyan media, occasionally by being transmitted live on the Libyan National TV.

The Recording Industry

As has already been remarked, in the 1969 post-revolutionary years Tripoli saw the proliferation of a number of recording studios. Some of these studios were set up and subsidized by the state while others were home-based and, therefore, run privately. In the 1980s renowned Libyan pop singers, described by an informant as 'of the new generation', bought hi-tech equipment to set up their own home-based studios. This provided them with the chance to make recordings of their own songs, as well as those of other pop singers. Many youths at that time realized

[17] For further reading on Tuareg music and dance see Standifer 1988.

this was a good source of income; consequently, the number of such studios increased considerably. In time, home-based studios expanded into fully equipped ones with the potential to host and make recordings of large ensembles. In contrast with private studios, state-subsidized studios catered mainly for the production of classical Arab music, which genre also included professionally arranged pieces of Libyan folk music. Nevertheless, the recording industry generated plenty of work opportunities in this sector for both technical personnel and for professionally trained musicians and composers.

The emphasis of state-subsidized studios on the production of professionally arranged Libyan folk music occurred in line with the sense of nationalism and 'Arabness' as advanced by the ideals of the 1969 revolution. During the Gaddafi era, professionally arranged Libyan folk music was broadcast on a regular basis on Libyan TV and radio; in itself it was a good replacement for Western pop music. Professionally arranged Libyan folk music was produced by ensembles affiliated to the Libyan Jamahiriya Television and Radio Broadcasting Centre. Such ensembles employed both Western and Arab musical instruments such as the clarinet, violin and cello together with the *darabukka*, *nāy*, *qānūn* (a trapezoidal zither) and *'ūd* (lute). Recording and rehearsing sessions were held regularly in the evening as some of the musicians had other jobs during the daytime. All the musicians whom I have seen rehearsing in these professional ensembles were musically literate with strong sight-reading skills. Since recording time was limited and needed to be cost-effective, professional musicians working in the recording industry were supplied with music parts from which they played without the need to memorize new material. This saved both rehearsal and recording time while at the same time increased productivity. Apart from that, some of the arrangements also employed harmonized sections that demanded a high degree of coordination and proficiency. In arrangements employing such sections, the lead violin player assumed the role of a conductor with his conducting emphasizing not only tempo but also balance and phrasing. Once everything was in place, the recording process began with the finished recording be ready on the same evening, as the broadcast of the song was scheduled for the day after.

Apart from its inclusion in the classical repertoire, Libya's folk music is also strongly present in Libyan pop music. The fusion of Libyan folk rhythms and melodies with Western pop gives to newly released albums a local tinge that facilitates sales of the album in Libya. Songs employing this style are known in Libya as *al-ughniyāt ash-shabābiyya* (youth songs). The style normally employs a full string section, Arab instruments such as the *nāy*, *darabukka*, *bandīr*, *qānūn*, as well as electric guitars and keyboards. The fast rhythmic beat emerging after a vocal improvisation, known as *mawwāl*, with several choruses leading to a rousing dance tempo makes the form of such songs ideal for both wedding celebrations and hotel entertainment, the latter gaining more importance with the building of hotels by Western investors. When the recording of songs in this style takes place in Egypt, due to the lower costs there, singers take with them Libyan percussionists knowledgeable in rhythms employed in Libyan folk music—an essential musical element that, according to informants, makes their songs in this style 'sound Libyan'.

The Libyan connection with Egypt in the domain of pop music goes back to 1974 when the young Libyan singer Hamid al-Shaeri fled to Egypt after witnessing the public burning of Western musical instruments as described above. Shaeri, who was born in Benghazi, studied aviation in Britain and music in Cairo before he settled permanently in Cairo where 'he steadily made a name for himself as Egypt's leading champion of westernized synthesizer pop, known as *Al-jīl* (generation music)' (Leon Jackson 2010). He became central to a movement of Egyptian youths who were 'in the 1970s fed up with listening to the Beatles, Abba and Boney M in a language they couldn't understand' (Lodge and Badley 2000: 343). They decided to do better by proposing the *Al-jīl* style with a distinct dance appeal generated by an array of samplers and synths producing Middle Eastern melodies. Shaeri's 1988 hit single *Lolaiki*, which was recorded in a back room, sold in the millions (Lodge and Badley 2000).

The tendency for Libyan pop singers to leave the country in order to make a name abroad has recently been facilitated by the state's recording industry. In fact, one of its important roles nowadays is that of airing festivals such as the annual Libyan Song Festival, which promotes the original compositions of Libyan pop songs. Another such festival is the Tripoli Festival of *Ma'lūf* and *Muwashshaḥāt* that promotes Arab classical musical forms. Festivals such as the former serve as a good opportunity for young singers to attain the public exposure that will eventually lead them to international recording contracts, especially with recording companies within the region. This is the case with internationally known pop singers, such as Cheb Jilāni (b.1976) (see Figure 1.5) and Ayman al Attar (b.1982). An online biography of the former, for instance, highlights the fact that Jilāni's fame flourished when he was ranked second at the 2001 Libyan Song Festival, and he now enjoys a pan-Arab following (Anon 2010c). Moreover, some of his songs present a distinct musical style that fuses classical Arab singing, such as the *muwashshaḥāt* and *qaṣīda*, with Western pop. In a separate online interview, Al Attar explains that he started singing at home when he was six years old. When he turned seven he was given the opportunity to sing live on Libyan Radio, during children's TV shows, at school and during music festivals (Abudaber n.d.). In general, the strong participating response to such festivals has sometimes led the organizers to spread a festival over a week or even a fortnight, with such festivals transmitted live on Libyan National TV, reaching all of North Africa. Such festivals sometimes also include, as additional entertainment, the participation of folk troupes and wind bands with the latter proving to have a very strong and diffused tradition in Tripoli.

Figure 1.5 Cheb Jilāni's album *Oyouni Sahara* [5285] EMI 2003

Music Education and Institutions in Tripoli

It has been noted above that by the end of the 1970s and the beginning of the 1980s the Libyan Authorities had implemented an extensive programme in music education spread over the different levels of the education system. Such a programme included the setting up of two music schools, one in Tripoli and another one in Benghazi, as well as the recruitment of more music teachers. Whilst the Benghazi music school has closed down, the one in Tripoli (called Maʿhad Jamāl Ad-Dīn Al-Mīlādī) is still active with a study programme that covers both theoretical and practical areas. In the 1980s two other educational music institutions were founded, also in Tripoli. One was a music programme within the College of Arts and Media at Al-Fātiḥ University and the other one was the High Institute of Music (known as Al-Markaz al-ʿĀlī lil-Mihan al-Mūsīqiyya w al-Masraḥīyya). The latter institution is considered as an intermediary college between the programme at Al-Fātiḥ University and the one at Maʿhad Jamāl Ad-Dīn Al-Mīlādī. Professional ensembles like the one described above employ only proficient musicians equipped with a sound instrumental technique and good sight-reading skills who have normally undertaken training at these institutions up to diploma or degree level (see Figure 1.6).

The Maʿhad Jamāl Ad-Dīn Al-Mīlādī Music School offers separate four-year diploma courses in both music and theatre. The music programme includes training in solfège, music theory (both Arab and Western) and instrumental tuition. The school also offers tuition in Arab instruments such as the *qānūn*, *'ūd* and *nāy*, as well as in classical Arab singing. Tuition in Western instruments is offered on piano and on all bowed string instruments. Most students opting for instruction in Arab instruments at Maʿhad Jamāl Ad-Dīn Al-Mīlādī would already have some basic knowledge of their instruments before they join the programme; such knowledge is acquired orally, normally in the context of *zāwiya* (a Sufi lodge next to the mosque). In the case of students opting for an Arab music instrument, they start tuition in Arab music theory from the first year of the programme. Such tuition includes theoretical knowledge of the Arab *maqāmāt* (melodic modes; plural of *maqām*) and *īqā'āt* (rhythmic modes; plural of *īqā'*); tuition in Arab theory is continuous throughout the four-year course. Students receiving tuition in a Western instrument start tuition in Western theory from the first year of their course. Solfège classes are taken up by all students throughout the entire four-year course.

Many graduates from Maʿhad Jamāl Ad-Dīn Al-Mīlādī Music School remain in touch with the School, mainly by attending rehearsal sessions and performances held by the School Ensemble. The Ensemble's repertoire consists of classical Arab music and, therefore, graduates and students of Western instruments might find this a good means of being introduced to this musical genre. Before such rehearsals, one would be able to hear graduate violinists playing extracts from Monti's *Czardas* and Vivaldi's *The Four Seasons* to show off technical ability. Proficiency on the violin is sometimes demonstrated through the playing of Western masterpieces like the ones just mentioned. Within the premises of the

Figure 1.6 Professionally trained musicians in rehearsal

School one also finds a very active workshop for the maintenance and making of Arab instruments under the direction of an Egyptian instructor residing in Libya.

Hāfa, the person in charge of the School's workshop, like so many Egyptian workers, had to leave his family behind in Egypt when he moved to Libya in order to make a living out of making and repairing instruments. He was given accommodation within the premises of the School and, therefore, there was little disparity between his life at work and after work. Hāfa could not make a decent living for himself and his family in his home country due to the many instrument-makers and repairers there, which led to fierce competition and severe price cuts. Therefore, he moved to Libya where his trade is much more profitable. He sometimes visits Jamāl's workshop in the Madīna, exchanging a word with him and, eventually, both explore ways of collaborating in the business of instruments with selling ventures that range from the supply of their instruments to nearby vendors in the open market of the Old City, to music shops and to educational music institutions in Cairo.

Graduates from Ma'had Jamāl Ad-Dīn Al-Mīlādī Music School are normally recruited by ensembles catering for the Libyan recording industry. Promising graduates who intend to further their musical studies are admitted to the music programme at the College of Arts and Media at Al-Fātiḥ University without having to follow the intermediary three-year diploma course at Al-Markaz al-'Ālī lil-Mihan al-Mūsīqiyya w al-Masraḥīyya Music School. Apart from the music programme, the College offers programmes in theatre, art and the media. The four-year music course mainly concentrates on academic aspects such as harmony, music education and history; however, it also provides instrumental tuition in a number of instruments. Apart from that, within the College there is a strong research interest in Libyan folk music, with a good number of students opting to take up related research topics for their undergraduate and postgraduate research projects.

Most music graduates from the above institutions find jobs as music teachers in state schools, taking part-time work as professional players in the evenings. Others are involved only in the professional ensembles described above, with a daytime job unrelated to music. 'Making a living solely out of music is really hard here, especially if you have a family', one of these graduates explained to me. He continued:

> Musicians are not adequately paid here! Therefore, I decided to set up my own business. But this is leaving me no time to practise my instrument and attend regular rehearsals and, you know, the music business is like being a professional athlete—you're either fit and flexible or else do something else. I have reached a point where I have to decide now either to resume with a career in music or to dedicate all my time to my own business. For sure, I can't continue doing them both. Life's demands are pressing me to opt for the latter.

Music teachers in Libyan music schools are expected to teach general music with a programme that during the Gaddafi era accentuated the singing of patriotic songs (known as *anashiyd waṭaniyya*) at both the primary and secondary levels. The tradition of patriotic songs in Libya goes back to the presence of the Italians. Elderly Libyans, who received their primary and secondary education when Libya was under Italian occupation, still remember their teachers teaching them Italian songs such as *La Giovinezza* and other songs in praise of Mussolini and Fascism. Italian song tunes, such as the one just mentioned, even had Arabic words set to them and became *qaṣā'id* (plural of *qaṣīda*). Furthermore, *qaṣā'id* tunes have sometimes been turned into Turkish and Italian military marches during the respective occupations. The singing of patriotic songs in schools has endured in the post-revolutionary era, albeit with text honouring the Gaddafi administration and the new developments in modern Libya.

The impact of military music in Libya even influenced the tuition of woodwind and brass instruments. Such tuition is not part of the curricula of the above-mentioned educational music institutions. In Tripoli only military bandsmen teach such instruments, either privately at home or at the Islamic Arts and Crafts School in downtown Tripoli (see Figure 1.7). This institution has a renowned marching band affiliated to it, which was set up with the foundation of the School in 1898. Apart from this band, one finds in Tripoli several other bands either affiliated to other cultural institutions or else formed ad hoc by individual bandsmen to perform in one-off events. Wind bands in Libya trace their origin to the Turkish and Italian military parades frequently seen marching in the streets of Tripoli

Figure 1.7 Young bandsmen playing informally at the Islamic Arts and Crafts School in downtown Tripoli

during the times when these nations had conquered the country. As with other forms of ensemble playing mentioned above, gender segregation is not applicable to wind band playing, as these bands are sometimes composed of both male and female musicians (see Figure 1.8 below).

Conclusion

Transitional processes between traditional and modern social structures and values can be noticed in all spheres of contemporary Libyan society. The growing sense of individualism amongst the younger generation led newly married couples to establish residency away from their parents rather than residing in the same family house as in the past. Moreover, the strongly increased diffusion of Western media facilitated easier access to internet and satellite TV programmes from all over the world, with the result that these contributed greatly towards more social change and the assimilation of values alien to the traditional layers of Libyan culture.

At the same time, the coexistence of the 'modern' and the 'archaic', 'innovation' and 'sameness', 'change' and 'conformity' are present in Libyan life as much as

Figure 1.8 A Tripolitan wind band composed of male and female musicians

they are present in the different domains of Libyan music including the *ma'lūf* tradition, as we will see in the coming chapters. Whilst the Libyan Authority was implementing new projects in the field of music education, the traditional oral teaching of music in *zāwiya* continued and, in a way, complemented that provided by the above-mentioned music institutions. As I will argue later on in this book, the *ma'lūf* lives in this dynamic of transmission and its survival is sustained by both performances held in *zāwiya* and in professional settings.

Turning to rural music, one notes Libyan rural music heard both in its 'authentic' contexts and as transformed by professional ensembles in recording studios, with some parts even harmonized. CDs and DVDs featuring *raï* music and Western pop music can be seen displayed in record shops next to CD collections of famous Qur'ān reciters such as Sheikh Abdul Bāsiṭ 'Abd uṣ-Samad from Egypt or Sheikh Mishary Rashid Ghareeb Mohammed Rashid Al-Afasy from Kuwait. This is the kind of coexistence that occurs within a social context that values strongly the 'conventional', the 'familiar', the 'old' and the 'known' whilst at the same time absorbing the 'new', the 'unfamiliar', the 'modern' and the 'imported' with a great deal of caution within a framework deeply rooted in the socio-historical experiences of the past and the values of Islam in general. In a way, this matches Brandily's comment that 'most of Libyan society is now open to change but also that there are limits and to go beyond them is not considered acceptable' (1982: 212). Such limits are especially present, for instance, in cultural areas intrinsically linked to Islamic practices; these include rituals and ceremonies in which *ma'lūf* plays a central role and, therefore, resilience to change in those domains would also impact the rate of change of the *ma'lūf* itself as practised in that context. More limits show up in areas where prestigious legacies from the past are conceived as not being treated with enough cautiousness and sensitivity. As I will argue in Chapter 3, this factor was central to the acceptance and rejection of a national project that had seen the *ma'lūf* as experienced and perceived in *zāwiya* being transformed into a musical experience that at that time seemed unfitting to the richness of an artistic legacy embedded in centuries of tradition.

Chapter 2
The *Nawba* in North Africa and in Libya

Talking to people about 'their own' musical tradition may lead the researcher to construct a pattern, or even patterns, of musical discourse most characteristic to that music tradition. Borrowing from the French writer Michel Foucault, Turino (2008: 103) notes that discourse may be defined 'as a relatively systematic constellation of habits of thought and expression which shape people's reality about a particular subject or realm of expression'. Such pattern/s, or as Turino puts it, this 'systematic constellation of habits of thought and expression', can say a lot about the nature of the body of continuous thinking that accompanies music and, by extension, about the musical tradition of our concern. With renowned musicians, used to interviews and public speeches, and, moreover, aware of the importance of structured speeches for the sake of clarity, this kind of patterning may occur quite explicitly, usually starting on a level which can be described as 'pan-Arab', proceeding to a phase that can be termed as 'regional' and finishing on the 'national'. This may even emerge during informal discussions with both musicians and other people, although with more flexibility and fusion of the three levels of discourse just mentioned. What music means to certain music cultures and what, in turn, these cultures mean by it, must be understood in the widest possible framework, one that possibly exceeds 'national' and even 'regional' boundaries.[1]

This is the kind of experience I have had since my first steps in Libya, eager to explore what the *ma'lūf* means in today's Libyan society. 'The *ma'lūf* is not Libyan but Arab music', my taxi driver insisted, when I explained to him what I was there for. 'It is found in other North African countries … although the sweetest (*l-aḥla*) is found here … because in Libya the *ma'lūf* remained faithfully Andalusian', he continued with an assured tone, probably unaware of the many changes that this tradition had passed through over the years. His statements were forged within the above three levels of discourse: mainly, that the Libyan *ma'lūf* belongs to the much wider concept of *al-mūsīqā al-'arabiyya* (Arab music) [pan-Arab]; it is an offshoot of the classical Arab musical tradition known for its 'official' origin in Andalusian Spain (*al-mūsīqā al-'andalusiyya*) and transmitted to North Africa [regional]; and, thirdly, the Libyan tradition of *ma'lūf* is 'authentic', existing now as it existed in Medieval Spain [national].

[1] I had the diametrically opposite experience during fieldwork experiences with Maltese folk singers (see, for instance, Ciantar 1996). The way they speak about *għana* (Malta's folk singing; pronounced *āna*) reflects their sole and focused interest in the musical tradition they represent, with hardly any references to other neighbouring folk music.

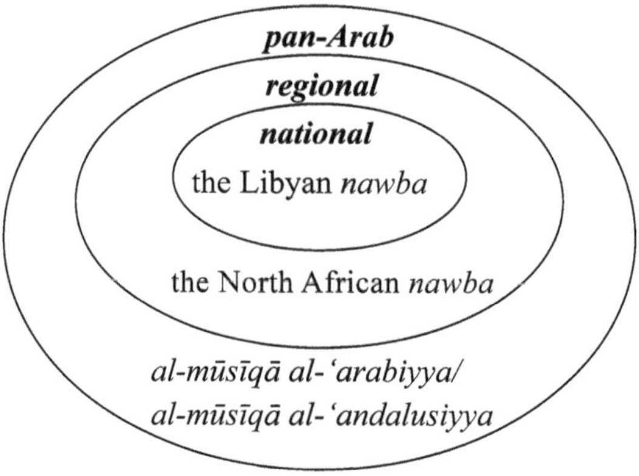

Figure 2.1 Modes of musical discourse

Interviews with established and renowned Libyan musicians were, in most cases, characterized by extensive preambles on what Arab music is, who is the Arab musician, comparisons of Arab music to Western music with a strong emphasis on memorization, and general statements about and explanations of the North African *nawba* (song cycle; the formal structure of the genre *ma'lūf*). Finally, after some insistent questions requiring focused answers, discourse about the Libyan *ma'lūf* in particular would emerge, including comparisons with North African music of the same genre. The overall message was consistent: the Libyan *ma'lūf* must be understood in the wider framework of Arab musical history, theory and practice, with frequent references to the musical genre as it exists in neighbouring North African countries. Reading from the outside toward the centre, the diagram of concentric circles (see Figure 2.1) shows the narrowing-down from pan-Arab to national modes of discourse as evolved during most of my interviews in Libya. This equitable approach to discourse about the Libyan *ma'lūf* presents a somewhat different position from that proposed by Langlois (2009: 226) when asserting that *al-mūsīqā al-'andalusiyya* 'is presented in each of the Maghreb countries as an inclusive symbol of national identity'. In the case of Libya, what is considered as distinctly Libyan in the *ma'lūf* is mostly blended in the wider discourse of Arabic music and the North African *nawba*.

There are three things that led my informants to avoid speaking of *ma'lūf* as a distinctly Libyan tradition: the fact that the *ma'lūf* is conceived according to the two most distinguishable musical elements in Arab music, that is the *maqām* (melodic mode) and *īqā'* (rhythmic mode), a reliance on a widely disseminated poetical genre believed to reveal its origin from a common source, and its basis in the formal structure of the North African *nawba*. However, as we shall see later in this chapter, the Libyan *nawbāt ma'lūf* (that is, 'the *nawba* of *ma'lūf*' as it is sometimes called in Libya) has particular characteristics, most evidently in its form, that distinguish it from the *nawba* of Morocco, Algeria and Tunisia. At this stage, one can briefly define a *nawba* as a song cycle containing sections that unfold in different *īqāʿāt* (plural of *īqāʿ*) and where the overall music progresses gradually from a slow to a fast tempo.

The present chapter sheds light on the traditional performance of the Libyan *nawba* with particular emphasis on its social, religious and cultural role in Libyan society, its history and its structure, as well as its musical and poetical content. The way the present chapter unfolds resembles the way most of my interviews in Libya were shaped during my fieldwork there. The two outer levels of the above concentric diagram, that is, discourse about Arabic music and the North African *nawba*, are dealt with in the first section. A discussion focusing on the Libyan *nawba* in particular, mainly its traditional performance context, will then be explored in the sections that follow, leaving the scrutiny of the newer performance style for the subsequent chapter. For the sake of conciseness, discussion of Arab music as it unfolds in the first section is restricted only to historical and musical aspects that in some way relate to the *nawba*. The second section will highlight the social, religious and cultural dimensions of the traditional Libyan *nawba* with special emphasis on its role in Sufi celebrations. This will then lead on to a focus on the history of the Libyan *nawba*, and therefore of the *ma'lūf*, and the important role played by deceased renowned Libyan *shuyūkh al-ma'lūf* in the making of the same history. The fourth section will discuss aspects related to music and text as employed by the Libyan *nawba*.

The North African *Nawba*: Dissemination, Regional Variations and Developments

Whilst between 750 and 1258 Baghdad became the capital of the Abbasid Caliphate, the years between 920 and 1031 had seen the emergence of Córdoba as the capital of the Spanish or Western Caliphate. The invasion of Spain by North African Muslims, also known as Moors, led to the collapse of the Visigoth kingdom in 711. In Spain the Moors had introduced improved methods of agriculture, manufacturing, stockbreeding and metallurgy. Moorish Spain became noted for art and learning, with Córdoba as its great intellectual and artistic centre. At that time Spain was known by the Arabs as *al-andalus*. It was during this period, in 822, that a freed Persian slave and court lute player known as Ziryāb (a nickname for Abū'l-Hasan 'Alī ibn Nāfi') allegedly left the court of 'Abd al-Rahman Harun al-Rashid in Baghdad and took refuge in the court of Sultan 'Abd al-Rahmān II in Córdoba (Poché 1995: 35). According to the tradition it was in Córdoba that Ziryāb founded a music school in which he taught singers how to sing a *nawba* in accordance with a set of rules (Guettat 2001: 447). Accounts of Ziryāb's teaching initiatives in Spain highlight the fact that his teaching spread to newly established music schools in other parts of Spain, including Toledo, Seville, Valencia and Granada.

The Christian reconquest of Spain that began in the 900s marked the beginning of the exodus of the Muslims and Jews from the Peninsula to North Africa, even though the *andalusī nawba* continued to flourish for some time still. The Muslims came under increasing pressure to convert to Christianity or leave Spain. Those who left the country established residency in different parts of the Maghreb. When referring to the migration of Jews and Muslims from Spain, Davis (2004: 2–3) notes that:

> The first migration, from the 10th to the 12th centuries, was from Seville to Tunis; in the twelfth century, refugees fled from Córdoba to Tlemcen (Algeria) and from Valencia to Fez (Morocco); then, with the fall of Granada in 1492, a further wave of migrants made for Fez and Tutuan (Morocco).

Their presence in the Maghreb was historically considered as providential for a region that was then stagnating; it was also beneficial from the musical point of view, as observed by Jones (2001: 433):

> [These Andalusian refugees] had a generally higher level of culture and technology than the Maghreb … and their innovative contributions were admired, to the extent that even today anyone who claims Andalusian descent is asserting a certain nobility. The music they brought enriched and vitalized cognate genres in the Maghreb, particularly 'classical' art music, which subsequently came to be called Andalusian. This should not be taken to mean that the entire genre is an importation. The Andalusian endowment was substantial, in terms of both textual and musical material, but it merged with an existing repertoire and other influences to form a uniquely North African idiom, with important regional variations.

The expulsion of Muslims to North Africa had supported the strengthening of a movement within Islam, known as Sufism, through the manifestation of intensive exaltation of religious sentiments. In the context of Islam, Sufism came to be understood as 'the interiorization and intensification of Islamic faith and practice' (Chittick 1995: 102). The movement evolved into several Sufi brotherhoods that spread throughout the Maghreb to the extent that Sufism became the most influential Islamic practice in the region. The Sufis contributed immensely towards the survival of the original *nawba* repertory, mainly through its dissemination in the centres established by them and its inclusion in their rituals. Predominantly in this domain, one may mention the orders of the *'Īsāwiyya* and the *Qādiriyya* with the latter considered as the oldest Sufi order.[2] The *Qādiriyya* order was founded by the followers of Abd al-Qādir al-Jīlānī (1078–1166) in Baghdad and later spread by his sons into North Africa, Central Asia and India. The *'Īsāwiyya* brotherhood was founded in the sixteenth century by Sidi Muhammed Bin 'Aysa (d.1518), who came from the city of Meknes in Morocco (El-Mahdi 1978: 10). As in the case of the *Qādiriyya* before it, the *'Īsāwiyya* established centres in several North African cities and villages, from Morocco to the Egyptian border, to centres in the Sahara of

---

2 A Sufi order is known as *ṭarīqa* (path or way).

Fezzan, in Mauritania and in Libya. Groups belonging to this brotherhood offered practical instruction on melodic modes and rhythms as well as tutoring in the playing of percussion instruments. Music played an important role in Sufi life as it came to be understood as 'a means to draw the soul closer to God' (Schimmel 2001:11). The brotherhoods also included spectacles in their religious rites, such as dancing leading to ecstasy, the rubbing of the body against a cactus without feeling pain, and even the swallowing of nails (El-Mahdi 1978: 10). However, many of the stern, Sharia-bound Muslims objected to such spectacles and the music included in these rituals (Schimmel 2001: 11). Consequently, up to the present day, while some of these orders accept the practice of music, others—the so-called sober orders—prohibit it.

As has already been indicated, these Sufi orders contributed enormously towards the dissemination of the musical and poetic Andalusian repertoire. This is still done, with the *'Īsāwiyya* at the forefront in the teaching and transmission of the Andalusian *nawba* in particular. On first impressions, Sufi mystic songs that form part of the corpus of *nawba* text, and which exalt Allah, the Prophet Muhammad, or even the holy founder of the order, might literally be understood as profane love songs without any spiritual connection. Indeed, it is essential for one to understand that in these songs the profane aspect of Andalusian lyricism acquires an elevated religious connotation. For instance, the carnal love of men and women becomes sublimated as divine love, and the intoxication of wine (proscribed by the Qur'ān) becomes a metaphor for the exaltation of the Divine. In Sufi poetry the imaginable realm of unveiled knowledge, the vision of union and oneness, are most frequently found in expressions referring to drunkenness (Chittick 1995: 106). When referring to this aspect of Sufi poetry, Benbaabali (2006: 49) notes that wine is for the Sufis that which allows the accomplishment of unification; it abrogates the sense of plurality. Moreover, the ego is annihilated and everything comes into unity. The tavern as employed in such text can be a reference either to the place where the Sufis meet or to the entire world in its unity (Benbaabali 2006: 49). In addition, the cupbearer can be a reference to God pouring his grace or mystical initiation on man in order to communicate with him (Benbaabali 2006: 49). All this shows that there is a poetic licence in Sufi poetry that permits Sufi poets to say things that could not be expressed in prose form (Chittick 1995: 106).

The poetic stanzas of the Andalusian *nawba* belong to two sister-genres of Arabic strophic poetry known as *muwashshaḥ* (also called *tawshīḥ*) and *zajal*. When referring to the origin of both poetic genres, Zwartjes (2006: 1) asserts that they were particularly developed in *al-andalus* and soon became extremely popular in North Africa and the Middle East, 'not only within the Arabic literary tradition but also in Hispano-Hebrew literature and in Hebrew literature outside Muslim Spain'. Both the *muwashshaḥ* and *zajal* are composed of stanzas with a variable number of hemistichs in each. Although there are various differences between the two, such as optional introductory strophes in *muwashshaḥ* and obligatory ones in *zajal*, the main distinction lies in the fact that the *muwashshaḥ* is a strophic poem written in classical Arabic, while the *zajal* is written in colloquial Arabic. Structurally, the fundamental scheme of the *muwashshaḥ* is AA bbbAA cccAA or

AB cccAB dddAB while that of the *zajal* is AA bbbA cccA (Stern 1974: 53) or its more involved variant ABAB cccABdddAB (Alvarez 1998: 819). *Muwashshaḥ* poetry has been sung and accompanied by instruments ever since its development in Muslim Spain (Al Faruqi 1974: 154). In this respect Stern (1974: 42) notes that 'more than the *qaṣīda* (the most classical and the most formal Arabic verse form), the *muwashshaḥ* was destined—by its very nature as a poem to be *sung*—to be an ornament of the courtly assemblies'. Some of the themes treated by both *muwashshaḥ* and *zajal* poetry are love (*ghazal*), the description of nature (*waṣf*), praise (*madīḥ*), mourning (*marthiya*), satire (*hijā'*), wine-songs (*khamriyya*), frivolity (*mujūn*) and asceticism (*zuhd*).

The *nawba* tradition was perpetuated along different lines in Tunisia, Morocco, Algeria and Libya. The melodic and poetical repertoire, both claiming an Andalusian origin, underwent several transformations when combined with local social, cultural and aesthetic values and tastes. This is evident even from the way this repertoire is diversely known throughout the region. For instance, in Tunisia, Libya and Eastern Algeria it is known as *ma'lūf* (familiar, customary, usual, well-known), in Algiers it is called *san'a* (work of art), in Western Algeria it is known as *gharnāti* (from Granada) while in Morocco it is known as *āla* (instrumental music). More subtly, these North African schools also differ in the tuning of melodic modes and the articulation of rhythmic modes, both when employed in *nawba* and in Arabic music more broadly. These differences, at times scarcely perceptible to an outsider, are the musical equivalents of dialects.[3] However, irrespective of all these regional differences and all the variants that these might imply, the two musical pillars that shape the structure of the North African *nawba* are the *maqām* and *īqā'*.

In Arab music the term for a melodic mode is *maqām*. However, in Libya the term *tab'* is sometimes employed for *maqām* in the folk music domain. The intervallic distance between the notes of a *maqām*, when superficially understood in terms of scale, might be of a tone, semitone, three-quarter tone (slightly larger than a semitone) and five-quarter-tone (slightly larger than the Western whole tone). The other aspect of a *maqām* is the order in which melodies appear in it and their rate of emergence. Moreover, every *maqām* is known by a name; therefore, one finds *maqām sabá*, *maqām sīkā*, *maqām bayyātī* and others. In Morocco, Algeria and Tunisia a *nawba* takes its name from the *maqām* in which it unfolds. The 13 most performed Tunisian *nawbāt*, for instance, have titles such as, *nawbāt al-sīka* or *nawbāt al-aṣbahān*, that is, a *nawba* that unfolds in *maqām sīka* in the former and in *maqām aṣbahān* in the latter. However, in Libya, a *nawba* gets its name from the opening hemistich. At this stage it is worth noting the fact that a hemistich in a *nawba* corresponds to the *īqā'* (that is, the rhythmic mode) in which that particular section unfolds, in a way that one can infer the *īqā'* from the length of the hemistich itself.

---

[3] In this regard, El-Mallah (1997: 25) rightly notes that Arab music is rich in musical dialects due to close ties between regional schools of thought.

Each rhythmic mode in Arab music is known by a name. Examples include *īqā' barwal*, *īqā' maṣmūdī kabīr* and *īqā' samā'ī thaqīl*. Arab musicians remember these rhythms by employing two mnemonic syllables resembling the two characteristic sound-strokes of the *darabukka*: the *dumm* and *takk*. The *dumm* denotes the lowest sound produced on the centre of the membrane whilst the *takk* denotes the high-pitched sound produced on the rim of the same instrument. The rest is known as *ess*. For instance, *īqā' maṣmūdī kabīr* (see Example 2.1) can be mnemonically represented as:

Example 2.1 *Īqā' maṣmūdī kabīr*

In most instances the different cycles that make up a *nawba* bear the name of the *īqā'* in which the same cycle grows. The Moroccan *nawba*, for instance, comprises five cycles called *mayāzīn* (singular, *mīzān*), each with its own rhythmic mode, in such a way that each cycle is named after its respective rhythmic mode. Therefore, *mīzān basīt* refers to the first cycle of the *nawba* on the rhythmic mode that bears the same name. Moreover, apart from vocal sections a *nawba* may also include instrumental sections, the most common of which amongst the Maghreb traditions is the instrumental opening known as *mīshāliya* in the Moroccan *nawba*, *mustahbār al-san'a* or *mīshāliya* in the Algerian *nawba*, and *istiftāh* in the Tunisian and Libyan *nawba*.

The *nawba* repertoire is strongly marked by regional variations even within the same country. In Morocco, for example, the existing repertoire of 11 *nawbāt* exists in several schools, each school disseminating and teaching according to its own particular tradition, such as those in Fez, Rabat and Tetuan. The Algerian *nawba*, whose repertoire is organized into 12 complete *nawbāt*, is another case in point. This repertoire is taught in three main schools: Tlemcen, Algiers and Constantine. Constantine and Tlemcen are the two oldest centres with Algiers emerging as the third in terms of importance. Due to its geographical position between these two centres, the Andalusian repertory in Algiers absorbed influences from both traditions. When referring to regional variants in the Algerian *nawba*, Elsner (1997: 468) notes several distinctive elements, such as regional preferences with respect to tempo, timbre and performance practice. While in Algiers, for example, a moderate tempo is preferred, in Tlemcen there is a stronger tendency towards a slower tempo. In addition, a faster tempo is normally employed in the Constantine tradition.

Whilst the *nawba* continues to be performed in Sufi lodges, mainly by male choruses singing in unison and accompanied by hand and/or percussion instruments and, in some cases, by a melody instrument, performances outside traditional Sufi contexts are also very common. In the latter case an ensemble may vary from a small group of singers and instrumentalists to extensive ensembles consisting of both Western and Arab instruments, as well as male and female voices. An Algerian *nawba* ensemble, for instance, performing outside a Sufi lodge may include an *'ūd ʿarabī* (a four-stringed lute), *rabāb* and *kamanja kabīra* (viola).[4] The Algerian ensemble (or *jawq*) that accompanies a *nawba* expanded from a small ensemble into a large ensemble, a development that had taken place by the 1930s. This expansion continued after Algerian independence with the introduction of other European instruments that eventually changed the more traditional sonority of the *nawba* ensemble in Algeria (Reynolds 1995). A somewhat similar path was followed by the Tunisian *ma'lūf*, which initially was performed in *zawāyā* by Sufi brothers 'both for recreation and entertainment' as well as 'an act of duty to conserve the Andalusian heritage' (Davis 2004: 42). However, with the setting up of the Rashidiyya Institute in Tunis in 1934, the entire *ma'lūf* repertoire was transcribed from its oral tradition into Western staff notation (Davis 2004: 42). Eventually, these and other alternative transcriptions that emerged later aided instrumental ensembles, composed of both Western and Arab instruments, in the dissemination of the *ma'lūf* in Tunisia. Apart from the inclusion of Western instruments, such ensembles had also been extended to include numerous instrumentalists together with an extensive choir composed of male and female voices. When such ensembles contained fewer members it was up to the instrumentalists themselves to provide the singing. It became very evident, though, that performance practices employed by these innovative ensembles were modelled on Western performance practices, the most evident of which being the presence of a conductor directing the ensemble from the front as in Western orchestral conducting. The same fate affected the Libyan *nawba* when in 1964 it emerged out of Sufi lodges and was 'modernized' in line with developments that had previously occurred in the Tunisian *ma'lūf*.

The Traditional Libyan *Nawba*: Religious, Social and Cultural Functions

As has already been mentioned in the first chapter, the *ma'lūf* tradition in Libya is most strongly found in Tripoli. In other parts of Libya, such as Benghazi, Sabha and Misurata, this tradition is much less diffused. The Libyans distinguish between *ma'lūf az-zāwiya*, sometimes also called *ma'lūf at-taqlīdī* (*taqlīdī* means 'traditional') and *ma'lūf al-idhāʿa*, referring to performances of *ma'lūf* in the traditional contexts of *zāwiya* in the former and those performed in the context of the modern recording industry or broadcasting (*idhāʿa* means 'broadcasting') in the latter. Recordings of the former only exist in private collections. On the other hand, the somewhat limited recording market of the *ma'lūf* is predominantly taken up by examples of the *ma'lūf al-idhāʿa*, recorded in professional recording studios with larger ensembles that also include Western musical instruments such as the

4 In Constantine, the *rabāb* has been entirely replaced by the viola (Elsner 2002: 470).

violin, cello and double bass. *Ma'lūf al-idhā'a* performances are also featured regularly on national Libyan TV.

The *ma'lūf az-zāwiya* is predominantly 'context-based'; that is, strongly embedded in traditional *'Īsāwiyya* Sufi ceremonies and rituals. According to informants, the *ma'lūf* was also sung by Libyans on their caravan journeys to Mecca, a practice that is no longer in existence due to modern transportation. *Ma'lūf* sessions are held in *zāwiya* during *ḥaḍra* (a Sufi religious ceremony), at wedding celebrations, during circumcision ceremonies, at the inauguration of a new house and, occasionally, during burial rites. At all such events the *ma'lūf* is integrated within a ritual that in itself provides a level of stability to the same tradition both in terms of performance practice, as well as a degree of change. According to Libyans I interviewed, the true preservation of the *ma'lūf* is in its functional role in *zāwiya* and related activities. Contemporary initiatives to preserve this tradition are sometimes looked at by the same interviewees as 'superficial', providing only a relatively short-term safeguard for the continuation of the tradition.

The present section focuses on the *ma'lūf az-zāwiya* and its role in three Sufi celebrations or events, namely during the *mawlid* (in this sense understood as the Muslim period during which Muslims celebrate the birth of the Prophet Muhammad),[5] wedding celebrations and funeral rituals. Although, as I said, the *ma'lūf* may also be performed during circumcision rites, people I interviewed consider the inclusion of the *ma'lūf* in circumcision ceremonies as no longer common in today's Libya. The *mawlid* event highlighted in the present section, and which I attended, occurred on 1 May 2004 in Tripoli's Madīna al-Qadīma. That day marked the beginning of the *mawlid* period and related Sufi celebrations. The role of *ma'lūf* in funeral rituals was explained to me by the Libyan music scholar El Sibaei. The same informant provided me with videotapes of a wedding celebration that included *ma'lūf*; I watched and scrutinized these tapes on my return from fieldwork. Unfortunately, I never had the opportunity to attend funeral or wedding celebrations during my periods of stay in Libya, and therefore the explanation that follows for these two events relies on close examination of videotapes and descriptions provided to me by my informants.

Considering the various events in which the *ma'lūf* is employed in Libya, reaching a conclusion on whether it is sacred or secular music would be a difficult task indeed. Whenever I asked my informants about this, I could always sense an overall non-committal attitude to my question. The discreet answers of some accentuated the fact that whether the *ma'lūf* is sacred or secular depends on distinct but interrelated factors, such as the intention of listeners and performers and their knowledge of Sufi arts and traditions, and the kind of occasion or event at which performance occurs.[6] Nevertheless, others were more

[5] This is specifically known as *mawlid an-nabī*–the Birth of the Prophet.

[6] See also During 1992: 285 for more insight into the issue of the sacred/secular distinction in Islamic music.

specific if not also clearer in their answers. For instance, some asserted that a *ma'lūf* session in *zāwiya* is considered as sacred whilst a *ma'lūf* session on stage during a festival is believed to be secular, as if what makes the *ma'lūf* secular or sacred is the context in which it occurs. For instance, the *ma'lūf* as performed during the *mawlid* celebrations was definitely considered by my informants as sacred music, not only because its singing commences in *zāwiya* but, moreover, because its performance continues in processional form as part of a ritual along the streets of the Madīna al-Qadīma.[7]

The *mawlid* falls on the twelfth day of the third month of the Islamic lunar calendar (*rabī' al-awwal*). The Muslims celebrate this day with a holiday characterized by popular festivities and ceremonies. In Libya the *mawlid* is celebrated with grandeur over a period of a month or so following *mawlid* day. Throughout this period of celebrations all the *zawāyā* of Tripoli are decorated with lights on the outside as a sign of celebration. Many consider the *mawlid* period as that time of the year in which the art of *ma'lūf* reaches its peak, due to its widespread inclusion in several indoor and outdoor ceremonies organized by Sufi brotherhoods. The common religious sentiment that prevails during these days attributes a sense of sacredness to *ma'lūf* performances and, by extension, to the *ma'lūf* itself; that is what the *'Īsāwiyya* Sufis of Libya believe. On the other hand, *Qādiriyya* and *Ārusīyya* Sufi brotherhoods refrain from including *ma'lūf* in their *mawlid* celebrations. Some of the most orthodox Sufi members within these two Sufi confraternities oppose even its performance in *zāwiya*, as they believe that the *ma'lūf* is solely *fulklūr* (folklore) and, by extension, 'secular' and, there is therefore nothing religious about it.

Nevertheless, on the morning of *mawlid* day, Sufi brotherhoods meet in their respective *zāwiya* in Tripoli's Madīna al-Qadīma. They meet for a *ḥaḍra* that includes readings from the Qur'ān, praise songs (*madīḥ*) and *dhikr* (pronouncement or remembrance). The *ḥaḍra* that I attended that morning took place at the *zāwiya l-kabīra*. When I arrived at around 8.30 a.m. the congregation had already started that part in which passages from the Qur'ān are read. After came the *dhikr*, which can be briefly described as 'the ritual invocation of god and divine authority and power by Muslims through the repetition of the Most Beautiful Names of God, and usually accompanied by the performance of chanting and bodily movements known collectively as *samā'* (audition)' (Shannon 2006: 112). The *dhikr* rite involved two choruses: one standing along the walls of the *zāwiya* and another one sitting in the middle. The standing chorus started invoking the name of Allah *la ilāha illā Allāh* (There is no god but Allah) on a motivic ostinato initiated by the sheikh leading the *dhikr* (known as *sheikh dhikr*) (see Figure 2.2). The members of the standing chorus swung

[7] It is worth noting here that much ethnomusicology scholarship seems to agree that the issue of whether something is 'sacred' or 'secular' (or even defined as 'music') in the Islamic world is essentially a question of context and intent (and more of a Western preoccupation than a local concern).

Figure 2.2 *Dhikr* at the *zāwiya l-kabīra*

their bodies from right to left and backwards and forwards in tempo with the ostinato singing. The other group sat in a circle singing a *madīḥ* and, later on, a *qaṣīda*.[8] The ostinato singing intermingled with the singing of the sitting group, together making a melody and ostinato texture. Later on, the participants started moving joyfully around the *zāwiya*, singing and accompanying themselves on the *bās* (small hand-drum) whilst another member moved around playing a pair of cymbals (see Figure 2.3 below).

After the *dhikr*, the members left the *zāwiya* for a *ma'lūf* parade in the narrow streets of the Madīna. Each of the three *zawāyā* in the Old City holds its own parade according to a programme agreed in advance by the same three confraternities.[9] At the front of the parade the *dhikr* group continued with the ostinato singing and playing initiated in *zāwiya*. At some distance behind, a *ma'lūf* ensemble moved slowly singing a *nawbāt ma'lūf*. The first *nawba* sung by these parades is always *nawba ya muhammad* (Oh Muhammad) as it fits nicely

[8] A *qaṣīda* I heard during the present account is called *tala' l-badir alina* (The Moon has Risen for Us). It is traditionally known that this *qaṣīda* was sung by the women of *Madīna* on greeting the Prophet Muhammad on his arrival from Mecca.

[9] In Tripoli's Madīna al-Qadīma there are three *zawāyā*: *az-zāwiya l-kabīra* (the great *zāwiya*), *az-zāwiya as-saghīra* (the small *zāwiya*) and *zāwiyat Muknī* (*Muknī*'s *zāwiya*).

Figure 2.3 Sufi members playing hand-drums and cymbals in *zāwiya*

with the spirit of these *mawlid* celebrations. As has already been indicated, in contrast with the other *nawba* traditions in the region, the Libyan *nawba* gets its name from the text of the opening hemistich; *nawba ya muhammad* is a case in point. The *sheikh ma'lūf* was leading the singing surrounded by a group of singers known as *raddāda* and accompanied by the *ghayṭa* (shawm) player and *kinjī*[10] (the second; the sheikh's assistant) (see Figure 2.4). Behind the sheikh stood the *naqqārāt* player playing two small kettle drums suspended on the shoulders of someone who had volunteered to carry them along the parade (see Figure 2.5). The *naqqārāt* provided an added rhythmic filler to that provided by the *nawba* and *bandīr* (single-headed frame drum) players (see Figure 2.6 below), who all stood at the back of the parade. At the very end, a carriage carrying a brass stove (*kānūn*) containing burning charcoal was being pushed by hand. When the *bandīr* players felt that the membrane had softened, they would approach the stove to warm their drum (see Figure 2.7 below) so the membrane would be stretched again; this would produce a better sound quality.

The way the parade was set up conveyed acoustic considerations. The *dhikr* group moved ahead and at a distance from the *ma'lūf* group so that their singing remained distinct from that of the *nawba*. On the other hand, the percussion

[10] This is a term derived from Turkish.

Figure 2.4 The *ghayṭa* player, *sheikh ma'lūf* (centre) and *kinjī*

Figure 2.5 The *naqqārāt* player

Figure 2.6 *Nawba* and *bandīr* players

Figure 2.7 A *bandīr* being heated on a *kānūn*

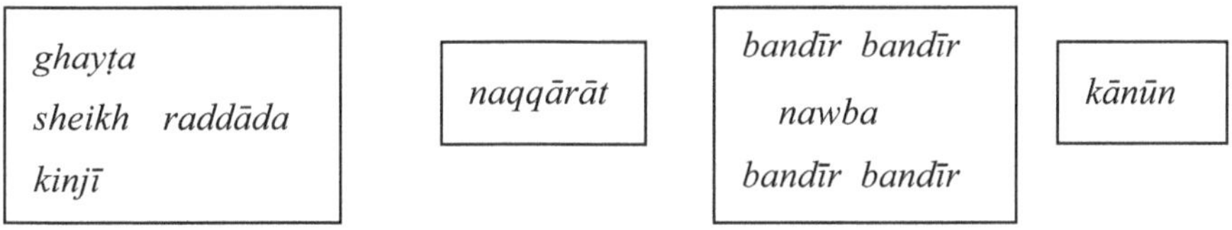

Figure 2.8 Outline of a *ma'lūf* parade

section stood at a distance behind the sheikh so that it would not overwhelm the singing, making it difficult to comprehend. Figure 2.8 shows an outline of a *ma'lūf* parade as just described.[11]

The performers taking part in the parade swung their bodies to the rhythm of the percussion. Everybody seemed to be united by the same religious sentiment, and the *ma'lūf* enhanced that sentiment. Every now and then the parade would stop in front of the house of a distinguished family residing in the Madīna. A male member of the family appeared on the main doorstep holding a censer with burning incense signifying *baraka* (blessing) (see Figure 2.9 below), whilst women of the same

[11] Descriptions of *mawlid* parades in Tripoli found in Cerbella and Ageli (1949: 31–43) match contemporary practices.

Figure 2.9 The *ma'lūf* parade greeted with incense and orange blossom water

Figure 2.10 An *Ārusīyya* ensemble

household sprinkled orange blossom water from atop the balcony. Occasionally, these families would also serve mint tea and almond biscuits to all participants in the parade. Along the parade, women were standing by the side of the street enriching the entire celebrative atmosphere with ululations they shrilled out from time to time.

In a parallel street, an *Ārusīyya* Sufi group marched and made music on the *zukra* (bagpipe) and *bandīr* (see Figure 2.10). They were not performing *ma'lūf*, as in Libya it is only performed by 'Īsāwiyya Sufis, as I have remarked earlier. The sound of the *Ārusīyya* ensemble became clearer as the brotherhood performing *ma'lūf* took a short break between one *nawba*, which normally takes three-quarters of an hour or so, and another. The long and slow-moving parade resumed and went on until nine or so in the evening when the confraternities returned to their respective *zawāyā*.

At around ten in the evening, the brotherhood again met in the *zāwiya* for another *ḥaḍra*.[12] The sheikh of the *zāwiya as-saghīra*, which is situated on the other side of the Old City, welcomed the members of the confraternity and Sufi members from other *zawāyā* as well as people who only attended as observers to share in the communal spirit of the *mawlid*. *Zāwiya* members gave out mint tea, Arabic coffee and other beverages to all those present. In contrast with the morning session at the *zāwiya l-kabīra* I was not allowed to take pictures or video there. As the *sheikh az-zāwiya* (i.e. the sheikh in charge of the *zāwiya*) noticed me taking out my photo and video cameras he stopped me at once, explaining to me that whatever occurs in that place should remain strictly within the confines of the confraternity and not be dispersed publicly. However, I was allowed to make audio recordings and meet *zāwiya* members afterwards.

During the *mawlid* period each *zāwiya* would organize a *ḥaḍra* for seven consecutive evenings at its own expense. That evening's *ḥaḍra* followed the same sequence as the morning session, that is, readings from the Qur'ān, the singing of *madīḥ* and *qaṣīda*, the *dhikr* and, finally, the performance of a *nawba*. The atmosphere during *dhikr* became overwhelming with members participating in the ritual rocking their bodies abnormally to and fro as in a trance. They were eventually calmed down by the sheikh of the *zāwiya* and brought back to consciousness by his tapping on their back and wetting their faces with fresh water. After the *dhikr*, the *ghayṭa* player blew a few notes as an indication that a *ma'lūf* session was going to start soon. This time, instead of marching out of *zāwiya* to sing *ma'lūf* the brotherhood remained in *zāwiya*, waiting for some to join in and others to leave. While some of the men attending the *dhikr* remained seated on the floor waiting for the *ma'lūf* session to begin, others left the place where the session was going to be held and preferred to stay outside the *zāwiya*, chatting with friends and sipping coffee or mint tea.

Inside, the *sheikh ma'lūf* initiated a *nawba* accompanied by a *ghayṭa* player and a *kinjī* (sitting one on each side) and four to six *bandīr* players sitting round a lighted *kānūn*. A group of *raddāda* were sitting in a circle slightly away from the *bandīr* players and the *naqqārāt*. Other *ma'lūf* singers were sitting around that part of the

---

12 This part of the account occurs in the *zāwiya as-saghīra*.

zāwiya in which the session was being held, supporting their backs against the walls (see Figure 2.11 for an outline). Apart from leading the singing, the *sheikh ma'lūf* was also playing the *darabukka,* which in *zāwiya* performances replaces the *nawba* drum in the marking of the *dumm* stroke of the *īqā'*. The *sheikh ma'lūf* is considered as the most knowledgeable in this oral tradition, recognized for the huge amounts of *ma'lūf* texts that he has memorized and pronounced during such sessions.

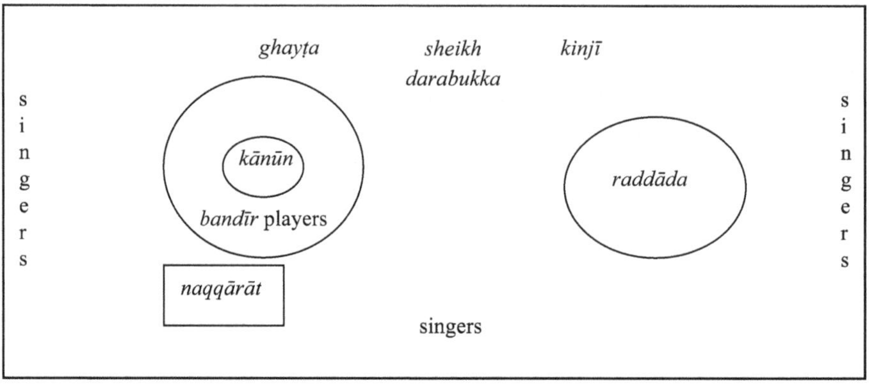

Figure 2.11 The set-up of a *ma'lūf* ensemble in *zāwiya*

According to informants to whom I had the chance to talk after the above session, the seventh such reunion signifies the farewell evening. They pointed out to me that the seventh *ḥaḍra* would follow the sequence of the previous ones with the difference that drinks and sweets would be much more plentiful than on the previous evenings. Also, for the final evening the *zāwiya* would invite a guest of honour from the neighbouring area. This might be a respected sheikh living in the vicinity or a member of the top echelon from the administrative authority. The same informants had also remarked that the final *ḥaḍra* would take longer than the previous ones, so much so that it might not even come to an end until the early hours of the following day. For this conclusive session the ensemble would perform the *nawba* called *nāḥ al-ḥamām* (The Pigeons' Lament), a *nawba* very central in the Libyan *ma'lūf* repertoire as it marks the end of any event involving *ma'lūf* both in *zāwiya* and outside. After this *nawba,* all those present would bid each other farewell, promising one another a similar appointment for the following year.

At this stage it is worth noting the fact that towards the end of the 1980s and the beginning of the 1990s there were instances when *mawlid* parades as organized by the three *zawāyā* of the Old City were prohibited by the Libyan authorities. Such a measure was a response to the opposition that had emerged in Libya during the course of the 1980s, which opposition had led to clashes with the Libyan forces. Religious groups such as the Sufis were considered by the Libyan authority as a threat to political stability and, therefore, they were not allowed to hold public events such as *mawlid* processions (Joffe 1988: 628). Moreover, incidents such as the *coup d'état* occurring in Tripoli in April and May 1980 that had resulted in a pitched battle in the streets of Tripoli close to Gaddafi's residence (Joffe 1988: 627) intensified the state's prohibition of and resistance to mass public manifestations. Nevertheless, other *ma'lūf* events taking place away from the above *mawlid* celebration continued without interruption.

As already indicated above, the *ma'lūf* has an important role in mainstream Tripolitanian weddings.[13] In Tripoli, weddings are normally held in August and September due to the fine weather at that time. A Tripolitanian wedding takes a week of celebrations in which folk music provided by *zamzamāt* (mentioned in Chapter 1), *ma'lūf* and other religious music are incorporated. The *ma'lūf* in a Tripolitanian wedding is still a very popular tradition and its absence marks the lack of something very much valued in these weddings. It is a tradition in Tripoli that on *laylat ad-dakhla*—that is, the wedding night that normally falls on a Thursday—the groom is taken to the *zāwiya* where he joins in a religious service that includes religious singing provided by a male choir accompanied by percussion and an *'ūd*. Towards the end of the service the congregation commences with *ma'lūf* singing that resumes outside in a kind of parade (or *tūsīla*) led by a hired *ma'lūf* ensemble, a parade which is gradually augmented as more friends and relatives, sometimes amounting to hundreds, join in. The *tūsīla* moves slowly and takes the longest route to the bride's house. Relatives and friends of the groom join in the singing or drumming of *ma'lūf*, their acquaintance with the repertory and overall performing aspects being the only prerequisites for them to join in. Wedding events in Tripoli, as in other North African countries, are commonly transformed into a neighbourhood event. Such ceremonies convey a semblance of family honour and prestige and, in the case of Libya, the *ma'lūf* adds to that sense. A *ma'lūf* ensemble in such a context would have the same set-up as the one during a *mawlid* parade. The *tūsīla* leads the groom to the house of the bride, who will be waiting for him together with her parents, relatives and guests. After the encounter of the couple and the reading of the *fatīḥa* (that is, the first chapter of the Qur'ān), the bride and the groom, accompanied by their families, leave for the *zaffa* (parade) that will take the couple to the hotel hosting the reception. At the hotel, men and women will continue celebrating in two separate halls. The *zaffa* takes about an hour, after which the *ma'lūf* ensemble gets paid and leaves.[14] Several sheikhs of *ma'lūf* in Tripoli have their own ensembles to provide this kind of service when requested.

A somewhat related ceremony in which *ma'lūf* may also be included is during a burial ceremony. *Ma'lūf* in funerals is normally employed when the deceased is a sheikh, a renowned Libyan scholar or a young bachelor. In such circumstances the coffin of the deceased is carried to the cemetery accompanied by *ma'lūf* singing. The processional ceremony is known as *tidrīsha*, during which religiously oriented parts of some *nawbāt* are sung without instrumental accompaniment. These parts

13 For more information regarding weddings in Tripoli see Abdelkafi 1994.

14 Such a service would normally cost the couple about 450LD (c.255 GBP).

would normally include verses traditionally attributed to Abū al-Hasan 'Alī ibn 'Abd Allāh al-Shushtarī (1212–69), a mystic Sufi poet known for his composition of *muwashshaḥ* and *zajal* verses. In the case of a young bachelor, the inclusion of *ma'lūf* would serve as a pseudo-*tūsīla*; in other words, the young deceased bachelor would be given the *ma'lūf* that he never had the chance to enjoy at his wedding.

History and *Shuyūkh al-Ma'lūf*

The continuation of the *ma'lūf* tradition in Libya has been possible thanks to the commitment of dedicated sheikhs who knew the tradition intimately and passed it on to others during performances in *zāwiya*, privately at home and sometimes even during extensive conversations in the middle of a market.[15] These were eminent artists who had sometimes contributed by adding their own texts and melodies to the core repertoire claimed to be of Andalusian origin. Each sheikh had his own way of teaching by heart the texts and melodies of the *ma'lūf*. Some sheikhs could hardly read or write, but still they preserved and transmitted huge quantities of *ma'lūf* texts and melodies, mainly through performance and teaching. Some sheikhs are still remembered for their particular fields of expertise; for instance, the quality of their voice or their skill in matching new and adapted words to *ma'lūf* melodies.

The history of the *ma'lūf* in Libya mainly evolves round the lives and deeds of deceased eminent sheikhs. Its early phases are mostly speculative while the more recent ones are somewhat overshadowed by accounts revolving around the lives of these sheikhs. Most of the accounts are anecdotes with the figure of the sheikh as the protagonist. For some *ma'lūf* aficionados, and other people as well, these accounts are the only history they know of the Libyan *ma'lūf*. These are anecdotes passed on orally from father to son and from sheikh to student. They are also recounted to receptive audiences during state-sponsored festivals , and retold to friends before and after a *ma'lūf* session in zāwiya. Such anecdotes are sometimes sentimentally intensified with personal memories expressed with a deep sense of nostalgia—the kind of nostalgia that embraces a past that will never return but which should nevertheless be an inspiration for the present.

The history of the *ma'lūf* in Libya may be divided into two main phases. The first phase covers the period preceding the setting up of the first modern *ma'lūf* ensemble in 1964 by the renowned Libyan musician Hassan Araibi, whilst the second one covers the period following that event, a period mainly characterized by state-subsidized projects intended to revive and preserve the *ma'lūf* tradition. Whilst the present section sheds light on historical aspects from the former phase, the latter phase is discussed in more detail in the subsequent chapter. The same

---

[15] This section served as the basis for a paper that I presented during a conference on Arabic and Jewish strophic poetry held in London at the School of Oriental and African Studies (SOAS) between the 8 and 10 October 2004, which paper was eventually published in the proceedings of the same conference (see Ciantar 2006).

section aims to show how the history of *ma'lūf* in Libya is a history of individual lives and, therefore, is strongly marked by sheikhs highly committed in transmitting this art. For this purpose, I rely on accounts that were narrated to me by *shuyūkh al-ma'lūf*, by aficionados who regularly participate in every *ma'lūf* activity both in *zāwiya* and outside, and by both amateur and professional researchers, some of whom are themselves involved in *ma'lūf* performances. These are people whose enthusiasm for this art has been unceasing since the time they were first introduced to it. Some were even instructed in *ma'lūf* by sheikhs who will be mentioned here; they were always keen to mention their masters at any opportunity. In the Libyan *ma'lūf*, as in many musical traditions, who you learn your music with is extremely important, because it enhances your musical status through a variety of means that may include the evocation of exceptional performances, models of commitment and, sometimes, even perceptions of unique vocal timbres and interpretations.

The advent of the *ma'lūf* in Libya is still subject to speculation. The general opinion is that no one knows exactly how and when this tradition reached the country. What has been written on the matter thus far reiterates what has been passed on orally from one generation to another and, eventually, what I was told during the interviews that I conducted in Libya. Some Libyan scholars of *ma'lūf* attribute the beginning of this art in Libya to the presence in the country of the *'Īsāwiyya* Sufi brotherhood related to Sidi Muhammad Bin 'Aysa (c.1535). The preservation of this tradition has been maintained by this brotherhood since the arrival in Tripoli of Sheikh Muhammad Alam Banram el-Fasi in the mid-sixteenth century. It was at this time that the first *zāwiya*, known as the *zāwiya al-kabīra* (the grand *zāwiya*), was founded in the Bāb al-Huriya neighbourhood of Tripoli.[16] Over the years it was the *'Īsāwiyya* brotherhood who maintained the tradition of the *ma'lūf* in Libya, as argued above.

A popular Libyan belief attributes the early traces of *ma'lūf* text in Libya to the presence of the Sufi poet Shushtarī (mentioned above) who, according to popular legend, spent some time in Libya on his journey to Egypt. It is believed that Shushtarī was the first to compose *zajal* verses on religious themes (Scheindlin 1998: 716). *Zajal* poems found in two of Shushtarī's manuscripts in Cairo and Aleppo include the melodic and rhythmic modes in which the same verses had to be sung (Farmer 1957: 476).[17] When referring to Shushtarī's poetry, Alvarez (2006: 23) writes that his songs 'bring the imagery of secular Hispano-Arabic poetry into a religious context, constantly calling on the listener to look beyond the illusions and deceptions of this world and perceive the divine in all of its manifestations'. The following are three *ma'lūf* lines from Libya sung to *maqām hussayn* attributed to al-Shushtarī:

ja't bil-āḥtuqār *aliy al-mālik al-'āliy*
yāmaqīyl al-'athār *muwlāy ajbar hālīy*

[16] Nowadays this *zāwiya* is situated in Tripoli's Madīna al-Qadīma.

[17] For more information about Al-Shushtarī's *zajal* verses see Stern 1974: 89.

I humbly appeal	to the supreme King
To lift me	from my pitfall and restore me

[author's translation]

Whether religious *zajal* verses found in the Libyan *ma'lūf* and attributed to Shushtarī were brought to Libya by him or by someone else is not yet determined. What is certain, though, is the fact that these verses are amongst the most treasured and beloved verses in the Libyan *ma'lūf*. It is as if their possible source of attribution enriches them both with the aura of the 'authentic', as well as with all the sentimental nuances that whatever is believed to be 'authentic' owns.

Another more generalized and more popular speculation for this transmission claims that the *ma'lūf* entered Libya through the presence of Andalusians who had moved into the country from Tunisia, Libya's closest neighbour, during the seventeenth century. This is considered as very possible in Libya, since Libya always served as a route of transit between Tunisia and Egypt. Evidence of this musical cross-fertilization includes some melodies found in the Libyan *ma'lūf* that are either very similar or identical to melodies in the *ma'lūf* of Tunisia. This has sometimes led scholars of Arab music to believe that there is no *ma'lūf* in Libya, and that any traces of it are entirely Tunisian. For instance, on proposing a doctoral thesis on the Libyan *nawba* at the University of Arts in Cairo towards the end of the 1980s, El Sibaei was told by the thesis committee that there was no *ma'lūf* in Libya and that 'any Libyan *ma'lūf* was not Libyan but Tunisian'; eventually, his work proved the existence of a repertory evidently distinct, even though with some commonalities, from the Tunisian one. Such an instance reveals how the Libyan *ma'lūf* was sometimes placed by some non-Libyan music scholars on the periphery of the core Andalusian tradition.

For musically proficient listeners acquainted with this art, the Libyan *ma'lūf* may be seen as an aggregate of Tunisian, Turkish and Egyptian influences. Discussion in this vein adduces geographical evidence (such as the positioning of Libya between Tunisia and Egypt) and historical facts (such as the colonization of Libya by the Ottomans); it also involves accounts of sheikhs having borrowed texts and melodies from colonizers and neighbouring countries. For instance, Sheikh Jamāl ad-Dīn al-Mīlādī (1881–1963) is known to have composed verses to Tunisian and Egyptian melodies; these verses eventually became part of the repertoire of Libyan *ma'lūf*. Sheikh Jamāl worked as an administrator with the Ottoman Military in Tripoli. He was also a jurist and a follower of the *Qādiriyya* dervish order, as is apparent from a *ma'lūf* poem allegedly composed by him with the title *ya jilānī ṭūl mā 'ishtu* (Oh Jilāniy, as Long as I Live). Sheikh al-Mīlādī composed this poem in honour of Abdulkader al-Jilāniy, the founder of the same *Qādiriyya* order. The melodic source of this poem was a Tunisian song beginning with the words *a'zah wa al'ab* (Jump and Play). Sheikh al-Mīlādī also composed *ma'lūf* texts based on Egyptian tunes in the form of *mu'āraḍāt* (plural of *mu'āraḍā*; pastiche verses).[18] As understood here, the making of a *mu'āraḍa*

[18] Information provided by Sheikh Hakim Yahya, 18 July 2003.

implies the making of a new poem that follows the rhyme, metre and melody of another well-known song.[19] In this regard, Stern (1974: 45–6) observes that this was a well-established literary practice in classical Arabic poetry, as I shall also show in the case of Libya. With reference to the setting of new text to existing tunes, which we may also hypothesize as applicable to the Libyan *mu'āraḍāt*, Wright (1993: 1042–3) notes the following:

> A degree of flexibility would in any case be required in a situation where an existing tune was used for a new poem which might not always fulfil the *mu'āraḍa* ideal of complete correspondence. Verse might tug at melody but, equally, musical imperatives could prevail, especially with the injection of sections of semantically void syllables, and even if this occurred but rarely, the fundamental independence of the melody would rule out the possibility of adducing musical factors in deciding between the respective merits of quantity versus stress in prosody.

The employment of non-sense syllables in the Libyan *ma'lūf*, evident in some *mu'āraḍāt*, had in more recent times led some Libyan sheikhs to substitute the same syllables with religious text that they thought was more appropriate to the rites in which the same text would be sung. As I shall show later on in this section, the substitution of text with religiously oriented text was quite a common practice amongst Libyan sheikhs of the *ma'lūf*.

Some sheikhs are still recalled for their *mu'āraḍāt*. One whose name crops up frequently in discussions about *mu'āraḍāt* is Sheikh Ali Amin Sayala. Sheikh Ali was born in Tripoli in 1860. He was a man of letters who occupied several high-ranking religious and civil positions. According to the well-known *muwashshaḥāt* Libyan singer Ali Mansūr al-Ghannay,[20] Sheikh Ali was unpretentious in claiming authorship for his writing. His aspiration was to compose *mu'āraḍāt* for all the love-poetry texts found in the *ma'lūf*, changing them into texts in praise of the Prophet. He also wished to add some of his own verses to existing verses praising the Prophet, as he did in a *ma'lūf* text starting with the words *ya muhammad* (the same words of the *nawba* mentioned above). However, he was prevented from composing more *mu'āraḍāt* by Sheikh Muhammad Abdulsalam al-Faituri al-Misurati, who ordered him to cease tampering with the text of the *ma'lūf*; with due humility Sheikh Ali accepted al-Misurati's advice and stopped.

Historical accounts of the Libyan *ma'lūf* tell of sheikhs preserving and retrieving the 'authentic' repertory, and, paradoxically, contributing to the continuity of this tradition by composing and adding their own verses and melodies. In some instances, however, the inclusion of the 'new' was seen by some sheikhs as liable

---

19 For an insightful discussion on *mu'āraḍāt* see Almbladh 2006.

20 At the time of this research Ali Mansūr al-Ghannay was a teacher of *muwashshaḥāt* singing at Mā'had Jamāl Ad-Dīn Al-Mīlādī School of Music. This information was provided to me during an interview with him on 21 April 2003.

to distract attention from the 'old'; innovation was sometimes viewed as a threat to tradition, something that had to be opposed and possibly strongly resisted. The lives of two brothers, Sheikh Jamāl Muhammad and Sheikh Kamel Muhammad al-Ghādiy, are sometimes mentioned as examples of this particular tension. Sheikh Jamāl (born in Tripoli in 1903) was a skilful carpenter and learned *ma'lūf* under the tuition of Sheikh Muhammad Abu Rayana. He was known for his strong memory for *ma'lūf* text and his ongoing efforts in the dissemination of a great deal of extinct text. He used to send unknown *ma'lūf* texts, which only he had knowledge of, to a committee established by the Libyan Ministry of Culture in 1964 to compile and make recordings of *nawbāt* (see Chapter 3 for a detailed discussion regarding this committee). He supplied texts preserved only in his memory to this committee through Sheikh Ali Mankusa, who at that time was one of his *ma'lūf* apprentices. Sheikh Hassan Araibi, who at that time was also a member of this committee, remarked to me that the verses sent to them by Sheikh Jamāl were sometimes entirely unknown even to the eldest members of the committee.

A story related to this sheikh says that, in 1960, the followers of the *zāwiya* he used to attend asked him to meet in the evening to teach them *ma'lūf*. He showed no hesitation at all, so much so that he began to meet them twice a week (on Saturdays and Wednesdays). More than twenty followers used to attend his teaching sessions; he had veneration for the old heritage. Whilst he was always disposed to teach and share 'authentic' text with others, he used to strongly reject what he considered as the 'unscrupulous' attitude of some sheikhs in adding their own verses to the *ma'lūf*. This is reaffirmed by an anecdote about Sheikh Jamāl that is quite well known amongst *ma'lūf* aficionados. The story goes that one day some of his students brought him *ma'lūf* verses that they had been taught by his brother, Sheikh Kamel. He looked at them and told the students: 'If these verses are composed by him, then tell him to look for other places to make them popular, but if they are old texts, bring them to us to learn and make them known to the people.' As in the case of al-Misurati, Sheikh Jamāl used to tell his brother to stop adding his own text, because by doing that, Kamel would be working to the detriment of the 'authentic' text.[21]

Further accounts that concern the inclusion of 'new' text in the Libyan *ma'lūf* bring to the fore Sheikh Ali Hanka (1865/6–1959) who had allegedly composed *ma'lūf* verses in honour of the Prophet to be sung in *ma'lūf* wedding parades. As in the previous case, Hanka's initiatives were met with severe criticism, mostly from sheikhs who strongly rejected this practice.

Sheikh Jamāl's brother, Sheikh Kamel Muhammad al-Ghādiy (b.1908), was a goldsmith known for his fine engravings on jewellery, copper and brass. He mastered writing in both Arabic and Roman scripts and was known in Tripoli as a leading *zajal* poet, able to improvise extended verses with detailed descriptions of the circumstances of the event at which he would be singing. He was also a *qānūn*

---

21 Information provided to me during an interview with Ali Mansūr al-Ghannay on 5 August 2003.

(trapezoidal zither) and *'ūd* player, having learned to play the former under the instruction of a Jewish player who lived in Tripoli's Madīna al-Qadīma and the latter under the tuition of Mahmoud Shawkat al-Mabrouk, a renowned *'ūd* player at that time. Sheikh Kamel is also remembered for his *mu'āraḍāt*. Some *ma'lūf mu'āraḍāt* composed by Sheikh Kamel have been attributed to another renowned Libyan *sheikh ma'lūf* by the name of Sheikh Muhammad Abu Median. In order to avert criticism, Sheikh Kamel preferred not to claim these works as his own. He used to show his verses to Sheikh Omar el-Arabi al-Zanzuri, a language and religion scholar, so as to avoid falling into language errors or anything that could be considered abusive of religion.[22] Part of the aesthetic experience of the *ma'lūf* lies in the beauty of its text. A good performance of *ma'lūf* relies on verses that are fine in construction, pleasant in words and meanings, and enriched in beauty by elegant melodies. In this context the 'new' is only considered as acceptable within the 'old' if the former fits agreeably within it and maintains its identity.

The military march-like melodies of certain *nawbāt* (such as *nawba nāḥ al-ḥamām*) have led El Sibaei to attribute these melodies to Ottoman military music. According to him, some of these melodies suggest sources of 'expert' music-making such as that of the military bands regularly heard marching in the streets of Tripoli during the Ottoman occupation. The inclusion of Ottoman melodies in the Libyan *ma'lūf* evokes the figure of Sheikh Gheddur Afandi, known for having included such melodies in *ma'lūf*. He was a prominent *sheikh ma'lūf* and Qur'ān chanter who served as *imām* (religious leader) to a battalion of the Ottoman Army in Tripoli. Accounts related to this sheikh refer to the fact that he was also married to a Turkish woman. This is sometimes said to emphasize the close links that the sheikh had with Turkish culture, and that he was exposed to its assimilation. Sheikh Gheddur used to take his annual leave in the month of the *mawlid*, during which period the followers of the *zāwiya al-kabīra* always prepared a residence (*waqf*) close to the mosque, to be occupied by the sheikh and his family. It is said that one evening, when Sheikh Gheddur attended the evening's *ma'lūf* session, he said to those around him: 'I didn't come to drink your tea', referring to his commitment to passing on the tradition and being of service to the *zāwiya* rather than just having a good time at its expense.

Anecdotes related to these sheikhs abound, with some of them emphasizing the memory required by this art. Particular sheikhs are still remembered for the huge amounts of *ma'lūf* text they possessed. *Ma'lūf* text in Libya is considered infinite—so much so that there is a popular Libyan saying: *al-ma'lūf kelma 'andek wa miyya 'and jārak* (the *ma'lūf*: a word belongs to you while a hundred words belong to your neighbour). Such a saying highlights the huge repertoire of poetic material in this tradition. One anecdote relates the story of Sheikh Khalifa Imhammed Farhat al-Rammash, born around 1893. He was fond of collecting texts, and had them written down. On one occasion Sheikh Khalifa met Sheikh Hassan al-Kamiy in a cattle market. Sheikh al-Kamiy greeted him and asked Sheikh Khalifa for

---

22 From an interview with Ali Mansūr al-Ghannay, 7 August 2003.

some *ma'lūf* verses that might be new to him. The latter recited verse after verse until there was no one left in the market. Then Sheikh Hassan, with his sense of humour, said: 'What shall I do tomorrow? What shall I slaughter?' 'Perhaps I should slaughter you!' replied Sheikh Khalifa with a possible indirect reference to his friend's relatively minimal knowledge of text when compared to his.[23] At this stage, it is worth mentioning the fact that what Sheikh Khalifa did in the market was rooted in an old Sufi practice and, therefore, the sheikh was possibly reviving a practice that had an old Sufi legacy. In this regard, Alvarez (2006: 24) notes that several literary Sufi writers explain the old Sufi practice of reciting and/or singing poetry in the market in terms of 'a spiritual discipline imposed on the future poet by Ibn Sab'īn, who was known for his extreme practice of poverty'. According to a modern account written by the Moroccan Sufi leader and scholar 'Abd al-'Azīz Ibn al-Siddīq, this practice was eventually imposed by Ibn Sab'īn on Shushtarī, who was also ordered by his master 'to take a *bandīr* … and sing among the lowly and the scorned in the souks' (Alvarez 2006: 24). Understood more widely, the renouncement of the material world will consequently provide to the illiterate or semi-literate rural mystic the 'unfathomable wisdom through God's grace which will then result into [sic] mystical and poetic inspiration' (Alvarez 2006: 24).

In the Libyan *ma'lūf*, stories that link particular texts with specific events may be more personal and therefore more nostalgic. For instance, Shushtarī verses sung unaccompanied during burial rites brought to Hassan Araibi's mind the vision of the moribund Sheikh Khalifa al-Rammash the day before he died. When Araibi was visiting him at the hospital, the sheikh turned to him and said: 'Tomorrow, Hassan, the funeral will be in the afternoon. I want a Shushtarī poem.' Araibi answered that the sheikh was still needed, and wished him to be well again. But the old man's words were right because, as he had anticipated, he died the day after. His burial rite included the singing of *ma'lūf* Shushtarī verses as he had requested. At this stage it is worth noting that the most common themes sung at funerals are songs of supplication like the ones quoted from Shushtarī in the previous section. Funeral *ma'lūf* poetry also includes verses of invocation, of longing for the place of the Prophet Muhammad, as well as songs of prayers and obedience to the Prophet.

Another eminent deceased sheikh often mentioned in the interviews I carried out in Libya was Sheikh Muhammad Abu Rayana (1906–1968). Hassan Araibi, who worked closely with Sheikh Abu Rayana in the above mentioned committee established by the Libyan Ministry of Culture, described him as a humble and enduring man. He used to say that 'Whoever wants to commit himself to *ma'lūf* must be like a straw mat with everybody walking upon it', a statement that refers to the strong commitment required by this art and the disposition it entails for the needs of others. Although Sheikh Muhammad is mainly mentioned for his brilliant memory of *ma'lūf* text, his sweet vocal tone and his dedication in teaching *ma'lūf* accentuates the fact that he used to keep the *nawba* going for not more than half an hour. Hassan Araibi remembers Sheikh Muhammad saying that he wanted to see

23 From an interview with Sheikh Sālem Stuka, 2 August 2003.

the participating *bandīr* players and singers longing for more *ma'lūf* rather than leaving the session exhausted and displeased. This shows that the shortening of the *nawba* in Libya was not only the consequence of aesthetics imposed on it by the recording industry, as I shall highlight in the next chapter, but it was also the result of intrinsic aesthetics, moulded in traditional contexts like that of *zāwiya* and, therefore, based on the feedback of in-house musicians. This and other anecdotes are not only seminal components in the history of the *ma'lūf* in Libya but, more than that, provide a deeper meaning to the musical tradition of our concern, one that shows the *ma'lūf* as more than merely an activity of performance.

Musical and Poetical Content

The Libyan *nawba* exists in two forms: the short *nawba* form called *barwal nawba*, and the longer, more elaborate *nawba* known as *muṣaddar nawba*. Such a distinction is somewhat similar to that found in Algeria, where the Algerian *nawba al-inqilābāt* is considered as a kind of mini-*nawba* that, like the Libyan *nawba*, borrows some of the rhythmic modes from the large-scale *nawba* whilst excluding others.[24] The present section deals first with the formal structure of the *muṣaddar nawba* and then with that of the *barwal nawba*, both as performed by a *ma'lūf az-zāwiya* ensemble. It also includes a brief discussion of the poetical content of the *ma'lūf*, intended only to provide a background for this aspect rather than as an in-depth scrutiny. To illustrate the structure of the *muṣaddar nawba* I take as an example *nawba nāḥ al-ḥamām*, already referred to above. The transcribed extracts are taken from a live performance by a *ma'lūf az-zāwiya* ensemble called Firqat ash-Sheikh Mustafiy Abu Jirād (Sheikh Abu Jirād Ensemble).[25] This performance took place during the Tripoli festival of *ma'lūf* and *muwashshaḥāt* held at the Markezia Gardens in central Tripoli. Here, a traditional ensemble (in this case employing an indoor *zāwiya* set-up) refers to an ensemble consisting of a sheikh assisted by a *kinjī*, a male choir (*raddāda*), *ghayṭa*, *bandīr*, *darabukka* and *naqqārāt*.

The most performed *nawbāt* in Libya total eighteen in number. Compared to the number of commonly performed *nawbāt* in other *nawba* traditions of the Maghreb the Libyan case shows a lower rate of decline. The eighteen Libyan *nawbāt* are categorized into 10 *muṣaddar nawba* and 8 *barwal nawba* (Rajūba 1993: 3). In the Libyan *nawba* one finds four *īqā'āt*: *muṣaddar* (8/4), *barwal* (8/8), *murabba'* (6/4) and *'allājī* (6/8) (see Example 2.2 below). *Ma'lūf* in *īqā'āt murabba'* and *'allājī* are hardly performed nowadays.

---

[24] When referring to the Algerian *nawba* Reynolds (2000: 73) notes that 'in Tlemcen … it is commonly asserted that the "great suites" [*nawbāt*] represent the oldest material while a secondary repertory known as "transformations" or "rotations" [*inqilābāt*] represents more recent additions'.

[25] The performance was held on 4 August 2003.

Example 2.2 The *īqā'āt* of the Libyan *ma'lūf*

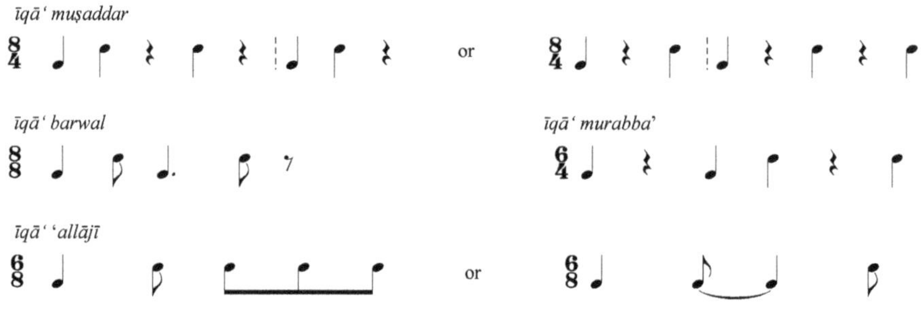

The *maqāmāt* employed by the Libyan *ma'lūf* are *rāst*, *muhayyar*, *hussayn*, *nawā*, *asba'ayn* and *sīkah*. For instance, *nāh al-ḥamām* unfolds in *maqām muhayyar* (see Example 2.3) and initiates on *īqā' muṣaddar*. Since the first song in this *nawba* belongs to *īqā' muṣaddar*, the entire *nawba* is categorized as *muṣaddar nawba*. When compared to the other *nawba* traditions of the Maghreb, as we shall see later on in this section, the Libyan *nawba* emerges as somewhat simpler in structure and employing fewer *īqā'āt*.

Example 2.3 *Maqām muhayyar*

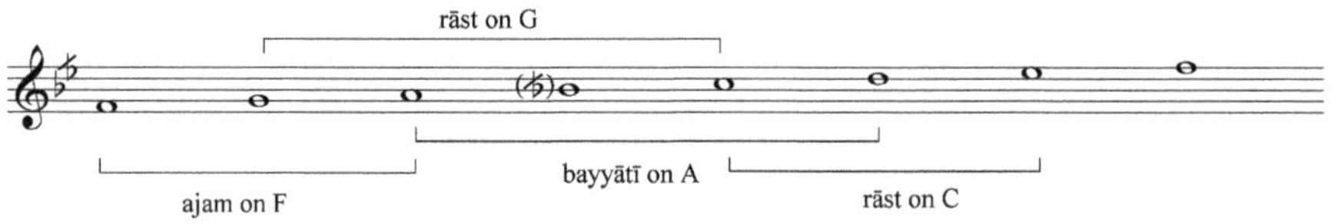

The *muṣaddar nawba* begins with an introductory section consisting of alternating solo instrumental improvisations on the *ghayṭa* and the vocal improvisations of the sheikh. While an improvisation on the *ghayṭa* is known as *istikhbār* (announcement), the vocal improvisation of the sheikh is called *istiftāḥ* (opening). At this stage it is worth noting that the *istiftāḥ* is also found in the Tunisian *nawba* whilst the term *istikhbār* is used in the Algerian *nawba al-inqilābāt*. In the *istikhbār*, the *ghayṭa* player introduces the *maqām* in which the entire *nawba* unfolds. As already stated, *nāḥ al-ḥamām* belongs to *maqām muhayyar*—a *maqām* that takes its name from the central note d^2, called *muhayyar* in Arab music. Emphasis on this note is then followed by a descending movement; in fact, in Arab music theory this *maqām* is known as a 'descending *maqām*'. As Example 2.3 shows, *maqām muhayyar* comprises four *ajnas* (sets, plural of *jins*). Apart from an assemblage of notes, a *maqām* may also be considered in practice as a combination of *ajnas*. In the case of *maqām muhayyar*, for instance, one finds the lower trichordal *jins* known as *ajam* on f^1 and an upper tetrachordal *jins* called *rāst* on c^1. This *maqām* also includes two overlapping (or secondary) tetrachordal *ajnas*, namely *rāst* on g[1] and *bayyati* on a[1]. The dominant note (or *ghammaz* in Arabic) is the starting note of the upper *jins*, which in this case is c[2].

The *istikhbār* in Example 2.4 shows an undulating melodic movement starting on d[1], extending up an octave to d[2] and gradually descending back to d[1] after several soundings of d[2]. This *istikhbār* is mainly characterized by a continuous melodic line composed of several phrases uninterrupted by any breath-taking in between. The whole process is supported by a technique known as circular breathing. Through this technique the player uses the pressure of the puffed cheeks to expel air through the double reed while simultaneously inhaling through the nostrils (Stock 1996a: 53). Most of the phrases round up on g[1], which in itself is the key-note of the secondary tetrachord *rāst* on g[1]. Through these repeated cadential movements the note g[1] becomes a central pitch to which the whole structure of this improvised opening returns again and again. At this stage, one may also note the economy in the melodic material employed by the *ghayṭa* player throughout the *istikhbār*.

Example 2.4 The *istikhbār* to *nawba nāḥ al-ḥamām*

Following the *istikhbār*, the sheikh of the ensemble sings an *istiftāḥ* by employing material already sounded by the *ghayṭa* in the *istikhbār*. In the *istiftāḥ*, the sheikh improvises a verse of praise (*madīḥ*) along the *maqām* established by the *ghayṭa* (see Example 2.5 below). Traditionally, it is the sheikh who sings the *istiftāḥ*; however, the *istiftāḥ* is sometimes entrusted to that member of the

Example 2.5 The *istiftāḥ*

ensemble with the finest voice. The *istiftāḥ* is a good opportunity for the singer to show off his vocal qualities and his ability to explore the characteristics of the *maqām* through melismas and other vocal techniques. On certain occasions, such as during *ma'lūf* festivals, an *istiftāḥ* is sung as a free-standing improvisation by leading singers present amongst the audience who use this form to demonstrate their knowledge of the *maqām* and their skilful voices. The *istiftāḥ* in Example 2.5 employs material introduced in the *istikhbār*, such as the frequent cadencing on g^1, a stepwise melody with an overall undulating melodic movement, and the reiteration of certain motifs. The first cadential closure on g^1 is answered by a short phrase on the *ghayṭa*, after which the singer resumes his improvisation. Following an extensive *ghayṭa* interpolation (not transcribed), the singer continues with the *istiftāḥ* in a kind of singing that is both syllabic and melismatic. As his voice warms up, the overall rhythmic content gets denser and vocal 'ornamentation' becomes more frequent and elaborate. The resultant overall effect is that of an increase in tempo with note a^1 at the end serving as a lead-in for the *muṣaddar* section.

After the initial solos, the whole ensemble joins in for the first section known as *muṣaddar*. In this section, as in the sections that follow, the sheikh selects *ma'lūf* songs belonging to the same *īqā'* and *maqām* and spins them into a section. In the case of *nāḥ al-ḥamām* the *muṣaddar* rhythm is divided into 5+3. However, in other cases this rhythm may take the division of 3+5, either division being determined by the down-stroke *dumm* of the *darabukka*. Example 2.6 below shows the first hemistich of the first song in the *muṣaddar* section with the *muṣaddar* rhythm grouped into 5+3 underneath. The *nawba* makes use of the call and response form, with the sheikh singing a line (call) that is then repeated in response by the *raddāda*. In a way, the convenience of the call and response form lies in the fact that the sheikh may include in his singing lines which might be new to the *raddāda* but which could still be sung by them, as all that is involved is a repetition of the sheikh's pronouncement. The song is repeated, in strophic form, several times before the ensemble proceeds to another song.

The singing employed in the present interpretation of *nāḥ al-ḥamām* is mostly syllabic. When compared to the solo singing of the sheikh, the choral replies emerge as relatively less embellished due to the limitations imposed by the dimension of group performance. The *ghayṭa* accompanies the solos of the sheikh in a heterophonic style and drops out for the choral responses. Other songs will follow until the *muṣaddar* leads on to the *murakkaz*. This is the stage at which an increase in tempo is discernible. For instance, in the present interpretation the overall tempo accelerates from approximately 76 crotchet beats per minute in the *muṣaddar* to 115 crotchet beats per minute in the *murakkaz*. At this point, new songs are included while the rhythm remains that of the *muṣaddar*. Here the music becomes more rapid, preparing the listeners for the fast tempo of the *barwal* section that unfolds in a fast 8/8 rhythmic cycle.

As in the *muṣaddar*, the *barwal* section employs songs belonging to *maqām muhayyar* but this time unfolding in *īqā' barwal* (see Example 2.7 below). The tempo becomes progressively livelier until it reaches the delirium of the finale.

Example 2.6 The first hemistich of the *muṣaddar* section

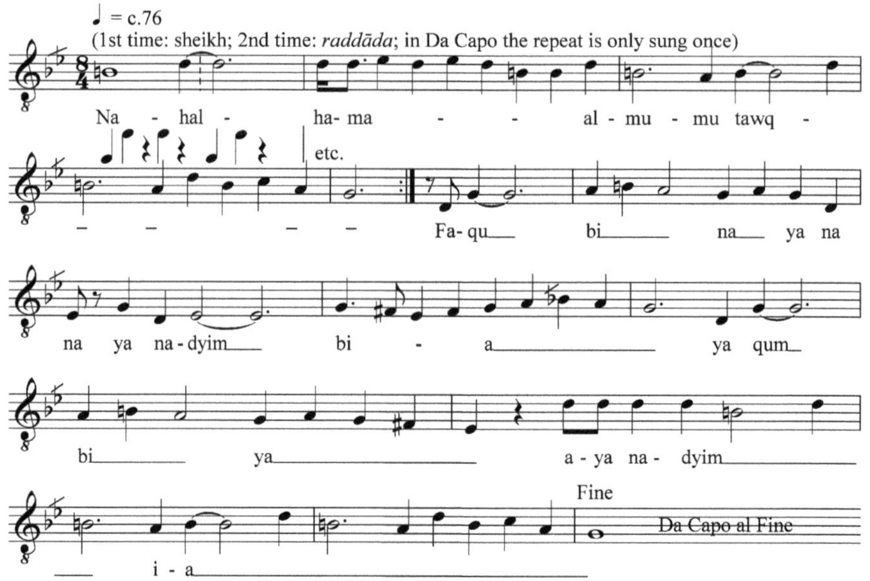

Example 2.7 The initial hemistich of the first song in *barwal*

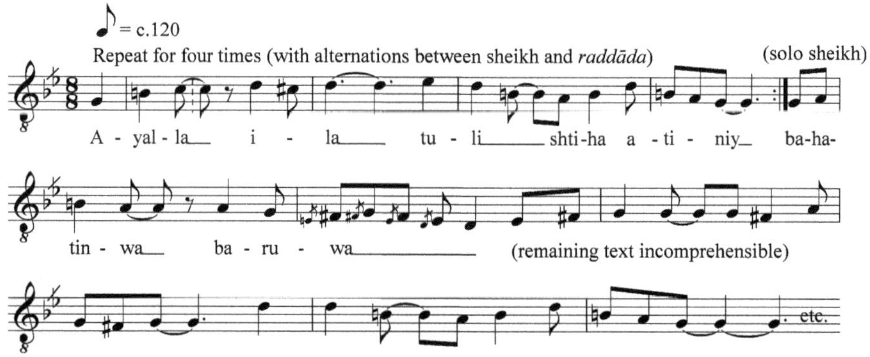

At this stage the same line is repeated several times and eventually comes to a *rallentando* that signals the last rendition.

As in the *muṣaddar nawba*, the *barwal nawba* opens up with an *istikhbār* and *istiftāḥ*. The latter leads on to the inclusion of an unaccompanied *qaṣīda* or *madīh* sung by the *raddāda*. After this comes the *barwal* section composed of *ma'lūf* songs belonging to the same *maqām*, with each line sung first by the sheikh, accompanied on the *ghayṭa*, and then repeated by the *raddāda*. Songs in this *īqā'* resume till the end of the *nawba*, with the music accelerating till the end. Such an increase in tempo is occasionally indicated, if not also initiated, by one of the *bandīr* players beating his *bandīr* in cross-rhythm with the consistent rhythmic pattern of the other percussionists. A *barwal nawba* may have the same duration as a *muṣaddar nawba* though with the deduction of the *muṣaddar* section and, as already indicated above, the inclusion of an unaccompanied *qaṣīda* or *madīh*.

When referring to the rapport between poetic form and music in the Libyan *ma'lūf*, Guettat (1980: 231) notes that the melodic structure is very much regulated by the demands of the poetic form and, therefore, the former employs several combinations of calls and responses to accommodate the demands of the latter in a predominantly repetitive manner. The text is highly enriched by detailed descriptions and the deep meanings that go with it. The text of *nawba nāḥ al-ḥamām*, for example, is very much appreciated for the way descriptions are portrayed and the meaning/s it conveys. The murmuring of the pigeons coming from the trees early in the morning, for instance, is understood as being either singing or lamenting; however, the text shows uncertainty in this. These are metaphorical descriptions that carry several meanings within them and, therefore, a full interpretation of them is not always possible. As already noted, in Sufi literature references to wine convey undiscovered knowledge, while intoxication refers to the exaltation of God. Due to references to wine, the opening lines of *nāḥ al-ḥamām* belong to that genre of Arabic poetry known as *sha'r al-faṣiyh*, that is, eloquent poetry. The text of the same song also includes lines of supplication (*ibtihāl*), a theme very common in Sufi literature; some of these lines are even taken from the Qur'ān. The following literal translation from *nāḥ al-ḥamām* illustrates the amalgamation of the above themes:

nāḥ al-ḥamām al-muṭawwaq	*fa-qum binā ya nadīm*
nashrubu sharāban murawwaq	*min ash-sharābi l-qadīm*
min khamra 'attaqūhā	*sahbā ṭabrā s-saqīm*
'arūsa qad jallūhā	*fī jinḥ al-layl al-bahīm*
Allāh qad qāla qawlan	*fī l-kitāb al-qadīm*
nabbī 'ibādī bi-'ānnī	*'anā al-ghafūr ar-raḥīm*
yā ghāriqan fī l-khaṭāyā	*wa al-qalb minhu saqīm*
qad qāla rabbī ta'ālā	*wa-qawluhu l-mustaqīm*
nabbī 'ibādī bi-'ānnī	*'anā al-ghafūr ar-raḥīm*
yā mani ghtarra jahlan	*fī kulli wādī yahīm*
lam yakhshā rabban 'aẓīman	*wa fī al-khaṭāyā muqīm*
qad qāla 'inna 'adhābī	*huwa l-'adhābu l-'ālīm*

The encircled pigeons lamented	stand by us Oh drinking companion
We drink a straying drink	from the old drink
From mature wine	the reddish gold of the sick
They have come for a bride	in the darkness of the night
Allāh had said a word	in the old book

I am the prophet of my slaves	I am the merciful forgiver
Oh you the one drowned in sins	(and) the heart is sick of it
He had said, 'Be He exalted'	(and) the saying of the righteous
The prophet of my slaves is my builder	I am the most merciful God
Oh who was ignorantly misled	in every valley he wanders
Why does he fear hostile interests	(and) in sins he dwells
About my anguish he said	it is a grievous torment

[author's translation]

As the above example shows, each line is divided into two hemistichs in a kind of strophe known as *bayt*. In this regard, Jalajel (2007) notes that:

> the metrical structure of the *bayt* is such that the two hemistichs produce a natural place for a caesura right in the middle of the line. The Arab poet has many options as to how to exploit this caesura artistically.

A Sufi theme featured frequently in the text of the Libyan *ma'lūf* is that of praise in honour of Sufi leaders (*madīḥ aṣḥāb aṭ-ṭarīq*). For instance, Sheikh Kamel Muhammad al-Ghādiy composed such verses in honour of Sidi Muhammed Bin 'Aysa from Meknas, the founder of the *'Īsāwiyya* Sufi order. The following verses are taken from *nawba ya Bin 'Aysa* (a *nawba* in *maqām nawā* and *īqā' muṣaddar*).

Yā bin 'īsā ya waliyy meknās	*ifza' w-hizz er-rās*
Yā bin'īsā yā quṭb el-āsrār	*ifza'-lnā bi-llāh*

Oh Bin 'Īsā oh guardian of Meknās	protect and excite the head
Oh Bin 'Īsā oh keeper of secrets	protect us through Allāh

[author's translation]

Another theme commonly found in the Libyan *ma'lūf* is that of love (*ghazal*). In his love poetry the poet expresses his deep passion for his fascinating sweetheart to whom he attributes all perfections, as in the following lines (performed on *maqām hussayn* and *īqā' barwal*):

na'shaq ma'shūq	*bi-ḥusn badī'*
ḥluww esh-shmāyil	*ẓarf wa- mashākil*

I love a sweetheart,	unique in her beauty,
With delicate traits,	charming and yet arrogant

[author's translation]

As argued above, the text of *ma'lūf* passed through several changes. When some sheikhs found explicit wooing and sensuous meanings unbefitting religious

Sufism, they tried to alter and 'improve' such texts to suit the Sufi meaning. One example is the following:

wa al-mā' lil hiffān	*wa al-yusr ba'd l-'usr*
wa-janntu r-riḍwān	*ba'da l-'adhāb al-'ākbar*
Water for the dead thirsty	comfort after difficult times
The pleasant paradise	after the great suffering
	[author's translation]

These lines were modified as follows in order to attain religious meaning:

al-'afuw lil raḥman	*wa al-yusr ba'd l-'usr*
wa-janntu r-riḍwān	*ba'da l-'adhāb al-'ākbar*
The Supreme is merciful	wealth will follow poverty
The pleasant paradise	after the great punishment
	[author's translation]

All these instances show how the 'authentic' *ma'lūf* text changed over the years so as to meet Sufi and religious aspirations. In a way this eased the inclusion of such text in the Libyan *nawba* and, consequently, its ubiquitous employment in Sufi rites and ceremonies.

Conclusion

The present chapter unfolded in accordance with how I came to understand the Libyan *ma'lūf* tradition, mainly in the context of the theory and practices of Arab music, its various links with the North African *nawba*, and also recognition of the unique traits in the Libyan tradition as continuously evaluated within the wider framework described above. The way the *ma'lūf* was presented to me was very much supported by the aura of 'authenticity', even though the anecdotes sketched out above of sheikhs believed to have tampered with *ma'lūf* text and melodies could mar this seemingly 'smooth' link with the 'authenticity' of *al-andalus*. 'The *ma'lūf* is an "old heritage" (*turāth qadīm*),' was the common aphorism—a statement that in most cases developed into extensive discussions unfolding within a blurred distinction between the present and the past, what is 'typically' Libyan and widely Maghrebian, and what is 'faithful' to the tradition and modified and, therefore, dubious. Even if the subsequent chapter deals primarily with the *ma'lūf* out of its *zāwiya* context, a proper understanding of it is not possible without a discussion of the remote past, the more recent past and the amalgamation of both in the tradition of the present as practised nowadays in the *zāwiya* context.

The tradition of *ma'lūf* as portrayed in this chapter should serve as a frame of reference for questions raised in the subsequent chapters, questions such as: To what extent are 'modern' performances of *ma'lūf* linked to the practices in *zāwiya*-related performances? How do aficionados and performers mediate their involvement and artistry between 'old' and 'modern' sonorities and practices? Is traditional practice a point of reference for 'new' practice? Answering these questions will require an in-depth enquiry into the meanings endorsed in the *ma'lūf al-idhāʿa*; answers that will partially refer to the content of this chapter as the present work progresses.

Chapter 3

The *Ma'lūf al-Idhā'a*: Change, Continuity and Contemporary Practices

The year 1964 marks a milestone in the history of the *ma'lūf* in Libya. It was the year during which the *ma'lūf* stepped into the domain of musical 'professionalism' and, therefore, significant change was generated and made plausible. In the Libyan *ma'lūf* change generated processes and mechanisms that in themselves supported continuity, and in this sense change should be seen as the counterpart of continuity rather than its opposite. Here one notes that innovation came not to overshadow 'traditional' practices but rather to propose new musical performances and sonorities in line with the developments that had taken place years before in the *mūsīqā al-'arabiyya* (Arab music), or *al-turāth* (the heritage), of neighbouring Maghreb countries. Most of these innovations were modelled on Western musical practices, sometimes considered to symbolize musical 'progress' and elevation. Such developments included the rise of bigger ensembles, performing venues mostly associated with Western art concert venues, adherence to performing norms practised by Western symphony orchestras and the inclusion of Western instruments, as well as the placing of more emphasis on the role of the leader in the ensemble. Until the beginning of the 1960s these practices were inconceivable in the context of the Libyan *ma'lūf*, or, if thought of at all, those concerned lacked the necessary know-how for their implementation. Then, in 1964 Hassan Araibi, a well-known Libyan musician, began to put forward ideas of enriching the musical tradition with the hallmarks of 'high art', which he felt were not being reached in performances in *zāwiya*. This dovetails nicely with Merriam's (1964: 313) assertion that changes are sometimes welcomed 'because existing mechanisms do not provide enough of something that is valued'.

The Libyan *ma'lūf* tradition presents a situation in which the 'old' and the 'new' have their own respective niches and do not exist in opposition to each other, but rather coexist within complementary frameworks. For instance, no one in Tripoli expects a wedding *tūsīla* (the traditional parade described in Chapter 2) to be performed by a 'modern' *ma'lūf* ensemble; the sonority of *ma'lūf* expected at such an event is that of the *ma'lūf az-zāwiya*. On the other hand, it is normal practice for the Libyan *ma'lūf* to be exported abroad by the state and marketed by the recording industry under the stamp of 'classical' Arab music, that is, as performed by 'modern' ensembles with norms of performance practice modelled on Western practices. As noted in Chapter 2, the strong connection of this style of *ma'lūf* with the recording industry and broadcasting has given it the name of *ma'lūf al-idhā'a* (the broadcasting *ma'lūf*). Such equilibrium in importance maintained by a particular society can easily be missed by researchers alien to the music tradition under their investigation, who are sometimes very much influenced by the circumstances in which they find themselves carrying out fieldwork. Such circumstances are sometimes shaped by subtle or unconscious pressures exerted on the researcher, not only by what people think and say about their music but also by the several signifiers (or forms) of change that surround the researcher and the emphasis put on them.

The first time I visited Libya I was treated as if I were a diplomat, with a pre-planned programme of formal visits, and a driver and a mentor at my disposal. The first commitment was a visit to the National Centre for the Research and Study of Arabic Music (based in Tripoli), a state-subsidized institution that has affiliated to it a 'modern' *ma'lūf* ensemble called Firqat al-Ma'lūf wa al-Muwashshaḥāt wa al-Alḥān al-ʿArabiyya (The Ensemble of *Ma'lūf*, *Muwashshaḥāt* and Arab Melodies). There I met Hassan Araibi, chair of the Institute and music director of the ensemble. During my first meeting with him he explained to me how in 1964 he founded a new *ma'lūf* ensemble different from the traditional *zāwiya* ensemble. He explained how this offered an alternative to the 'traditional' sonority by the inclusion of instruments such as the violin, cello and double bass, and how listeners at the first concert of his newly established ensemble rejected these instruments. During that meeting the *ma'lūf* was presented to me as something that had changed drastically over the years. My first impression was that in today's Libya the *ma'lūf az-zāwiya* was just a relic of the past, with a very minimal place, if any. His discussion, focused on the post-1964 innovations, led me to think that in Libya there was currently only one *ma'lūf*, that is, the *ma'lūf al-idhā'a*, as recorded in studios and broadcast on radio and TV, not the 'raw' one as performed in *zāwiya*. After the meeting I was led to the rehearsal room downstairs, which was equipped with an amplification system, music stands with music on them in preparation for the next rehearsal and photographs on the wall accentuating the 'new' with very few traces of the 'old'.

Our subsequent meeting took place during a recording session that Araibi was holding with his ensemble at Qatar al-Fajr al-Jadīd recording studio (see Figure 3.1). The sound engineer was busy balancing the music in the control room, while Araibi and his ensemble were performing in the studio. After each take Araibi would put his *'ūd* on a chair and approach the sound engineer to discuss with him balancing matters and possible resetting of microphones for an enhanced sound quality. Here, I was given an explanation of the recording process, and how the members of the ensemble are paid for their rehearsing and recording sessions. I was told that the ensemble was recording music for Libyan TV and that everything had to be ready within a week so that a TV programme on the *ma'lūf* of Libya, in which the ensemble would have a prominent role, could be aired as scheduled.

A month after that, I was invited to travel with the same ensemble to the Tunisian town of Testour, where the ensemble was to participate in a week-long festival of *ma'lūf*. On the afternoon following the day of our arrival there the ensemble gathered in the refectory of the hostel where we were staying for a rehearsal in preparation for that evening's performance. Hassan's son Yusuf, a young man in his mid-twenties and also a violin player in his father's group,

Figure 3.1 At Qatar al-Fajr al-Jadīd recording studio

led the rehearsal in the absence of his father. He conducted the ensemble from a standing position, taking the role of a Western orchestral conductor rather than leading the ensemble seated like his father. These early events emphasized change rather than continuity, an impression that was strongly accented not only by Hassan Araibi but also by the circumstances within which I initially found myself immersed.

During my ongoing fieldwork, people explained to me how certain prominent sheikhs of *ma'lūf* had rejected the *nawba* as restyled by Hassan Araibi and his newly established ensemble in the 1960s. In these conversations no one spoke of continuity; continuity was something left to me to look for and explore. The *ma'lūf az-zāwiya* and the *ma'lūf al-idhā'a* seemed to me so distinct from each other that, initially, I was given the impression that this ensemble founded in 1964 had not only proposed new performance practices and sonorities but had even created an entirely different kind of *ma'lūf* from that traditionally performed in *zāwiya*. My early perceptions of the tradition were that the *ma'lūf az-zāwiya* differed from the *ma'lūf al-idhā'a* in melodies, texts, rhythms and many other ways. It took me some time to realize that most of the new was actually a 'modernized' version of the old, and that there was a link between the two. But even after these considerations, Hassan Araibi and his ensemble continued to represent change to me, and since most of my fieldwork trips developed in constant rapport with this ensemble, I was somehow led to believe that there was a kind of tension between change and continuity, which, as I explained above, was not the case.

This chapter begins by presenting a survey of the modernization processes that had taken place in the domain of Arab music in Egypt, Morocco, Algeria and Tunisia prior to the modernization initiatives occurring in Libya. Such processes had their own impact on the modernization of the Libyan *ma'lūf.* The aim here is to put Araibi's efforts into the context of similar initiatives that had occurred previously in the region. Araibi's musical career and work will then be discussed in the second section, which will provide a context for his project within the wider scenario of Libya's social and political life in the early 1960s. At this stage, I shall also argue that Araibi's stature in Libya not only assisted him in proceeding with his innovations throughout the years, but also allowed him to gain prestige and power, which, in turn, he managed to exploit in order to maintain and nurture the changes initiated by him in 1964 and in other related projects. In this sense, the *ma'lūf* and the innovations brought to it transpired in an arena in which music, power, patronage and prestige were intermingled and manipulated—a kind of coalescence that, apart from self-benefit, also supported long-term subsidy and projects. The same section sheds light on Libya's cultural policies during the Gaddafi era and the impact of these on the *ma'lūf.* Such developments sustained the innovations initiated by Araibi. The subsequent section will then highlight issues such as: the individual musician vis-à-vis the formal set-up of both the institute and the ensemble to which he belongs; the *ma'lūf* as a commodity; recruitment and training; and rehearsal practices. Based on ethnographic commentary, this section will bring to light particular sonic and non-sonic worlds that surround the modern practice of the *ma'lūf* as it evolves within its institutional set-up. Such ethnography resumes in the fourth section in an attempt to analyse contemporary performance practices as they unfold within a sequence of events that precede and follow the actual performance. Finally, attention will shift to the music itself, with the main focus being Araibi's restyled *nawba* and the striking innovations brought to it.

The Modernization Process in Egypt, Morocco, Algeria and Tunisia

Hassan Araibi established the first modern *ma'lūf* ensemble in 1964 when he was head of the music section in the Libyan Broadcasting Centre. His initiatives were modelled on similar innovations that had occurred before in Tunisia with the foundation of the Rashīdiyya School and its ensemble, which were intended to preserve the Tunisian *ma'lūf* tradition. Araibi had undergone musical training at the Rashīdiyya, and his initiatives in modernizing the Libyan *ma'lūf* were modelled on what he had experienced there. Changes that had occurred in Libya and Tunisia in *al-turāth* were similar to changes noted in Egypt, Morocco and Algeria years before. In this sense, Libya's *ma'lūf* trajectory is very similar to those of its neighbours, yet also uniquely forged by its particular history.

El-Shawan (1985) explains how during the 1960s and 1970s Western music was strongly rooted in Egypt's musical life and how European residents had introduced Western music into Egypt during the nineteenth century. European music had been adopted and performed professionally by several generations of Egyptian musicians, one result being the splitting of Egypt's musical life by the 1960s into two domains: Western and Arab music. Each of these had its professional ensembles, educational institutions and respective audiences. This led each of these domains to compete for government funds, audiences and a more dominant role in Egypt's musical life (El-Shawan 1984: 285). The mobility of musicians between the two realms was minimal, even when their training permitted this.

The division between Western and Arab music became less evident in the mid-1970s. It was at this time that many Egyptian musicians who were trained in Western music became more involved in the gainful Arab musical activity that was flourishing in their home country. Some of these musicians had even dropped European music altogether. At that time Arab popular music was booming, with Cairo emerging as an important centre for recording studios and attracting many solo vocalists from the Arab Gulf States and Saudi Arabia. These recording initiatives generated jobs for many Egyptian musicians. Moreover, the fresh discovery of Egypt's national identity also led to less interest in Western music performances. Consequently, the demand for Western music performances declined and there was less funding for such performances.

It was in 1967 that the Egyptian Ministry of Culture established a new ensemble under the name of Firqat al-Mūsīqā al-'Arabiyya (The Arab Music Ensemble) (El-Shawan 1984: 271). The Ensemble was a strong attempt on the part of traditional musicians to provide *takht* ensembles 'with an official and constant presence and to counterbalance the broad government support given to Western music' (El-Shawan 1984: 285). A *takht* ensemble consisted of a solo vocalist accompanied by a small group of instrumentalists playing *qānūn*, *'ūd*, *nāy*, violin and *riqq* (a single-headed tambourine). A chorus of four or so male singers was sometimes employed when this was required by the genre. The newly founded ensemble was considered a developed form of the *takht*, due mainly to the inclusion of more instrumentalists and its reliance on practices of Western music that were viewed by the founders as symbolizing 'progress'. The new ensemble also had the responsibility of reviving performances of *al-turāth* and 'preserving its melodic and rhythmic essence and ridding the musical performance from the factors of distortion and improvisation by presenting a uniform rendition of each composition which is respected by all performers' (El-Shawan 1984: 278). The term *al-turāth*, as used in Egypt, is described by Davis (1997b: 97) as 'a relative concept, denoting a comparatively recent and open-ended repertory'. Davis (1997b: 97) ably notes that this repertory cannot be compared to the Tunisian *ma'lūf*, for instance; nor can it be exactly likened to other Andalusian *nawba* music in the other Maghrebi countries. The Andalusian *nawba* conveys a historical continuity that qualifies it as '*turāth qadīm*' ('old heritage').

Nevertheless, the Egyptian *takht* still became widely popular across the region. Apart from a larger scale ensemble, modelled on the symphony orchestra, other Western practices were also implemented in the *takht*. Among these were the presence of a conductor leading from the front, the use of musical notation, more orderliness in musician and audience behaviour, as well as more organized performances with a well-balanced programme of instrumental and vocal compositions. Due to this expansion, which also included a chorus and the other innovations mentioned so far, improvisation became less possible (El-Shawan 1984: 276). The subtle heterophonic style of the *takht* was replaced by a texture composed of parts moving in unison and in a relationship of parallel octaves (Racy 1982: 402). The strong inclination towards the call-and-response style characteristic of pre-First World War songs was superseded by collective singing, which many Egyptians considered a highly 'evolved' and 'dramatic' musical idiom (Racy 1982: 402). Choral innovations included the frequent alternation of men's and women's voices, or the mixing of both. Sufi-related religious forms, such as the *qaṣīda,* which in the early twentieth century used to be recorded with the accompaniment of a *takht* ensemble, began to be performed by a large male chorus accompanied by an ensemble modelled on Firqat al-Mūsīqā al-'Arabiyya (Racy 1982: 403). Other Maghrebi countries followed the Egyptian initiatives.

Morocco and Algeria, for instance, both colonized by the French, integrated Western instruments into their Andalusian ensembles. These innovations brought with them changes in the traditional sonorities characteristic of these ensembles. For instance, when referring to Andalusian ensembles in Morocco, Schuyler (1978: 36–7) reports that:

> … microtonal intervals typical of the Middle East do not seem to play an important role in Andalusian music. Most Andalusian musicians and conservatory teachers now maintain that there are no microtones at all. The disappearance of non-tempered intervals may be attributable to the piano, introduced by the French both as a tool for teaching *solfège* in the conservatory and as an instrument of the orchestra.

Schuyler (1978: 40) also observes that the growing size of the Andalusian ensemble, numbering up to 40 performers including choristers and instrumentalists, was a major factor that, as in the Egyptian case, restricted that heterophony most typical of Arab music. The presence of Western instruments such as the piano, clarinet and saxophone in these ensembles was a sign of great prestige. These enlarged Andalusian ensembles became popular in the spheres of television and radio recordings. As most literature concerned with these developments reveals, the reliance of the recording industry on these ensembles became a normal practice not just in Morocco but also in other Maghrebi countries. Meanwhile, and over the years, ensembles of Andalusian music also multiplied and flourished in several Moroccan cities, such as Marrakech and Casablanca. These ensembles are considered as more traditional than others due to the instrumentation they employ. Schuyler (1987: 177), for example, notes that the Fes Andalusian ensemble was deemed more traditional than the ensembles of Rabat and Tetouan due to the absence of instruments such as the clarinet and piano that were found in the other two ensembles.

The colonization of Algeria by the French in 1830 left an impact on the Algerian Andalusian tradition, especially on the composition of the traditional *jawq* ensemble. In Constantine, for instance, the *rabāb* is rarely used in these ensembles nowadays and instead is being replaced by the viola. Instruments that were not part of the *jawq* ensemble are now considered a legitimate part of the Andalusian ensemble. By the 1930s the traditional small *jawq* ensemble had expanded into a large ensemble, an expansion that continued after Algerian independence with the introduction of other Western instruments such as the violin, piano and fretted mandolins (Reynolds 1995). These and other cases bring forth a trend in the process of including Western instruments within the confines of traditional settings. As in Algeria, for example, such instruments were initially introduced for teaching purposes but eventually became part of the traditional ensemble formation. A similar case occurred in Morocco, where the piano, which was initially employed in the teaching of *solfège*, was eventually transferred to the renovated forms of the ensembles.

Modernization was also the fate of the Tunisian *ma'lūf*, which in turn had its own impact on that of Libya. As in the case of other *nawba* traditions in the Maghreb, *ma'lūf* performances were mainly held in *zāwiya* by Sufi brotherhoods. Such ensembles consisted of a unison male chorus accompanied by percussion. Other venues for *ma'lūf* performances outside *zāwiya* were cafés, private homes and wedding ceremonies (Davis 1997b: 81). The establishment of the Rashīdiyya Institute in Tunis by Muhammad al-Rashid Bey in November 1934 had two main objectives: firstly, 'to protect the *ma'lūf* from the overwhelming influence of Egyptian music' and, secondly, to elevate the social status of the *ma'lūf* 'by providing a respectable, public secular environment for its performance comparable to a Western music conservatory' (Davis 1997b: 81). Teaching and performance at the Rashīdiyya were shaped on the teaching methods at the French Conservatory, founded in Tunis in 1896. Davis (1997b: 81) describes the early initiatives taken by the Rashīdiyya as follows:

> In order to create an ensemble of the highest possible standards, the founders [musicians, poets, intellectuals, bureaucrats, politicians and prominent personalities of the Tunisian bourgeoisie] sent out invitations to the leading shaykhs of the capital. The initial response produced six violins, two rabābs, five 'ūds, three qānūns, a tār, naqqārāt, one female and six male vocalists. Unprecedented both in size and proportion, the new ensemble encountered difficulties from the start. Many of the shaykhs were unaccustomed to performing together and knew different versions of the orally transmitted melodies; at the same time, their spontaneous embellishments were obscured by the instrumental doublings. Evidently, for the new ensemble to be viable the musicians needed to conform to a standard version of each melody; to this end, the young Tunisian violinist Muhammad Triki, adept in European, Middle Eastern and Tunisian traditions, was invited to supervise the transcription of the entire repertory

of the *ma'lūf* into Western staff notation, teach the shaykhs how to read the transcriptions and lead them in performance.

Triki established conventions of performance and rehearsal that are still being practised today. In his early initiatives he was also very much inspired by both the sonorities of the Egyptian *firqa* (ensemble) and by the European symphony orchestra. Sonorities of the Egyptian *firqa* were evident in his use of bowed strings in parallel octaves. Western practices revealed themselves in Triki's leadership of the ensemble, which he conducted from the front with a baton; sectional rehearsals for instrumentalists and choristers; and the instrumentalists' adherence to Triki's musical transcriptions (although the choir, coached by a knowledgeable sheikh, continued to employ the repetition and memorization approach). Since the ensemble was subsidized by the state, the musicians were given a minimal remuneration for their services (Davis 1997b: 84). In 1944 the Rashīdiyya established a three-year programme that included solmization, recognition of notation, instrumental performances, Arabic music history and theory. Although the school had developed independently from the ensemble, by the 1940s the instrumental section of the ensemble accepted only students from the Rashīdiyya. The Rashīdiyya was instrumental in the dissemination of the Tunisian *ma'lūf* in its refined form through radio, public concerts and its presence in national formal events, where performances were characterized by a serious atmosphere and an attentive audience (Davis 1997b: 84).

Davis (1997b: 88) notes further developments with the foundation of the Tunisian full-time professional radio orchestra in 1958. The ensemble introduced practices such as the provision of parts for each instrument, strict adherence to those parts, contrasts in timbre and register, and bowing and phrasal marking specified by the same parts characterized the new performance of the Tunisian *ma'lūf*. Individual nuances were agreed during rehearsals and adhered to in the actual performance. The cello and the double bass had a dual role: that of emphasizing the *īqā'* provided by the percussion, and of coming up with a reduced version of the main melodic line. The production of the melodic line was entrusted to the *nāy*, *qānūn*, violin and newly introduced instruments such as the electric harmonium, flutes, clarinets and accordions.

With the setting up of the Tunisian Ministry of Culture in 1961, several other ensembles, not only in Tunis but also over the entire country, followed the model of the Rashīdiyya ensemble. Most of these ensembles used the musical transcriptions of the *ma'lūf* as collected in a series of nine volumes entitled *al-Turāth al-Mūsīqī al-Tūnisī/Patrimoine Musical Tunisien* (The Tunisian Musical Heritage). In this regard, Davis (1997b: 85–6) notes that the teaching methods employed by the Rashīdiyya were also employed both by the National Conservatory and by other state-subsidized educational institutions. All this helped in establishing the *ma'lūf* as the musical heritage of Tunisia, in comparison with the more diversified rural folk music. (Davis 1997b: 85–6). In order to monitor and encourage the participation of new ensembles, the Tunisian Ministry of Culture also started organizing *ma'lūf* festivals, the apex of these festivals being the one held annually in the Andalusian town of Testour. Several ensembles, both Tunisian and Maghrebian, are invited to participate in this festival. An ensemble invited frequently to participate in this festival was Firqat al-Ma'lūf wa al-Muwashshaḥāt wa al-Alḥān al-ʿArabiyya led by Hassan Araibi.

Whilst colonization had a degree of impact on the modernization of the Andalusian *nawba* in Tunisia, Algeria and Morocco, the Libyan case presents a somewhat different scenario. According to Araibi, the Italian colonizers were only interested in attaining land and Libya's wealth rather than assisting the Libyans to preserve and modernize their *ma'lūf* tradition. He even attributed the absence of a Libyan delegation in the 1932 Cairo Congress on Arab music to the Italians' disinterest in Libyan cultural affairs. Processes of modernization in the Libyan *ma'lūf* were engendered by innovations brought forth by Araibi in the 1960s and through the financial support he consistently managed to attain from the state during the Gaddafi era. Araibi's stature in Libya assured such financial backing and, consequently, not only maintained the modernization process initiated by him in the 1960s but also acquired for the *ma'lūf* further recognition both in Libya and outside.

Hassan Araibi, Music Professionalism, Politics and Power

During interviews with Araibi, he stated to me that the objectives of the changes he had brought to the Libyan *ma'lūf* were twofold: firstly, he wanted to popularize a musical tradition that until that time was only confined to the *zāwiya* and its related activities, and, secondly, he wanted to preserve the tradition, fearing that each time a prominent *sheikh ma'lūf* died, his knowledge of this art was buried with him. Both reasons echo in part the incentives that led to similar innovations in the case of the Tunisian *ma'lūf*. These objectives emerged from an Arab musician's love and reverence for Arab music and an upbringing that, as Araibi told me, 'valued this art form'. Through his innovations, Araibi not only gained popularity but also moved to the core of power and authority in his country.

The benefits that musicians gain from implementing innovation within a musical tradition can be several. For instance, over the years Araibi became a highly esteemed and influential person in Libya capable not only of ensuring an unceasing state subsidy for his projects but also of influencing some of Libya's cultural policies. In addition, from the early 1960s Araibi became synonymous not only with the Libyan *ma'lūf* and the changes he had brought to it but also with Libya's entire musical and cultural spheres. Talking to Libyans about *ma'lūf*, they immediately mention Araibi and his contributions to this musical tradition. His frequent appearances on TV, whether performing in Libya or taking part in festivals of Arab music abroad as a member of a judging panel, continued to boost his popularity, not just in his own country but outside it as well. A visit to the section dedicated to Libyan music situated at the top level of the national Museum at Al-Ḥamra Castle in Tripoli takes one past a huge wall-to-wall photo

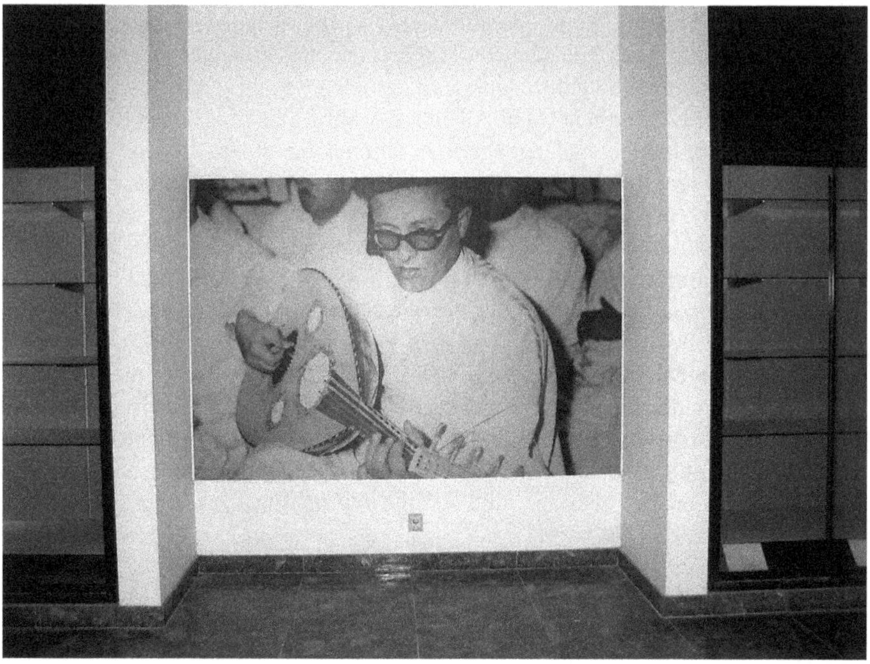

Figure 3.2 A wall-to-wall picture showing Hassan Araibi leading his ensemble

of Araibi performing on the *'ūd* (see Figure 3.2). Over the years Araibi has become an icon of Libya's musical heritage.

The innovations brought about by Araibi in 1964 and the power he was invested with in the years that followed might be better understood when viewed in the wider framework of Araibi's upbringing, training and overall career as a professional musician. Apart from placing his initiatives in a sequence of events and circumstances that preceded and followed his establishment of an ensemble in 1964 and its public appearance, this section must also help to identify some motivational factors that have not been highlighted so far. Given the existence of this order of events, the same section will scrutinize change and its implications not just for the tradition itself but also for its proponent.

Hassan Araibi was born in Tripoli in 1933 in the Sūq Al-Guima area. He received religious education in a mosque under the supervision of Sheikh Muhammad al-Sewidi and his grandfather. Hassan's awareness of *al-turāth* had started from a very early age. Both his father and grandfather used to take him with them to *zāwiya*, particularly during the *mawlid* period. Some brotherhoods also used to hold religious gatherings (*ḥaḍrāt*) at their house. Moreover, his grandfather, who was a chanter of the Qur'ān, used to sing a number of *ma'lūf* verses when finishing his chanting. As he asserted to me, 'I grew up in an environment that respected and valued this art form.' For him, the *ma'lūf* was not just an artistic activity but also an intrinsic part of his childhood environment and a congenial component of his upbringing.

He benefited greatly from sitting with his father and grandfather during his early instruction, and from all the questions he used to pose to them related to the *ma'lūf*. In his words, 'at an early age, I used to notice and peruse those details which formed my own background in this art and through which I started to gain knowledge of the Andalusian *maqāmāt*.' Like so many Arab singers, he gained knowledge of the *maqāmāt* by chanting the Qur'ān. Araibi vividly remembers his recitation from *Sura Yassin* (a chapter from the Qur'ān) in 1945, when the mosque of Bdairiy Square Area was rebuilt. By that time, although only 15, he was already acquainted with the *maqāmāt* even if he had not yet commenced playing a musical instrument. His instrumental instruction started in 1954, when he began taking '*ūd* lessons under Sheikh Al-Aref al-Jām and, later on, with Sheikh Khalil Alstarzi.

In the early 1950s he also started composing *ughniyāt* (songs). Since he was not yet acquainted with musical notation, he used to compose orally, remembering the music and then passing it on orally to the singer. That period witnessed the upsurge of the Algerian rebellion against the French and, inspired by that event, he composed his first song, entitled 'Along with You, Algeria'. The song was performed for the first time by the Libyan singer Abdullatif Hewail at al-Ḥamra Theatre in Tripoli. He composed several other songs for both Libyan and other Arab singers, an activity that continued until he was assigned the post of supervisor at the Benghazi radio station. There he set up a small ensemble, mainly to perform *ughniya* songs.

In 1960 Araibi joined the Rashīdiyya Institute in Tunis where he gained knowledge of and underwent training in the art of *ma'lūf*. It was from here that Araibi acquired new ideas in the modern performance practices of the tradition. During his year there he received instruction in *solfège* and had the opportunity to work with the pioneers of the Institute, people like Sheikh Khemais Tarnan, Salah al-Mahdi and Muhammad Triki. He went to the Rashīdiyya already possessing a good knowledge of the *ma'lūf*. Several times he was advised by the people mentioned above not to draw on the Tunisian *ma'lūf* when back in Libya because the Libyan *ma'lūf* was fine and represented another division of the Maghreb tradition.

This contrasts drastically with what El Sibaei (mentioned in the previous chapter) had experienced in Egypt on submitting a doctoral research topic on the Libyan *ma'lūf*. As explained in the previous chapter, El Sibaei had been told that in Libya there was no 'authentic' *ma'lūf* and that it was all Tunisian. These two contrasting views show the divergent opinions that people, including scholars, can hold of the same musical tradition even in the same region. Common elements shared by two neighbouring musical traditions are sometimes understood as, or confused for, complete assimilation. Strong historical, cultural and socio-political bonds between two neighbouring countries, as in the case of Libya and Tunisia, may lead to particular suppositions about a musical tradition. As most ethnomusicology shows, musical perceptions may be generated by processes that have (ostensibly) nothing to do with music.

By the end of 1963 Araibi was appointed head of the music section at the Libyan Broadcasting Centre in Tripoli. A year later he established a *ma'lūf* ensemble at the same Centre, composed mainly of employee singers and instrumentalists. Through his newly established ensemble, which was modelled on that of the Rashīdiyya, Araibi wanted to elevate the *ma'lūf* to 'classical' music, giving it the status he felt it deserved. The *ma'lūf* as it was performed in *zāwiya* was incomparable to that experienced by him in Tunis.

The first time the new ensemble performed in public was on 21 November 1964 at the al-Ḥamra Theatre in downtown Tripoli. At that time Araibi played the violin but later he changed to the *'ūd*. In the context of Arabic music the *'ūd* is considered the 'sultan of the instruments' (Shiloah 1979: 395), and playing this instrument was a move that allowed Araibi to affirm his position as the leader of the ensemble. The audience attending the first performance of the new ensemble disapproved of the inclusion of instruments such as the violin and cello. Other instruments conventionally used in *zāwiya*, such as the *naqqārāt*, *ghayṭa* and *bandīr*, were not included. The strong sound of six or so players striking their *bandīr* was substituted by the lighter sounds of the *ṭīrān* (plural of *ṭār*; a single-headed tambourine with a diameter of approximately 20 cm with jingles), *daff* (a frame drum with a diameter of approximately 30 cm and having nickel-plated cymbals inset all around, except for a space left to hold it) and *darabukka*. Conventional practices in *zāwiya*, such as the *bandīr* players heating up the membrane of the drum over a stove to keep it tightly stretched, were also excluded from this first performance and, eventually, from the modern performance of *ma'lūf* as both the *daff* and *ṭār* required no heating. The ensemble included instruments such as the *nāy* and *qānūn*, which, although belonging to Arab instrumentation, had never been included in *ma'lūf az-zāwiya* performances, as is still the practice today.

In response to all this, some members of the audience left the theatre while others ridiculed the musicians playing Western instruments. For Araibi and his ensemble, this first performance was a complete failure. The audience expected to hear the traditional sonority of the *ma'lūf az-zāwiya*. A member of Araibi's ensemble also pointed out to me that some of the pieces performed during that evening had serious faults, so much so that they had deviated extensively from what was already well known by audience members. The failure of this transitional performance led to the music section of the Broadcasting Centre holding a public lecture at which Araibi's innovations were clarified and explained. This initiative paved the way for a successful performance held a month later.

A similar performance was held on 24 December 1964 at the same venue. The concert was under the patronage of Khalif M. Tillisi, then Minister of Information and Culture. The presence of the Minister was interpreted by many of those attending as the Authorities' official support for Araibi's initiatives. High recognition attributed to musical concerts may sometimes depend not only on the high professional profiles of performers and/or their exquisite performances but also on who patronizes the concert and on the kind of audience attending. In this concert, and unlike the previous performance, the audience reacted positively, offering tremendous applause. According to Araibi, the people realized that the newly introduced instruments were supporting the revitalization of the tradition by making the sound of the ensemble, in Araibi's words, more 'appealing to the young generation'. Many people I interviewed were of the opinion that, through his innovations, Araibi brought more meaning to the *ma'lūf* as performed in *zāwiya* and thereby generated a renewed interest in it. This is a case in point where 'modern' trends assist in the regeneration, continuation and, therefore, preservation of the old. However, change in the *ma'lūf* could never have occurred if it had not found the right social base that permitted and, eventually, even nourished it.

In Chapter 1 it was noted how, in 1949 and 1950, the United Nations decided that Libya should become an independent constitutional monarchy, a declaration that was officially confirmed in 1951. Muhammad Idris Al-Sanussi, a former leader of the Libyan resistance movement against the Italians, became the first ruler of the new United Kingdom of Libya. Independence brought several challenges to the Libyans. To a certain extent, the king was able to expand the educational system. He also initiated development projects following Libya's discovery of oil reserves in the early 1960s. Vandewalle (1986: 30) observes that, during the 1960s, economically 'Libya moved from rags to riches'. He adds that during this decade Libya's economic growth rate 'was in excess of 20%, the highest in the world'. This was due to the country's incredibly fast development in the petroleum sector to the extent that by 1969 Libya had grown to be the fifth largest oil exporter in the world. This new wealth remained very unevenly distributed, most of it going into governmental and royal coffers, while foreigners and a small number of Libyans who had overseas work experience held the best jobs. Collins (1974: 14) notes that 'Libyans who worked in other Arab countries in the petroleum industries ... in many cases, had absorbed Arab nationalist views'. Due to the work generated by petroleum exploration during the late 1950s and early 1960s, Libyan workers from tribal areas moved away from home to urban areas in search of higher wages. Tripoli, for instance, doubled its population between 1954 and 1964 (Collins 1974: 14). The problems of the 1960s that led to the 1969 *coup d'état* are put in a nutshell by Collins (1974: 15):

> Idris' regime was being called upon to perform the functions of a national bourgeoisie—to generate and reinvest capital, and to develop the infrastructure. It accomplished this task in only minimal and half-hearted fashion, expanding the public service sector without modernizing it or establishing new industries. Idris' power base was not the bourgeoisie class, but feudal and tribal elements which consumed wealth rather than invested it. These elements favoured the continuing foreign exploitation of Libya's mineral wealth. There was no room for a national bourgeoisie to develop. The classes that moved in opposition to Idris in this period were the petty bourgeoisie (employees in the public service sector, middle-level military officers), the impoverished peasants and unemployed city migrants, and some tribal elements—all of whose positions deteriorated under Idris. It was the contradiction between the increasing wealth of the Idris clique

> and the rampant poverty of the rest of the population, plus the spread of Arab nationalist consciousness, that generated the coup d'état in 1969.

The above social circumstances coincided with Araibi's idea of renewing a tradition that, according to him, was on the verge of extinction. Araibi's project for the *ma'lūf* evolved within a fertile context sparked by the rise in Arab nationalist consciousness. Arab nationalism is here understood in the sense defined by Pfaff (1970: 149) as follows:

> a nationalism that is not fettered by the confines of any particular Arab polity, a nationalism that is more spiritual than political, a nationalism which is functionally efficacious in almost inverse proportion to its relationship to empirical reality.

Pfaff (1970: 157–8) states that Arab nationalism is a 'state of mind' or a psychological force 'that directs its "True Believers" toward a self-fulfilment that is shorn of the Hegelian imperative that the state be the fulfilling agent. Instead, fulfilment is gained merely by membership in the Arab community, the *'umma al-'arabiyya*' (emphasis added). Araibi's initiatives not only blended nicely with this rise in Arab nationalism but, moreover, signalled his personal commitment to the rediscovery of such consciousness in his own country through a new appreciation of the *turāth qadīm*. The importance of attention to such socio-political currents was regularly emphasized by John Blacking, and among his statements on this subject particularly salient to the present example is his assertion (1995: 172) that:

> musical change is important to watch because, owing to the deep-rooted nature of music, it may precede and forecast other changes in society. It is like a stage of *feeling towards* a new order of things.

In a way, the changes brought forward in the Libyan *ma'lūf* forecast the political and social upheavals that led to and followed the overthrow of Libya's King Idris on 1 September 1969.

In the process of reviving and rediscovering the *turāth qadīm*, Araibi was proposing a kind of modernization that, as had happened in the cases of neighbouring countries in the domain of Andalusian music, included Western musical practices and norms of performance. In the context of Araibi's efforts, the boundary between conformity and innovation needed very fine and sensitive handling. He had to Westernize without becoming Westernized, to propose the new without discarding the old, and to act discreetly within the spirit of a local rise in Arab national consciousness. Araibi's search for a balance between all the socio-cultural forces involved in his initiatives dovetails with Pfaff's assertion (1970: 156) that 'the Arab wants modernization, but has no desire to lose his own identity in the process'. In addition, one can also argue that prominent individual musicians such as Araibi, who may come to be remembered in society for their innovations (and whose deeds become history), do this in a forum of political–economic conditions and pre-established aesthetics not of their own making (Turino 1991: 130). All this explains the several considerations that pressed Araibi along the path of innovation. Had he contradicted or underestimated any one of these considerations, his whole initiative might have failed. His cautious handling of change not only helped him to strengthen his musical stature but, moreover, earned him support even from orthodox quarters in the domain of *ma'lūf*. Indeed, it was the 'unprecedented' success of the second appearance with his ensemble that paved the way for the formation of a committee made up of several Libyan sheikhs of *ma'lūf* under the chairmanship of Araibi himself.

The committee was set up to work on the preservation and revitalization of this tradition, with Araibi convening meetings three times a week. Together with Araibi's ensemble, the committee managed to record 272 reel-to-reel tapes, with the inclusion of Western instruments in most of these recordings. The music was transmitted and performed orally with a strong input of new melodies and texts from renowned sheikhs. Some of these were members of the newly formed committee, others were members of the ensemble, while others, featured in the previous chapter, contributed as outsiders. Regarding the value of the work carried out by the committee and its associates, Araibi asserted:

> At that time I was the head of the music section of the Broadcasting Centre. When I was appointed to a different position I left this heritage in the hands of someone else. It was a really rich heritage because most of the people who participated in this project were over sixty years old and, therefore, they brought with them old texts and melodies. These were energetic and honest people who were doing all this work from the heart.

According to Araibi, the sheikhs who were members of the ensemble were highly disposed toward the innovations he had proposed. Nevertheless, criticism of Araibi's initiatives never ceased over the years and, even now, his innovations are still seen by some as a threat to the 'authenticity' attributed to *ma'lūf*.

A common critique regarding Araibi's efforts revolves around the opinion that Araibi treated the *ma'lūf* as if it was a 'normal song'; as an informant told me, 'the *ma'lūf* is much deeper than just a song ... It's *turāth*, and therefore it should be treated with reverence.' Others criticize Araibi for the changes he brought to certain texts of this tradition. Araibi explained to me that he had made these modifications to improve the meaning of certain words. According to him, certain texts contained language mistakes committed by sheikhs who, in some cases, could hardly read and write. This meant that some words were added just to fit the music; these were words that Araibi had omitted due to their 'nonsense'. Other words were modified by him to fit more precisely with the music. These modifications, Araibi claimed, could help the people understand and, therefore, better appreciate the meaning of what they were singing or listening to. Critics, meanwhile, countered with the charge that Araibi's textual changes ruined the meaning of those very words and revealed his ineptitude at understanding their deep meanings.

The debate over Araibi's initiatives is still ongoing. Some admire him for his innovations while others resent what they see as his tampering with an old and valuable heritage. These two main views continue to polarize ongoing debate about the *ma'lūf* in Libya. However, despite all the criticism levelled at him, Araibi's career flourished and he gained substantial support, especially during the Gaddafi era. These years consolidated Araibi's position in Libya's musical life. The inclusion of Libyan folk music arrangements in the repertoire of his ensemble attests to the man's submission to proceed in line with the strong sense of Arabness propounded by the Gaddafi administration.

As explained in the first chapter, towards the end of the 1970s and the beginning of the 1980s the Libyan educational authorities worked on a plan intended to prepare and train an adequate number of Libyan music teachers, who would gradually replace foreign teachers. This plan included government scholarships for promising Libyan students to further their musical studies abroad (even at American universities) and the foundation of music schools to provide formal music training. These post-revolutionary developments had a strong impact on the work initiated by Araibi. For instance, Araibi's state-subsidized ensemble attracted musicians equipped with formal music training who could read musical notation. This permitted the inclusion of more and more instrumental arrangements of Libyan folk music that would have been hard to include when rehearsal relied entirely on oral transmission. Furthermore, with the setting up of these educational institutions, musical tuition became accessible to both men and women. Nowadays, advanced students attending music schools in Tripoli are organized into ensembles composed of both male and female instrumentalists and choristers. Some of these ensembles are even composed solely of teenage girls. The repertories of these ensembles include *nawbāt ma'lūf* from the Libyan repertory as well as *qaṣā'id, muwashshaḥāt* and songs from the repertory of Egyptian singers such as Umm Kulthūm and Muhammad Abd al-Wahhāb. This changed the tradition of the *ma'lūf* from an activity dominated by men to one in which women could participate actively. Such initiatives provided a different timbre from that heard in all-male ensembles. It was another innovation on top of those that had already been made. The creation of mixed choirs occurred concurrently with the efforts made by the Libyan authorities to create equal job opportunities for both men and women.

In the post-1969 revolutionary years the recording industry in Libya proliferated immensely. In Chapter 1 we saw that in the years following the 1 September revolution more recording studios were established, whilst at the same time the Broadcasting Centre continued subsidizing ensembles to supply it with original recordings, with a strong emphasis placed on arrangements of Libyan folk music. Araibi and his ensemble benefited greatly not only from exposure in the Libyan media but also from the supply of recordings of classical Arab music for Libyan TV. Popularity and public exposure consolidated Araibi's position, not just as an influential figure in Libya's musical life but also in assuring him a continuous subsidy from the state for both the ensemble and his institute.

This patronage and popularity are somewhat at odds with one another. For instance, some Libyans were surprised to see Araibi performing on television during a stately dinner for the diplomatic corps given by Gaddafi in a leading hotel in Tripoli. 'Have you ever seen Pavarotti performing with the diplomats dining? Never ... have you? By the same token ... how can you expect us to accept Araibi performing while the guests dine? He has debilitated his dignity and stature!', one member of his ensemble replied promptly to my comment that I had seen nothing wrong with that. Another member commented: 'How could we refuse when the invitation came directly from the Leader?' Such an incident highlights the fact that occasionally musical performances are not only the outcomes of official deals between performers and organizers but also of subtle obligations that only a restricted number of people can fully understand. Incidents such as these, while revealing how the media can bring into the public domain the concealed links between music and politics, account in part for Araibi's continuous backing from the state over the years. State support included the recording of a master collection of 14 cassettes in 1992, the financing of rehearsals and concerts undertaken by the ensemble and the funding of tours outside Libya. Countries toured by the ensemble included Morocco, Qatar, Kuwait, Algeria, Tunisia, Lebanon, Gambia and Egypt.

In the post-revolutionary years the new administration subsidized several Libyan folk groups to enable them to participate in folk festivals abroad. Such tours were in themselves an index of Libya's professional efforts to preserve and disseminate its cultural heritage. Araibi's ensemble benefited greatly from this policy, so much so that it toured abroad quite frequently. For Araibi, this was a means by which his innovations could gain appreciation and prestige outside Libya and his international artistic standing in the domain of Arab classical music could be consolidated. Araibi vividly recounted to me how, during the ensemble's performance at the Cairo Opera House, a retired colonel had stood up and publicly called out words of praise to the ensemble. This case was probably brought up by him to highlight the prestige that his ensemble had gained over the years both in Libya and abroad. It was significant, firstly due to the prestige associated with the venue where this incident occurred, and, secondly, because it took place in Egypt—the 'cradle' of modernization in the domain of classical Arab music. A similar anecdote by his son Yusuf reaffirmed what Araibi had in mind when he mentioned the Cairo incident. Yusuf explained to me how, in 1998, when he was participating in his father's ensemble in Qatar, a member of the audience came up to him after the performance and told him, 'Now I can say that Arab classical music does exist.' This may be understood in light of what the Libyans believe about the *ma'lūf* and its classical rendition, that is, that their *ma'lūf* tradition is *l-aḥla* (the sweetest), and therefore superior to the other neighbouring versions, and that its 'classical' presentation is the best in the Maghreb and, therefore, the most representative of the other neighbouring classical *nawba* traditions.

Araibi's cautiousness in the process of innovation, referred to above, persisted in the post-revolutionary years. Indeed, the scenario of the early post-revolutionary years was, if anything, even more complex as an environment for Araibi's work in this domain. Now it was no longer a matter of simply proposing the 'new' without discarding the 'old' or 'Westernizing' without becoming 'Westernized'. More than that, in the first years of the Gaddafi governance Araibi was 'modernizing' and 'classicizing' at the same time that revolutionary squads, as already noted in Chapter 1, were looting and burning Western musical instruments in Tripoli's Green Square (nowadays known as the Martyr's Square), with all this broadcast live on TV. In that particular scenario, Araibi was formulating his role in reconciling 'modernization' and 'classicization' of an Arab music tradition treasured by so many in Libya for its potential to evoke the glory of a nostalgic past and for integrating them into the wider history of Arab civilization. Within these parameters, Araibi's preambles and statements during public appearances and interviews, accentuating the value of the Arabness so much promulgated and stressed by the Gaddafi administration of that period, resonated long in the years that followed.

The National Centre for the Research and Study of Arab Music

Experiencing the field involves understanding what members of the music tradition under investigation think of their music, how they speak about it and, consequently, how they make it. Through such interactions, which also include the sharing of everyday life with the people in question, the researcher enters 'into the matrix of meanings with the researched, to participate in their system of organized activities, and to feel subject to their code of moral regulation' (Wax 1980: 272–3). As I have already remarked, most of my fieldwork with Libyan musicians evolved in almost constant rapport with members of Araibi's ensemble. Although other ensembles similar to Araibi's exist in Tripoli, these meet less regularly. That could have hindered me from observing musical and extra-musical processes evolving over a continuous span of time and establishing firm and friendly relationships with the musicians themselves. While my observations provided me with ample opportunity to attain more knowledge of practices related to rehearsing and performing, my close relationship with the musicians supported me in acquiring more insight into the musicians' world apart from that of the *ma'lūf*. Over time, I learned that it would work against the interests of my research if I moved around from one ensemble to another, as that could hinder the rapport I established with Araibi's ensemble through painstaking time and effort. My 'loyalty' to them was a means by which I could gain the trust and support needed for my research; in fact, a frequently expressed statement directed towards me by the musicians was, 'You're one of us.' The more I interacted with the ensemble, the more I realized the deeper meanings within this statement. At first it merely meant: 'Come to our rehearsals whenever you feel the need to do so', 'Ask as many questions as you like', 'You're most welcome to join us on our trip to Testour' and other expressions of goodwill. As my trips to Libya became more frequent, after two consecutive summers travelling to Testour with the ensemble and staying with them in the same hostel for a week or so, and after the three articles I had published about them, the original statement began to include not only the above but also 'the appreciation and support of a Western music researcher through whom our work can acquire recognition in the West'. The fact that I (as a Western researcher) had chosen them to collaborate with had its own bearing. This was sometimes interpreted as a 'privilege' over other ensembles and, therefore, that 'privilege' had to be solely enjoyed by them and by no one else.

The significance of a Western researcher examining the Libyan *ma'lūf* must be understood in light of the following considerations. My research trips coincided with the country's diplomatic normalization with the West and the lifting of international sanctions imposed on Libya by the United Nations. Moreover, in contrast with what many ethnomusicologists have experienced when dealing with extensively researched music traditions, the ensemble had never collaborated with a Western researcher before. My presence at rehearsals and for other activities was sometimes seen as 'beneficial'; as Muhammad, Araibi's assistant in charge of the choir, once told me: 'Your presence among us breathes refreshed interest among our musicians.' For some, my research into the Libyan *ma'lūf* carried plenty of significance, probably more than I had given it myself. It was precisely this sense of 'privilege' and 'loyalty' that I tried to care for throughout my trips. I began to understand that 'human relationships rather than methodology [determine] the quantity and quality of the information gathered' (Beaudry 1997: 68).

Concentrating on the activity of one particular ensemble also provided me with time and opportunity to re-evaluate observations I had made in the early stages of my research. For instance, a long phase of socialization that preceded rehearsals, mainly characterized by the drinking of Arabic coffee and mint tea and the smoking of cigarettes, with most of the musicians squatting on the fitted carpet of the rehearsal room, had sometimes been understood by me as a 'waste of time', especially when this overlapped with the time at which a rehearsal was scheduled to start. As time went by, I began to understand that the ensemble does not function simply on the level of music but also on the equally important level of fellowship and socialization, with the latter leading on nicely to my concept of the 'proper musical activity'. Through this and other situations involving time, I learned that I must temporarily be freed from my own cultural values as to time 'used' versus time 'wasted' and proceed according to my informants' pace of life. What initially seemed to me as defective rehearsing, sometimes stopping without clearly pointing out mistakes and giving specific instructions, later on revealed itself as a means by which a musician could gradually re-evaluate his playing through repetition until he could get his part right at his own pace and without excessive pressure.

Ethnographic commentaries presented in the discussion that follows are intended to link the music with the world in which it arises. It is the kind of ethnography that shifts its focus from the world of a group of people working together to the particular worlds of individual musicians making up the whole.

The portraits presented in this part complement the context of the processes of 'modernization' featured in the previous section, whilst occasionally attempting to establish both a contrast and a link with contemporary portraits of 'antiquity' raised in the previous chapter. My ethnographic reporting shifts from specific to recurrent occurrences, the depiction of which is, in my view, essential for the purpose of the present research. Through these ethnographic depictions, the individual musician is looked upon not only in relation to the musical genre he performs, and to which he devotes a substantial amount of his time, but also in connection with the institution that determines his actions not only as an individual but also as a member of an ensemble.

Arriving at the Furnāj Area in Tripoli, I directed my taxi driver (to his surprise) towards an area that at the time of research served as a barracks for the Libyan Army. I just needed to mention the name of Hassan Araibi to the soldier on duty at the gate to let us pass through. The Music Research Institute was situated inside this quiet, restricted area and covered hectares of land with ample space for parking in front. From the outside one could easily notice the several offices of the Institute and a banner on the main door with the words al-Markaz al-Qawmiya li-Buḥūth wa Dirasāt al-Mūsīqā al-'Arabiyya (The National Centre for the Research and Study of Arab Music). Libyan flags were draped all over the facade of the building. In a meeting with Araibi, he explained to me how the building was initially offered to him by the state as a private residence for himself and his family. Instead, he turned it into an institute that, despite its official name, served mainly to coordinate work related to Araibi's ensemble. On the inside, facing the main entrance, the Institute's library equipped with books that, although hardly used, gave the visitor an immediate feeling of entering an academic institution. On mentioning Hassan Araibi, the door attendant led me to the waiting area and went to inform Araibi's secretary of my visit. The waiting room was furnished with luxury sofas and, as in any Libyan public building of the time, a large picture of Colonel Gaddafi dominating the wall facing the entrance. After a few minutes waiting, Araibi appeared in his typical Libyan *jubba.*

He greeted me and welcomed me into his office. His desk was full of files and writing pads, while beside him there was a telephone system connected to the other offices in the Institute. A conference table stretched invitingly in front of him, instantly giving the impression that he chaired every meeting and committee held in that place. On the left-hand side of his desk the satellite TV, tuned to Al-Jazeera TV Station, was covering Gaddafi's visit to the European Union in Brussels. Sitting down, he commented on how Libya was opening its doors to new investment from the West and how, due to the setting up of new international hotels, more tourists were choosing Libya as a holiday destination. One moment he showed me a manuscript of *ma'lūf* text written by his grandfather (see Figure 3.3), and a few minutes later he took out from a drawer a sample jacket of a forthcoming CD collection that he was in the process of recording with his ensemble. Nevertheless, whatever lay within the 'present' always emerged as assimilating the most extensive attention by him, probably due to his leading role in its making.

Figure 3.3 Hassan Araibi showing a manuscript of *ma'lūf* text written by his grandfather

Our meetings covered various aspects, from discussions about particular *maqāmāt* to past successes of his ensemble; from his current commitments to comments about a transcription of a *nawba* that I had completed just before my visit. An extensive and formal interview with him was only held once, during my first visit. The other meetings were informal and lasted not longer than an hour or so. On my first visit to Libya my mentor described him as a busy artist with a tight schedule of commitments both in Libya and abroad. Keeping that in mind, I aimed for regular interviews without asking too many questions at once so that I would not interrupt him excessively and potentially infer disrespect. That approach also provided him ample time to say what he thought was most important for me to know about his own musical tradition. The main technique employed throughout my fieldwork trips was that of observing and recording naturally occurring talk and interaction (see also Emerson *et al.* 1995: 40). In this, I aimed to find a balance between the 'nonmodel approach' referred to by Beaudry (1997: 69), in which informants are given the chance 'to choose the manner in which they wish to instruct me and to decide in which directions they will channel me', and the pre-planned approach, where particular aims and objectives are established beforehand and struggled for at the right time, depending on the uniqueness of the situation. Within this framework, the concept of timing plays an important role; in other

Figure 3.4 The violin section in rehearsal

words, the sensitivity of the researcher to discern when to start talking about matters of the most personal concern, when to intervene with questions and comments and, most importantly, when to draw to a conclusion, while at the same time putting forward areas of probable interest in advance of the next meeting or appointment. Sometimes, such anticipation seemed very beneficial and informants came up with ideas that they suggested I should consider looking at during the next appointment.

Administrative work at the Institute took place in the morning. Rehearsals of the ensemble were held every evening except Thursdays and Fridays, starting at six and finishing at around eight. However, this depended on several factors such as the mood of the musicians, the level of attendance, long discussions on matters concerning the commitments of the ensemble and whether Araibi would be attending the rehearsal or not. The ensemble, which at the time of the present research numbered about 50 members, consisted of a male choir, a percussion section, a *nāy*, a string section composed of 8 to 10 violinists, a cello, a double bass and *qānūn*, and Araibi himself playing the *'ūd*.

The string players were young musicians who all held a diploma in their respective instruments, either from the Maʿhad Jamāl ad-Dīn al-Mīlādī or from the College of Arts and Media at Al-Fātiḥ University (see Figure 3.4). These used notated music for the performance of instrumental pieces. The music was kept in files with a picture of Hassan Araibi in performance on each front cover, placed on music stands. As previously noted, the amount of instrumental pieces has increased in the last few years as more formally trained instrumentalists have joined the ensemble, gradually replacing the musically 'non-literates' who needed much time to learn each composition. Notation was only used for instrumental arrangements of folk music, the rest of the repertory being played from memory. 'The *ma'lūf* would never be written, it should all be *maḥfūẓ* (memorized)', remarked Muhammad, implying not only the aura, or even the 'sacredness', surrounding the *turāth qadīm* but also the fact that through the memorization of the *ma'lūf* the Arab musician would acquire good knowledge of the *maqāmāt* and *'iqāt*. This recalls developments that had taken place in the Tunisian *ma'lūf* in the 1950s. At that time, the *ma'lūf* 'became the core component of the curriculum leading to the examination for the National Diploma of Arab Music' (Davis 2002).

Some of the instrumentalists were teachers of general music and/or instrument tutors, or freelance orchestral musicians in the recording industry. For most of the musicians, Araibi's ensemble was a part-time job that provided extra income on a regular basis. Salah, a music graduate from the School of Arts and, at that time, a percussionist in Araibi's ensemble, illustrates this attitude. His main musical passion was rock music; in fact, he had his own rock band in which he also played the drums. His band performed mostly cover versions of Black Sabbath, Metallica and Guns 'n' Roses. Being a member of Araibi's ensemble was for him another source of income. 'We only play rock in the garage where we meet to rehearse', he told me. 'Playing rock music in public is not allowed here both for political and religious reasons. In the case of the former, they might think of you as instigator of trouble while in the latter as the Devil (*shīṭān*).'

Tariq, at that time a violinist in his twenties, offered a somewhat contrasting position. He held a diploma in his instrument from Ma'had Jamāl ad-Dīn al-Mīlādī School of Music. He earned his living by playing in Firqat al-Mahrajān al-Ghinā'iyya (The Festival Singing Ensemble), an ensemble based in Tripoli specializing in the performance and recording of Libyan *ughniya*. He described this ensemble as 'huge', composed of 26 violinists, 4 cellists, *qānūn*, *nāy*, *'ūd*, 10 male and 10 female choristers, as well as 10 percussionists. Rehearsals were mostly held in the evening and continued until the early hours of the following day. He described rehearsing at the above ensemble as very demanding, with new music requiring technical dexterity coming up all the time. Prepared parts also involved some occasional harmony with violins divided into firsts and seconds. Tariq explained to me how the *ma'lūf*, through its broad bowing, has given him *rūḥ* (soul); in other words, an intense and deep feeling for his instrument. This contrasted with the kind of bowing employed in the other ensemble where most of the work required short, articulated bowing. This versatility from modern to classical Arab music was very common among these instrumentalists as it not only secured financial income but was also an important means by which they could project their own personality.

Figure 3.5 The choir section in rehearsal

In contrast with the instrumentalists, the choristers (numbering around 14) were less versatile in the styles they sung (see Figure 3.5). Their musical activities were mainly centred round the *zāwiya* and Araibi's ensemble. Their singing was somewhat restricted to traditional Arab classical musical genres such as the *muwashshaḥāt*, *qaṣā'id* and *ma'lūf*. They also considered the *ma'lūf* less of a commodity than did their instrumental colleagues. While the instrumentalists earned their living through music teaching and playing, the main income for the choristers came from jobs unrelated to music. Their occupations ranged from clerical duties, library attendants and bank cashiers to aviation engineers and pensioners. The choir included around five sheikhs, all very much renowned for their extensive knowledge of *ma'lūf* text, their insight into the *maqāmāt* and their apt voices in *ma'lūf* singing. Although unable to read music, their knowledge of the nuances that characterize each *maqām* was impressive; their public vocal improvisations in any *maqām* requested by the compères of the annual Tripoli Ma'lūf and Muwashshaḥāt Festival affirmed this. Their choral singing emphasized correct pronunciation and proper accentuation of words with the rhythm, as well as coherent group singing backed by a solid knowledge of the text and its meaning. Some of them also had their own *zāwiya ma'lūf* ensembles and were active in wedding *ma'lūf* parades. During the *mawlid* celebrations one could see them next to the *ghayṭa* player leading *ma'lūf* parades in the streets

Figure 3.6 Hassan Araibi rehearsing his ensemble

of Tripoli. A prominent member in Araibi's choir at the time of the present research was Sheikh Abu Sama. Sheikh Abu Sama was both a *sheikh ma'lūf* and a *sheikh dhikr*, that is, one who through his extensive knowledge of *dhikr* text and melodies could undertake the responsibility of leading this rite. A highly respected sheikh in Tripoli, Abu Sama was admired for his knowledge in both *dhikr* and *ma'lūf* arts. For both Abu Sama and the other choristers, the *ma'lūf* was a sacred experience as much as it was an aesthetic experience—an intense component through which they felt they could enrich their Muslim identity.

In between the instrumentalists and choristers sat Hassan Araibi behind a desk, marking the '*iqā* with the palm of his hand on the desk in front of him (see Figure 3.6). The ensemble employed a hierarchical set-up that distinguished not only the sheikh from the rest of the ensemble but also 'first'- from 'second'-class vocalists and instrumentalists, section leaders and assistant musical directors. In performance, Araibi used to play the *'ūd,* leading the ensemble from the front, but during rehearsals *'ūd* playing was entrusted to his son Yusuf, who sat next to his father. This gave Araibi more chance to concentrate on specific aspects such as the correct and exact matching of words with the *'iqā'*. Whilst in *zāwiya* a *ma'lūf* performance employs a call-and-response structure, in modern ensembles, as in that of Hassan Araibi, the singing is mostly choral, with calls and responses employed minimally. In itself this has reduced considerably the traditional practice of making many repeats, a change also requested by the recording industry. The recording industry has its own agenda, which in most instances relies not on what is appropriate or 'authentic' for the musical tradition in question but on market forces, budgetary restrictions and listeners' current aesthetics.

The inclusion of a new *nawba* in the repertory of the ensemble occured in stages, with Araibi introducing the *nawba* followed by the choristers repeating his singing while the instrumentalists remain seated, listening to both the sheikh and the choir. The singing and interpretation were considered by the ensemble members as extremely important and, therefore, they deserved an appropriate instrumental accompaniment that should by no means overshadow the words. This first stage could take several rehearsal sessions. This was then followed by another phase in which choir and instrumentalists rehearsed separately, and they were only reunited when their respective section leaders considered that as possible. A new *nawba* may or may not be completely new to the members of a modern ensemble. Also, the melodic content of the songs comprising a *nawba* may be identical, or almost identical, to that already performed in *zāwiya.* The opening lines of a *nawba*, however, remain the same in both contexts.

As already stated, a *nawba* takes its title from the opening lines, but what else is included in the text is decided by the sheikh. The sheikh selects *malūf* songs from the vast poetical material traditionally sung in the *maqām* of that particular *nawba*. Only the sheikh who happens to be leading might know these new songs. One of the factors that distinguishes the sheikh from the rest of the choir is his exceptional knowledge of text; nevertheless, new texts may occasionally arise even for sheikhs. In *zāwiya* performances it is up to the sheikh to decide which songs to include in the course of performance. In contrast, in the ensemble of our concern it was Araibi who determined the choice of songs at the precompositional stage; such selection would hardly be changed after that. The proficient *sheikh mālūf* is one who knows exactly which songs to choose and which to leave out in an attempt to establish a coherent line of thought throughout the selected songs. This is only possible after years of experience and training.

Rehearsals were occasionally attended by recruits, who sat at the back of the rehearsal room, observing what the experience would be like if they had to join in. From my observations in the domain of singing, the ensemble appealed more to young singers from the traditional environments of *zāwiya* than to formally trained singers from the music schools previously mentioned. The most probable reason for this could be the restricted musical genres making up the ensemble's repertory, a repertory that excluded genres like the *ughniya*, with its dance-like tempos, and *mawwāl*, which gave talented singers a chance to improvise extensively and show off their voices. Choral singing was somewhat unfulfilling for those ambitious young singers whom I have heard, with admiration, singing and improvising at the Tripoli festival, as well as in more informal venues such as on the doorstep of a recording studio, in an attempt to show off their versatility.

Since the *ma'lūf* is a very widely diffused tradition in Tripoli, many were those recruits who approached Araibi's ensemble already holding a good knowledge of a number of pieces they could have learned in *zāwiya* and/or from Araibi's cassette collection. Love for and knowledge of the *ma'lūf* most commonly begins at home, grows in *zāwiya* and is 'refined' in one of Tripoli's modern ensembles. New recruits intending to join Araibi's ensemble were normally asked to attend a number of rehearsal sessions as observers before they undergo a period of training. This reflected Araibi's insistence on listening before one actually starts making music. 'Arab music involves a lot of listening', he told me once when I expressed to him my desire to learn the *'ūd*. 'If you want to learn an Arab instrument, you need to listen a lot first. We have many Arab musical sounds that must get fixed in the mind through a long time of listening. After that, you start establishing a connection between your fingers and your emotions.' This initial period of listening was followed with Araibi auditioning the new recruits, asking them to sing something whilst at the same time assessing their voice quality, their listening ability, their vocal range and their ability to sing in tempo. 'A voice can have a harsh timbre', he told me, 'but it would still be considered as special.' Instrumentalists were normally asked to play a classical Arab piece for their audition. When accepted, the recruit was then put through a period of training under Araibi himself until he has assimilated most of the repertory of the ensemble. Such assimilation is normally quicker for instrumentalists, as the music relies on repeated melodies and motifs sometimes reiterated an octave higher. On the other hand, vocalists have to memorize extensive texts, sometimes given to them in print, or by copying it out themselves during rehearsals. The making of a singer depends on the personal ability of the individual and his disposition to learn. According to Muhammad, 'One can learn the text of *ma'lūf* expected of him to get along with us in two months or in a year. It depends entirely on the individual and his willingness to learn.'

A typical rehearsal began with the violins tuning up their instruments, normally to g^0, d^1, g^1, d^2, a tuning reflecting the frequent use of motivic reiterations at an octave higher. The *qānūn* player could be seen adjusting the tuning pegs of his instrument according to the *maqām* of each individual piece. The *nāy* player selected an instrument corresponding to the *maqām* of the piece from a case full of *nāys* of different lengths. The repertoire of the ensemble included instrumental arrangements of Libyan folk music, *muwashshaḥāt* pieces with music composed by Hassan Araibi on *muwashshaḥāt* text, claimed to be of Andalusian origin, *qaṣā'id* and *ma'lūf*. Among the instruments excluded by Araibi in his ensemble were the *naqqārāt* and *ghayṭa*. As Araibi pointed out to me, the *naqqārāt* had been left out of his 1964 ensemble for two principal reasons: firstly, its frequent 'unfitting' cross-rhythmic patterns with the *iqā'*, and, secondly, due to a general tendency towards hard striking that dominates the overall sound of the ensemble. At this point it is worth noting that in contemporary Tunisian ensembles the *naqqārāt* is still employed. From performances of Tunisian *ma'lūf* that I have had the opportunity to attend, I noticed a well-balanced blending of the *naqqārāt* with the rhythmic texture and timbre of the overall ensemble.

The Ensemble in Performance

As most contemporary ethnomusicology reveals, musical performance evolves within a sequence of events that precedes and follows it, and should be investigated along with these events and not separately from them. For this purpose I rely on ethnographic accounts derived from the ensemble's participation in the Testour festival of *ma'lūf* held in July 2002. The ethnography presented here is based on my direct experience when accompanying the ensemble on that trip and staying with its members in the same hostel. This provided me with the opportunity not only to observe but also to participate in the events that preceded and followed the performances of the Libyan ensemble.

Testour lies some seventy kilometres north-east of Tunis, the capital of Tunisia. 'Its inhabitants claim to be descended from Andalusian refugees who founded the town in the early seventeenth century, and they maintain a strong sense of their Andalusian identity' (Davis 1997a: 8). The 13-day Testour Festival has been held every summer since 1968. Apart from Tunisian ensembles, the festival also hosts other ensembles from the Maghreb, and the Libyan ensemble has participated every year since 1968. This regularity of invitation was understood by the members of the ensemble as a sign of respect and appreciation that both organizers and the people of Testour in general have always shown for Hassan Araibi, his ensemble and their high performing standards. For the Libyan ensemble the Testour festival was like an annual 'pilgrimage' that allowed them to renew their sense of commitment and responsibility towards a highly valued musical tradition.

The Andalusian character of Testour with its alleys, a minaret in the style of a Toledo church tower, the warm character of the people and the smell of jasmine, provides the right environment for a *ma'lūf* festival. The place itself evokes a blend of nostalgia, pride and artistic creativity. Throughout the days of the festival a car drove slowly through the narrow streets announcing the programme of the day from two loudspeakers on top of its roof. The Libyan performances were given high prominence indeed. The 24-hour café in the *baṭḥā*, the main town square, played music from the Libyan *ma'lūf* collection of Hassan Araibi and his ensemble. With their strong conviction that their *ma'lūf* is the best in the Maghreb, the Libyan musicians felt that by their presence they were aiding in adding that unique feature to the festival that no other ensemble could provide. Rehearsals during their stay in Testour were kept to a minimum. Testour was not the place for rehearsing, but it was the locale where their performances could blend with long periods sitting in the *baṭḥā* until the early hours, chatting and renewing memories with the organizers of the festival and friends, lying for a long time on their beds in the hostel and doing some shopping in the capital, Tunis.

It was here that the rehearsal led by Yusuf, mentioned at the beginning of this chapter, took place, described by the musicians as a *brova khafīfa* (a 'light rehearsal'). That was the only rehearsal that took place during their stay in Testour. Actually, it was the only one held in the two consecutive trips I made with them to the same town. In that rehearsal they ran through some instrumental pieces and *muwashshaḥāt*, as if from the entire repertoire those were the most problematic. The rehearsal only took an hour, during which time attention was focused more on the instrumentalists than on the singers. For the formally trained Yusuf, the polishing of certain passages and the occasional lack of assurance on the part of some of the violinists were still a preoccupation. On meeting Hassan Araibi in the evening before the performance, I asked him what he intended to perform that evening. 'We go on stage and decide on stage. We never go up with a programme in mind. My musicians know the music well, and whatever I decide to play they play without any problem.' Although this seems to be the normal practice (similar to that in *zāwiya*), some performances seem to be more formal than others and a programme is not only agreed upon beforehand but also printed, as when the ensemble performs in the annual Tripoli *ma'lūf* and *muwashshaḥāt* festival. When I arrived at the *masrah* of Testour (that is, Testour's open air theatre) a Tunisian mixed *ma'lūf* ensemble was performing on a stage set up for the occasion. All performances were scheduled to start at 10 p.m., with one or two sessions each night. As soon as the first session came to an end, Araibi's assistants went on stage to place the chairs and the microphones in their correct arrangement. The other musicians were backstage, all wearing their typical Libyan *jubba*. Some of the instrumentalists were tuning and warming up their instruments, others were taking photos, whilst still others were standing quietly waiting for their turn to go on stage. Araibi was being interviewed backstage by a young TV interviewer with a camera focused on them. The widespread popularity gained by the Libyan ensemble through their participation in this festival was as important as the festival itself.

The seats in the first row were reserved for the organizers and special guests whilst in the rows behind sat an audience comprising people of every age and gender. While some had a lucid idea of what was going to take place on stage, with strong memories and judgements of past performances by Araibi and his ensemble, others were simply there to fill in some time on a summer's night. For some of the youths present it was a good occasion to meet and spend some time in the company of friends and away from the watchful eyes of their parents; it was as if the event was hardly making sense for them, considering the fact that it was not backed up by the required memories and nostalgias that could enhance its meaning. The bar attendant was busy serving drinks to members of the audience and making sure that the guests in front were lacking nothing. Some metres away from the stage the sound engineer was checking that all the microphones were on and in their proper place so as to avoid feedback during performance. Since this was not the main performance of the Libyan ensemble for the festival, the attendance was not that great when compared to the number of audience members present at the longer performance given by the same ensemble three days later.

As soon as the compère finished with her introduction, Hassan Araibi walked out slowly on stage. The shouts of 'Hassan! Hassan!' from members of the audience as soon as the man appeared reverberated across the place. He indicated to the ensemble to stand and receive the applause with him from the audience. Throughout the years Araibi's name became synonymous with the Testour festival. Some Tunisians travelled long distances to hear him singing there. His voice was sometimes described by the people of the town and those coming from outside as *mistrayḥa* (unstrained), naturally shaped for *ma'lūf* singing. Araibi moved towards the centre of the stage, held the *'ūd* and sat on a chair prepared for him in front of the choir (see Figure 3.7).

The set-up of the ensemble on stage showed aesthetic priorities related to what must or must not be heard most. However, that same ensemble set-up was being contradicted by microphones dispersed all over the stage, making the musicians at the back sound as loud as those in front. Nevertheless, Figure 3.8 shows not only the set-up of Araibi's ensemble during the performance but also the placing of musicians most commonly employed by similar ensembles in Libya. As the same figure shows, it was the intention to give primary importance to the singers, as supported by the clear sound of the *īqā'* on the *darabukkah* and *daff*, by positioning them at the front.

At this stage one can add that recent developments in this regard among modern Libyan ensembles are taking place as well. Among these one can mention set-ups relying more on professional sound balancing rather than on the central position of the sheikh in the ensemble. In some of these ensembles the sheikh sits in line with the choristers at the back and at a higher level than the instrumentalists, while in place of the sheikh sitting centrally in front is the conductor who, like a Western conductor, conducts the ensemble holding a baton in a standing position. Whilst such a set-up still signals the prominence of singing, it has now become more evident that contemporary aesthetic preferences in the course of performance as regarding sound are becoming the product of mediation between the aesthetic values of the conductor and those of the sound engineer. In a way, the placing of the choir high up at the back has also made possible and facilitated the inclusion of all-female choirs. Their position, standing high at the back, not in front, and in a way detached from the other male musicians, seems to be in line not only with the teachings of the Qur'ān that discourages the mixing of men and women, but also in accordance with the strong belief amongst some *ma'lūf az-zāwiya* aficionados I met that, since the *ma'lūf* comprises sacred text, it should mainly be the domain of men, at least at performance. Challenging that view, the effort towards more gender equality promulgated by the Libyan Administration in areas such as employment opportunities and education has had an impact on the participation of women in the *ma'lūf al-idhā'a* and, by extension, on the democratization of this tradition. The enrolment of female music students at Tripoli's music schools and their participation in mixed choirs established at the same schools to perform musical genres such as *muwashshaḥ*, *qaṣīda* and *ma'lūf* had engendered the participation of female musicians in *ma'lūf al-idhā'a* performances during events such as the annual Tripoli *ma'lūf* festival. All this has even generated a small number of all-female *ma'lūf* ensembles, modelled on *ma'lūf*

Figure 3.7 Hassan Araibi leading his ensemble in Testour (July 2002)

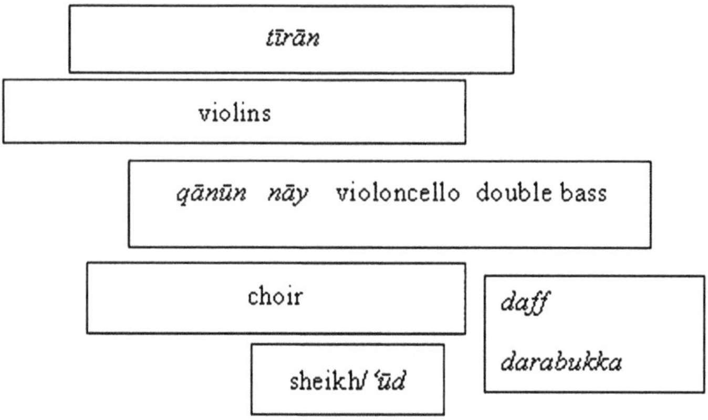

Figure 3.8 The set-up of a modern *ma'lūf* ensemble

al-idhā'a ensemble set-ups, with these having a somewhat restricted activity that mainly revolves around the days of the same festivals.

After a quite long preamble, Araibi played a few notes on the *'ūd* to indicate the first item on the programme. As was normal practice, the first item played by the ensemble was an instrumental piece that would also serve as a warm-up for the instrumentalists. Every item was introduced by Araibi giving the *maqām* and the *īqā'* of the piece together with some textual quotes. The quotation and explanation of the first few lines of the text as a means of introducing a piece, being a *qaṣīda*, *muwashshaḥāt* or *nawbāt ma'lūf*, is very common among sheikhs leading modern Libyan ensembles. In a way, this gives the text equal importance with the music. Araibi's introductions also often included long preambles on what makes Arabic music and what is causing its deterioration. Such introductions provided enough time for the *qānūn* player to adjust the tuning of his instrument and the *nāy* player to choose the appropriate instrument.

The selection of a programme item depended on various factors, including the particular musical tastes of a guest sitting in the front row, or whether a member of the organizing committee had requested a particular item from Araibi before the performance. Some *ma'lūf* songs were very popular among the audience attending the festival, as some members of the audience could be heard singing along. At this stage one must add that certain *ma'lūf* songs and verses are common to both the Tunisian and Libyan *ma'lūf* repertoire. As a result, the audiences in Testour liked some of the *nawbāt* of the Libyan ensemble more than others, even though they were interpreted slightly differently. For instance, the responsorial verse in the second *barwal* song in *nawba nāḥ al-ḥamām* (transcribed in Example 3.7c), is known in both Libya and Tunisia as *allif ya ṣultaniy*. Due to the affinity of the two repertoires, the performances of the Libyan ensemble during the Testour Festival accentuated the *ma'lūf* more than the other genres. Listening to music already known, even if given a different interpretation, not only deepens one's aesthetic

Figure 3.9 Araibi's ensemble in Testour (July 2002)

journey in the same piece but also enriches it with more meanings on the basis of past sensations and experiences related to it.

The second performance of the ensemble at the 2002 Testour Festival was held three days later (see Figure 3.9). Since it was considered to be the main performance for the Libyan ensemble, and the only performance for that evening, the programme lasted almost two hours. As in the above performance, the programme was all decided on stage. At one moment Araibi seemed to be attracting the attention of the double bass player whose pizzicato, according to Araibi, was not in exact time with the *īqā'*. As in the previous performance, the sound was consistently loud with some added reverb. Traditional performance practices typical of the *ma'lūf az-zāwiya* were also occasionally employed on stage by the ensemble. Among these one can mention the synchronized upward trills and solo cross-rhythmic playing on the *tīrān*, both typical of *zāwiya bandīr* playing, as well as synchronized choir-swaying at the final stage of the *nawba* also employed in *zāwiya* performances. All this shows old practices being included in new performance practices.

After the performance the musicians returned to the hostel to take off the *jubba* and put on some lighter clothes; then it was straight on to the *baṭḥā*. The performance that had just passed was hardly mentioned at the *baṭḥā*, as if an evaluation was unnecessary with a repertoire that hardly changes. It seemed that I was the only one interested in an evaluation of the performance; for the others, what had taken place was gone and only time would give it a value. Muhammad, who was always willing to assist me with my work, commented: 'Overall, it was a good performance … except for some weak entrances from the choir. If it were not for me to lead in, we could find ourselves lagging behind or, even worse, put off.' He was mainly referring to *attacca* passages at the beginning of songs and to immediate choral responses.

The arrival of Hassan Araibi for some rest at the *baṭḥā* brought our discussion to a halt. Some people approached him to congratulate him on that evening's performance while drinks were offered to him. A young man was introduced by his father to Araibi in an attempt to acquire Araibi's support in enrolling his son at a recognized institute for Arab music. Araibi asked the young man to sing something for him and listened attentively to him while the other men sitting round the same table stopped chatting and focused their attention on the young man and Araibi. The young chap sang a short improvisation with Araibi humming the *lawāzim* (plural of *lāzima*; instrumental fillers—see Chapter 5 for a detailed discussion), which made it possible for the man to continue. At first, the young man's voice trembled but it soon settled down well to give its best at such an important moment. As he stopped, Araibi promised him a letter of reference and urged him to include in his application that he was applying on Araibi's recommendation.

In some cases the time that follows a performance provides the right opportunity for performers to appraise for themselves the prestige and status gained during performance. In this sense, a *ma'lūf* performance, like any musical performance, is a means by which performers reaffirm their status not only as musicians of high calibre but also as personalities on whom the careers of others may depend. A musical performance is in itself a special occasion where so many processes are negotiated, mediated and intermingled with what seems to be mere musical experience. When performance is no longer possible, or seems to be very remote, so much that it would have already turned into nostalgia, the loss felt by a performer is not only a loss of opportunity to show off talent but it is also a loss of so many opportunities that can only be bestowed on individuals through performance. In this sense, performance is a means by which so many things can be achieved and which cannot be obtained otherwise in normal life circumstances.

Araibi's Restyled *Nawba*

As already mentioned above, Araibi underwent criticism for the changes he brought to certain texts of the *ma'lūf* and he was accused of 'insensitivity' towards the deep meaning of certain *ma'lūf* words and lines. Further criticism relates to the way he composed certain instrumental preludes to his repertory of *nawbāt*, which were held up for their incompatibility with the rest of the melodic content of the *nawba*. The present section will shed light on the musical structure of the *nawba* as restyled by Araibi. For convenience, I focus once again on the *nawba* already discussed in the previous chapter, that is, *nawba nāḥ al-ḥamām*, firstly, to avoid unnecessary repetition and, secondly, to facilitate the understanding of stylistic differences.

Whilst the *nawba* as restyled by Araibi follows the same divisions as the traditional *nawba*, its creation presents a somewhat diverse theoretical approach. For instance, whilst in the context of *zāwiya* performances *nāḥ al-ḥamām* belongs to *maqām muhayyar*, in its restyled form it is known as belonging to *maqām jaharkah* after the tonic note f^1, known in Arab music as *jaharkah.* As I shall show later on, such a shift in terminology also signifies an alteration from emphasis on a descending movement from d^2 (known as *muhayyar*) to the frequent cadencing on f^1 from the fourth or third note above, as is characteristic of *maqām jaharkah.* Although, theoretically, the tonic note in *maqām muhayyar* is f^1, its importance within the *maqām* is passed over by emphasis on d^2 and eventual descending movement from it. Moreover, in *maqām jaharkah,* the upper tetrachord *rāst* on C, as represented in Example 2.3 in Chapter 2, moves to below the tonic f^1 with c^1 serving as a secondary cadential note. As the examples in Chapter 2 reveal, this shift never occurred in the context of *maqām muhayyar*.

As already noted, the *nawba* under investigation, as recorded and performed by Hassan Araibi and his ensemble, begins with an instrumental prelude in 4/4 time (see Example 3.1a). It is worth noting at this stage that the use of Western analytical musical terms here, even if devoid of the terminology that Arabs use to describe their music or structural parts of it, may have facilitated a quick understanding of the techniques employed by Araibi and, therefore, his Western musical thinking in the process of composition. Techniques employed by Araibi included the use of sequences, clearly marked antecedent and consequent phrases within periods, phrase elisions, cadential delaying and the emergence of appoggiaturas from central notes, as well as the balanced splitting of phrases between different instruments (see Examples 3.1a, 3.1b and 3.1c). The initial bars of the prelude are followed by a choral section in free time and in fairly broad tempo, accompanied in unison and/ or at the octave by instruments. This reminds the listener of the improvised vocal *istiftāh* in the traditional *nawba* though, this time, constrained by group singing, even if this unfolds in free metre.

Example 3.1a Extract from the instrumental prelude

Example 3.1b Antecedent and consequent phrases

Example 3.1c Cadential delay

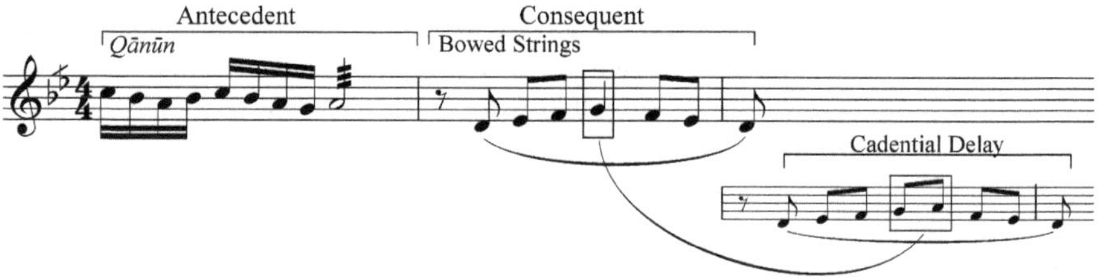

The melismatic vocal passage in Example 3.2 occurs on the vocable 'ah' since the pronouncement of the proper text commences at the initiation of the *muṣaddar* section. This choral section assimilates features from the traditional *istiftāh* most characteristic of this same *nawba*. A close look at both Example 3.2 and the first opening notes of the *istiftāh* in Example 2.5 of Chapter 2 (until the first *ghayṭa* interpolation) reveals similarities appertaining to rhythm, intervallic relations, temporal grouping of notes rounded up by pauses, as well as an instrumental interjection. All this brings forth attempts to maintain traditional features within the new. One difference that emerges between the two examples revolves round the fact that the music in Example 3.2 contains less 'ornamentation' when compared to the *istiftāh* as transcribed in Chapter 2. This is understandable, as 'ornamentation' is more freely employed in solo singing than in choral passages due to group restraints. Example 3.2 also includes instrumental interpolations reiterating cadential passages and their delaying through diminution techniques.

Example 3.2 The first part of the choral passage

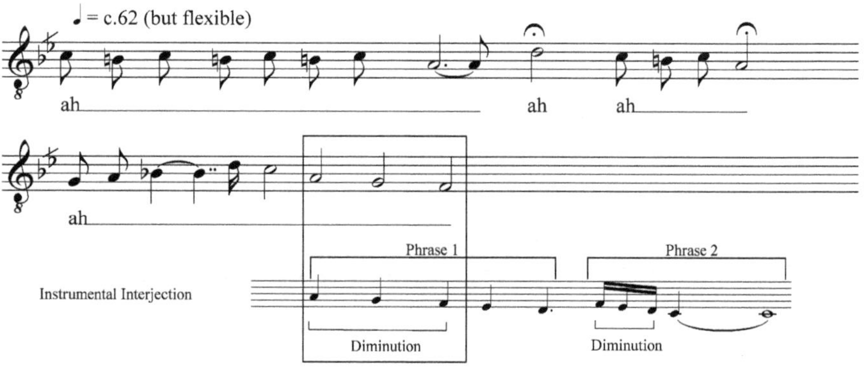

Example 3.3 The first song in *muṣaddar*

As already noted in the previous chapter, in the *muṣaddar* section a series of songs unfold at a fairly slow tempo in 8/4. While in the traditional *nawba* the role of the *darabukka* is that of producing the *dumm* stroke for the rest of the ensemble with the *bandīr* filling up the rest of the rhythmic cycle, in Araibi's restyled *nawba* the *darabukka* produces both the *dumm* stroke as well as the rhythmic filling that comes in between. In contrast to what occurs in *zāwiya*, the playing of this instrument is entrusted to another member of the instrumental section who might not be engaged in the singing. Such rhythmic fill-ins on the *darabukka* rely on personal nuances of the player, with some of these players emerging as technically more proficient than others on basis of these fill-ins.

The singing of the present *nawba* shifts from syllabic to melismatic with certain syllables acquiring more emphasis than others through embellished melismas. The strophic singing that evolves throughout is accompanied monophonically on the instruments, with occasional heterophony mainly provided by the *nāy* and *qānūn*. Example 3.3 shows the first statement of the first song in *muṣaddar*. The song opens with an instrumental verse based on the first repeat of the same song; this is followed by the choir singing. This first song establishes, as from the very beginning, the relationship between the tonic and the dominant notes of *maqām jaharkah* with this becoming further enhanced through the frequent cadencing on f^1 as the tonic note of this *maqām* (framed). The employment of the tetrachord *rāst* below the tonic f^1, as can be seen in section B, is another important aspect that adds to its identity as a melody belonging to *maqām jaharkah*. In addition, an aspect of *maqām jaharkah* also evident in the transcription is the strong tendency of the melodic line to move in a descending arc contour. More features of *maqām jaharkah* are also noted in Section A through the recurrence of an upward minor third interval between notes a^1 and c^2 with the b^1-natural leading towards the dominant c^2 with the latter note enhancing its importance as the dominant note of the *maqām* or the first note of the tetrachord in *rāst* on c^1. At this stage it is worth mentioning the fact that the upward minor third interval is quite common in *maqām jaharkah* melodies, especially between the third and fifth degrees of the *maqām*. In contrast with section A, the second section contains rhythmically denser material generated by a relatively heavier employment of 'ornamentation', which, as I noted during rehearsal sessions, becomes quite demanding in terms of group coordination. The 3–2–1 cadential movement most characteristic of *maqām jaharkah* is frequently employed here as well. Finally, section C leads on to the next song in *muṣaddar* through an *attacca* upbeat.

In the second *muṣaddar* song, the predominantly stepwise melodic movement and the minor third interval featured in the first song resume here, as may be noted in Example 3.4. Other frequently reiterated intervals are the perfect fourth and fifth with the tonic and dominant notes maintaining their centrality throughout. The 3–2–1 cadential progression (framed), apart from serving to bring the song to its conclusion, is mainly employed to complete phrase b and its variant phrase b1. The phrases that make up this song unfold in the following sequence: a b a_1 b c b_1 d e f b_1 with phrase b and its variant b_1 in most cases serving as recurring phrases.

Example 3.4 The second song in *muṣaddar*

As already remarked, the *murakkaz* serves as a bridge between the *muṣaddar* and the *barwal* sections. It is at this stage that a perceptible increase in speed announces the coming of the *barwal* section. The *murakkaz* transcribed in Example 3.5 shows elements already noted in the other songs, such as reliance on syncopation, the frequent use of the perfect fourth (c^1 to f^1) and minor third (a^1 to c^1) intervals, as well as the reiteration of phrases and motifs. The *murakkaz* pushes the *nawba* forward to the *barwal* section, a process that results in an accelerated tempo to almost double the speed of the *muṣaddar* (see Example 3.6).

Example 3.5 *Murakkaz*

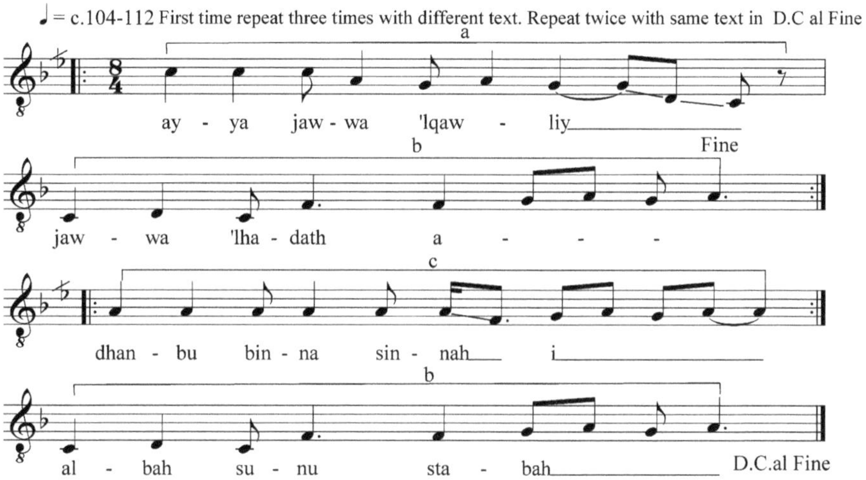

Example 3.6 The first song in *barwal*

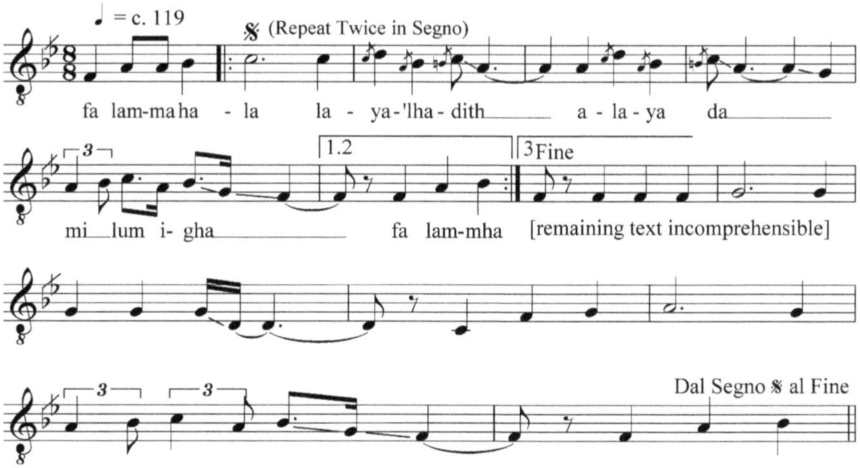

Features already noted in the *muṣaddar* section, such as the 3–2–1 cadential progression, re-emerge in this song as well, with the entire work gaining more coherence. The first song in *barwal* leads to two interlinked sets of calls and responses with a responsorial verse emerging after each rendition of the two interlinked sets. These sets, together with the responsorial verse, constitute the second song of *barwal*. Here we are reminded of the call-and-response structure of the traditional *nawba*. Examples 3.7a, 3.7b and 3.7c show the last occurrence of both the call and response sets, as well as of the responsorial verse. While some of the calls give the sensation of a quasi free-metered music, their corresponding replies evolve within a more rigid rhythmic and melodic set-up.

An answer as to how the musicians, and people in general, remember and interact with a musical structure like that of *nāḥ al-ḥamām* as restyled by Araibi may partially be found in the structure of the music itself and in the way the melodic material is organized within it. A strong element in this restyled *nawba*, as in other *nawbāt* recomposed by Araibi, is its strong repetitive element. According to Snyder (2000: 65), 'repeatedly returning to a particular pitch or pattern creates a closural effect.' Closure is here understood as 'the tendency of perceptual groupings to have beginning and ending boundaries' (Snyder 2000: 257). The above transcriptions show important closural points generally approached by the reiteration of familiar musical patterns and motifs, as if the 'familiar is more closural than the unfamiliar' (Snyder 2000: 65). Clear closures and groupings, as employed in the present recording, facilitate recollection processes and, consequently, serve as memory chunks. This applies not only to musicians, who will be able to perform a well-learned *nawba* on 'auto-pilot' as most frequently required by Araibi on stage, but also to listeners familiar with this music, or at least with its conventions. In this regard, Snyder (2000: 66) observes that 'music that does not exhibit clear patterns of closure is much more difficult to recollect: each detail must be remembered by itself, rather than as part of an organized memory chunk'. In Araibi's *nawba*, exact recollection on the part of musicians is of paramount importance since, compared with *zāwiya* practices, reliance on calls and responses is minimal. The organization of the different components of music into a hierarchical musical structure, as previously discussed, not only aids memorization but moreover supports the rapport between performers and listeners both in live and recorded performances. In a way, all this explains Araibi's claim that he has popularized the *ma'lūf* and its *nawba* repertoire in particular and brought it out of *zāwiya* reclusion. His claim that Libyans nowadays have a greater appreciation for the *ma'lūf* stems not only from his effort to 'professionalize' the sound of the ensemble but also from his own work in redesigning the *nawba* into a style with which people alien or unfamiliar to *zāwiya* can identify themselves, remember and, eventually, assimilate. In this sense, Araibi's 1964 project to revitalize the *ma'lūf* tradition implied the process of musical translation wherein music was given different shades to become more 'palatable' and, consequently, more comprehensible, meaningful and useful to the unfamiliar listener. Such a process takes place within a fabric of other interrelated processes that may vary from the initial formation and ongoing reshaping of

Example 3.7a The first set of calls and responses

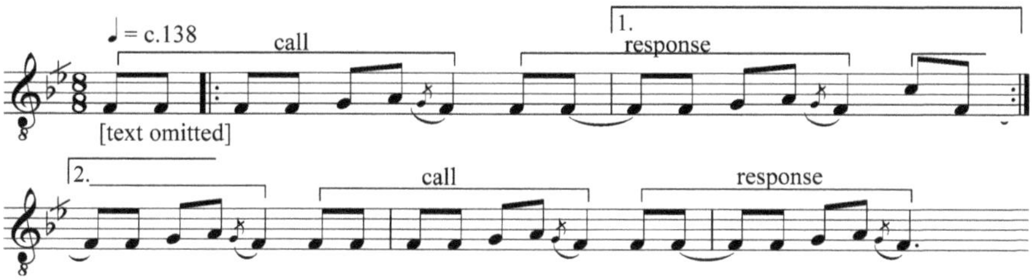

Example 3.7b The second set of calls and responses

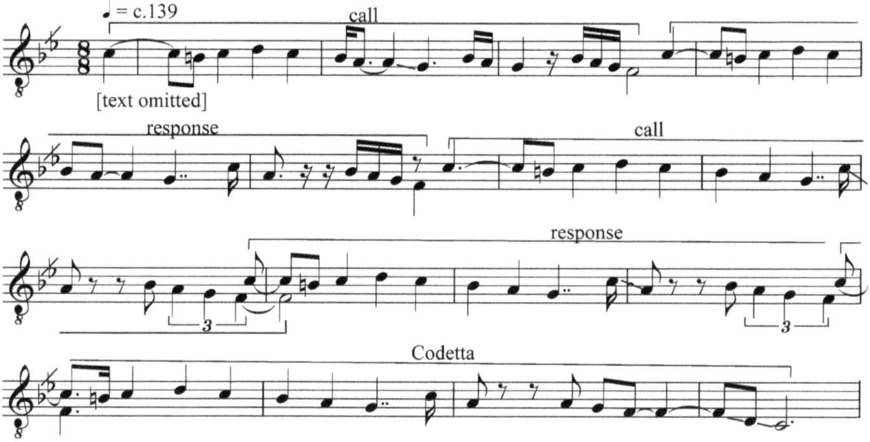

Example 3.7c Responsorial verse

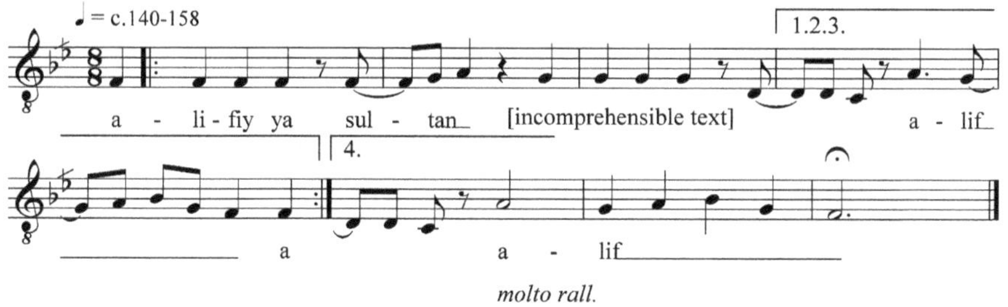

impressions in the listener's mind about a particular musical genre to political, economic and religious circumstances that nurture, reshape and/or constrain the same translation process.

Conclusion

This chapter has focused on aspects of change and continuity in the *ma'lūf* of Libya. Social, political and cultural conditions have supported the coexistence of the two styles, each within its distinct framework. Political change was to some extent anticipated in musical change with strong expression of Arabness supporting the safeguarding of the *turāth*. Moreover, the innovations proposed by Araibi and his long-term subsidized projects, and the consequent patronage bestowed on him over the years, maintained the process initiated by him in the mid-1960s. At this stage, it is worth noting that patronage and state subsidy are to the present time considered in the Maghreb as the sustenance of genres claiming an Andalusian origin. When referring to Andalusian music in Morocco and Algeria, for instance, Langlois (2009: 216–17) notes that this 'is a genre which requires patronage either from elites or from governmental structures' and, therefore, the implication of such a genre 'with regimes of power' is inevitable. He attributes this situation to sales of recordings being inadequate to enable the sustenance of a large industry, as is the case with more popular genres. Langlois' observation fits the Libyan case neatly, with ensembles like that of Araibi providing music for Libyan national TV and radio, and adapting their repertoires to meet expectations from patrons and governmental organizations. In addition, as noted above, the intermingling between politics, patronage, music professionalization and the implementation of post-1969 revolutionary policies has contributed towards an ongoing initiative to maintain continuity whilst at the same time popularizing the genre, as clearly evident, for instance, in the annual Tripoli festival of *ma'lūf*.

In terms of the 'music itself', the innovated *nawba* as proposed by Araibi has retained aesthetic features from the *ma'lūf az-zāwiya*, even if these are not always acknowledged by some *ma'lūf* aficionados for whom the 'authentic' is revered and, therefore, inimitable, since it leans heavily on cultural values that are intrinsically Islamic and, according to them, resilient to time and the change brought with it. At this stage, the question that comes to one's mind is whether the *ma'lūf al-idhā'a* will continue to change in the future, giving more space to innovative ideas both in terms of restylization and performance practice. This definitely depends on the socio-cultural context that will shape the Libya of the future and the extent to which the country will comply with or resist modern trends that consequently may generate further changes.

Chapter 4
The Musical Making of *Ma'lūf*

> In music, as in architecture, invention consists in constructing new works with the aid of material taken from the common domain.
>
> (Ferretti 1934, *Estetica Gregoriana Ossia Trattato delle Forme Musicali del Canto Gregoriano* [trans. Treitler 1975: 6])

An aspect mentioned in the previous chapters is the important role of the sheikh in *zāwiya* in selecting *ma'lūf* songs belonging to the same *maqām* and weaving them into a *nawba*. It has also been noted that *ma'lūf* songs, apart from belonging to a *maqām*, also belong to one of the four *īqā'āt* that regulate the rhythmic element of the same repertory, that is *īqā' muṣaddar* (8/4), *barwal* (8/8), *murabba'* (6/4) and *'allājī* (6/8). *Nawbāt* in the last two rhythmic modes are rarely performed nowadays, with their lack of usability leading songs in these two rhythmic groups to the verge of extinction. Whilst in the context of *zāwiya* performances the selection of songs for the making of a *nawba* takes place in the course of performance, in *ma'lūf al-idhā'a* performances a *nawba* is entirely pre-composed and, therefore, such a selective process takes place beforehand.

The present chapter will focus on the making of *ma'lūf* songs, with the technique of melodic criss-crossing at the forefront of such a process. In addition, the chapter will shed light on how such a technique nurtured and sustained the melodic identity and, consequently, pertinent stylistic features of this repertoire over time. When listening to *ma'lūf*, the consistency of style is evident and therefore worth scrutinizing, not only from a structural point of view but also from the extra-musical aspect that in itself complements the same practice. Melodic criss-crossing is a technique that refers, in this case, to the reuse of melodic material from one *ma'lūf* song in another—it is a kind of melodic intertextuality that for its realization relies on further techniques, such as those of omission, augmentation and truncation.

In the domain of ethnomusicology, the compositional technique of relying on the combination of material derived from different songs has been highlighted, for instance, by Merriam (1964: 177) when he asserts that 'one of the most frequently mentioned techniques of composition is that which involves taking parts of old songs and putting them together to make new ones'. On a more particular note, Nettl (2005: 27) states, for instance, that an Arapaho Indian takes a bit from one song, something from another and a phrase from a third to make a new Peyote song. Melodic construction techniques that follow the approach pointed out here have also been noted by Jeffery (1992: 93–4), referring to late Byzantine–Slavonic chants and how in recent centuries melodies inherited from the Middle

Ages within this repertoire 'have come to be understood as constructed from a finite series of short melodic phrases'. The overlapping of phrases within a song and from different songs in a complex and criss-crossing manner has also been noted by Wang (1992) when analysing the 'mosaic structure' of songs in a Chinese art music tradition called *nanguan.* In her analysis, Wang identifies a set of rules emerging from the construction of the same songs according to which elements are chosen and combined to form a structure appropriate to the *nanguan* song style. Similar processes, although on a somewhat larger scale, have been pointed out by Tenzer when referring to the repertoire of the Indonesian gamelan *Kebyar*. Tenzer (2000: 153) observes, for instance, that this repertoire 'absorbs, borrows from, and is engaged in continuing dialog with other gamelan repertoires'. The melodic criss-crossing scrutinized in the forthcoming discussion accentuates what Wang (1992: 24) describes as 'the aesthetic principle of diversity in unity, of creating the unlimited with the limited'.

Regarding the composition of new *ma'lūf* songs, there seems to exist in Libya a difference of opinion among the informants whom I interviewed on this matter. Some believe that *ma'lūf* songs can still be composed nowadays, while others are of the opinion that the *ma'lūf* repertory is now fixed and new songs are no longer composed and integrated. For instance, in an interview with Ali Munsur al-Ghannay, at the time of research a teacher of *muwashshaḥāt* singing at Mahād Jamāl Ad-Dīn Al-Mīlādī school of music, he described a kind of joint compositional process in which 'a sheikh composes the words and asks someone else to set his words to a *ma'lūf* melody'. His comment unfolded in the present as if the composition of *ma'lūf* songs were still in practice. He went even further to assert that he 'was the first in Libya who had composed an *ughniya* on the rhythm of *ma'lūf*' because, according to him, 'it is the rhythm that identifies *ma'lūf*'. Whilst one may or may not agree with al-Ghannay's former statement, his latter statement may be understood in light of the musical fusion so commonly employed in contemporary compositions and, therefore, it would be beyond the purpose of this chapter to elaborate on it. The possible link between *ughniya* and *ma'lūf* songs was also mentioned by Muhammad Elimam, who at the time of my research was an official in the Libyan consulate in Malta. He explained how well-loved tunes and themes from popular Libyan *ughniya* songs could have been brought into the *ma'lūf* repertory; only *ma'lūf* aficionados and followers with a strong knowledge of both *ma'lūf* and *ughniya* songs would note such blending. This sheds more light on the inclusion in this repertoire of musical material extraneous to *ma'lūf* apart from that featured in Chapter 2.

Expressing his opinion on the composition of new *ma'lūf* songs, Sheikh Muhammad Gebril El Ashhab (a member of Araibi's ensemble mentioned in the previous chapters) insisted that, nowadays, *ma'lūf* songs are hardly composed and that the repertory is fixed. Some active *ma'lūf* participants excluded all possibility of *ma'lūf* songs being composed nowadays. According to them, the practice of adding *ma'lūf* songs to the established repertory is no longer followed. Although they could not say when this practice had ceased, the accounts of sheikhs composing new *ma'lūf* songs as revealed in Chapter 2 show that such practice was still current in the mid twentieth century. In that chapter it was noted that certain sheikhs of *ma'lūf* are still remembered for the composition of particular *ma'lūf* songs and that they occasionally set their text to tunes borrowed either from the music of colonialists or from those of neighbouring musical traditions. This adds evidence to the fact that some *ma'lūf* songs found their place in the repertory much later than other songs labelled as 'authentic'.

The aura of the *qadīm* ascribed to this repertory and the anonymity attributed to almost the entirety of it make it impossible to talk to the composers of such songs and attain from them knowledge regarding the compositional techniques employed. The benefits of understanding the composition of a musical piece not only as it transpires in its sonic and/or written form but as it was crafted by its creator(s) are several. Such an insight, for instance, would enrich the researcher's analysis with more objectivity and allows for a more in-depth exploration of what Nattiez (1990) calls the *poietic* level, which is to say, what takes place at the phase of creation.

Although I attempted several times to gain insight into the musical making of these songs, the feedback I got from my informants always remained somewhat vague, with musicians either referring to 'inspiration' or straying off into illustrations of the wider phenomenon of the *maqām*. Sheikh Muhammad, for instance, emphasized to me the role of inspiration and how this generates the feeling required to compose *ma'lūf* songs. It seemed to me that the 'inspiration' explanation was a convenient answer to get away from an intricate subject that seemed to him hard both to think of and discuss. On the other hand, El Sibaei stressed the importance of the *maqām* and emphasized that the melodic content of these songs is regulated by the *maqām* to which each song belongs. He stressed the fact that the melodic criss-crossing that I had observed in my analysis of these songs, and which will be discussed in the forthcoming sections, was strongly regulated by the *maqām* phenomenon, mainly the characteristic melodic movements within individual *maqāmāt* and existing *maqām* interconnections.

In order to investigate such criss-crossing I rely on a collection of *ma'lūf* song transcriptions made at the beginning of the 1990s by El Sibaei (see Figure 4.1 below). El Sibaei collected these 178 songs for his doctoral thesis (later published as El Sibaei 2001) at the University of Cairo. The songs are categorized according to the six *maqāmāt* employed in the Libyan *ma'lūf* and sub-categorized according to the *īqā'āt* to which they belong, that is *muṣaddar*, *barwal*, *'allājī* and *murabba'*. The value of these transcriptions lies in the fact that they were done by a native researcher and therefore reflect an insider's conceptualization of the music.

Figure 4.2 below shows a classification of the 178 *ma'lūf* songs collected by El Sibaei, mainly, from *zāwiya* environments. As has already been argued in the previous chapters, the number of Libyan *ma'lūf* songs is incalculable, thus El Sibaei's work is only representative of such a vast repertoire; many other *ma'lūf* songs were extinct by the time these were collected. The small number of collected songs in the rhythmic modes *'allājī* and *murabba'* reflects the extinction of songs in these *īqā'āt*.

Figure 4.1 Professor Abdalla El Sibaei

Maqām	**Number of songs in each *maqām***	***muṣaddar* ($\frac{8}{4}$)**	***barwal* ($\frac{8}{8}$)**	***murabba'* ($\frac{6}{4}$)**	***'allājī* ($\frac{6}{8}$)**
rāst	30	14	11	3	2
hussayn	49	12	27	5	5
nawā	15	3	5	2	5
asba'ayn	35	9	19	4	3
sīkah	34	7	20	2	5
muhayyar	15	4	6	4	1

Figure 4.2 *Ma'lūf* songs classified according to their *maqām* and *īqā'*

Relying on El Sibaei's transcriptions, the present chapter investigates evident melodic criss-crossing in *ma'lūf* songs both within the same *maqām* as well as within other *maqāmāt*. For that purpose, the present inquiry unfolds in stages with analytical phases that lead from micro to macro levels of inquiry. In line with this, the present analysis begins by revealing how melodic material in one song reiterates, sometimes precisely and sometimes with modification, existing melodic material from within the same song and how all this relates to the *maqām* to which the song belongs—in this case *maqām rāst*. In light of this, a discussion of this *maqām* and its distinct features becomes central. This initial stage is then followed by further investigation into how melodic material emerging in one song is interconnected to songs belonging to the same *maqām* and *īqā'*, as well as to other *maqāmāt* and *īqā'āt*. Such enquiry is then followed by other sections aimed at investigating the correlation between melodic criss-crossing, stability and interpretation in the course of performance. What is meant here by melodic stability is the ability of a melody to maintain its 'essential selfhood' (Bronson 1951: 51) against an overwhelming number of factors that might change it intrinsically, such as individual interpretations, melody–text bonding and performance locale. All this aims at highlighting the safeguards for the melodic stability of criss-crossed material as well as the stylistic identity of the repertoire more widely. I will argue, for instance, that certain parts of songs or phrases in the repertoire of our concern are prone to variation while others need to be kept stable to maintain a song's identity. For this purpose, in the second section I discuss how melodic criss-crossing may also occur in performance and how this unfolds within certain parameters. This is then followed by another section focusing on the stability of criss-crossed material in the wider context of issues that arise from the interpretation of *ma'lūf*. Finally, I focus on extra-musical processes and how these assist the stability of melodic material in this repertoire and, by extension, of criss-crossed melodic content.

Melodic Criss-crossing in *Ma'lūf Rāst* Songs and Beyond

To illustrate melodic interconnectedness in *ma'lūf* songs belonging to *maqām rāst*, I shall start by taking one *rāst* song called *yā muḥammad* (referred to hereafter as YM), in *īqā' muṣaddar*, and analyse its internal melodic criss-crossing. The selection of YM emerges from its importance in the *ma'lūf az-zāwiya* repertoire, especially on *mawlid* day, when the first *nawba* performed during the morning parade is the one that bears the same title, that is *nawba yā muḥammad*. As its place at the beginning of such parades suggests, this song is intended to initiate an event that brings happiness, a mood supported by the *maqām* to which it belongs, that is, *maqām rāst*. In Arab music this *maqām* is believed to bring happiness and pride, two predominant elements in this Islamic event, as already noted in Chapter 2.[1]

[1] When referring to the development of this *maqām* over the years Plakhova (2006: 197) relies on various sources, pointing out the fact that this *maqām* underwent a long

Before discussing internal melodic criss-crossing techniques in this song, it would be beneficial to look at some characteristics of *maqām rāst* and how these eventually feature in *ma'lūf rāst* songs.

To start with, one may say that *maqām rāst* takes its name from its tonic note c^1, known in Arab music as *rāst*. In more recent Arab music theory books *maqām rāst* is represented as in Example 4.1 with the third and seventh degrees flattened by roughly a quarter tone in ascending form, and the latter degree fully flattened in its descending direction.

Example 4.1 *Maqām rāst*

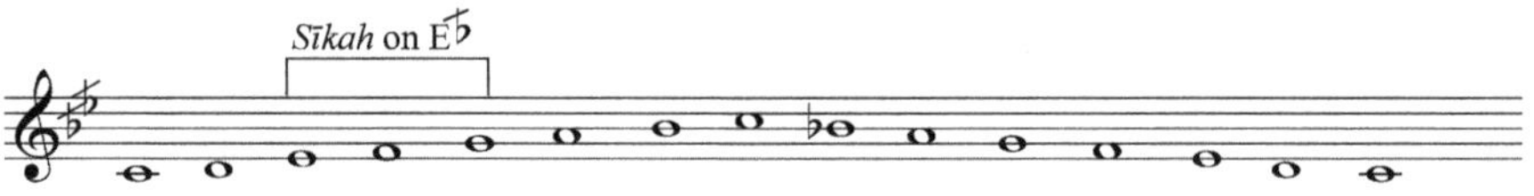

When referring to range in the 12 *rāst-muwashshaḥāt* in the Beirut *al-muwashshaḥāt* collection, Plakhova (2006: 199) presents the 'total range of *maqām rāst*' as it shows up in the same collection (see Example 4.2) with a range from g^0 up to g^2. Through her extensive representation of this *maqām* she could comment, for instance, that on average the c^1–c^2 range is the most 'active zone' of the *maqām* employed in the Beirut *rāst* collection and that, in general, the lower tetrachord g^0–c^1 is 'more actively present than the upper one, c^2–g^2' (Plakhova 2006: 200).

Example 4.2 The total range of *maqām rāst*

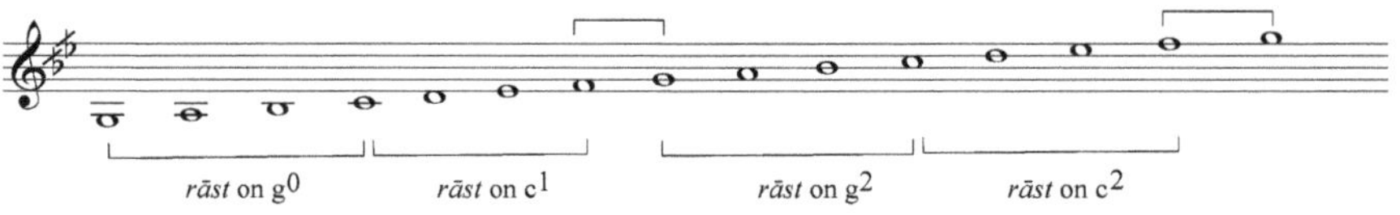

When Marcus (2007: 27) refers to the distinction between the theoretical and the performing dimensions of a *maqām*, he mentions 'individual notes that are occasionally used in performance but that are not part of a *maqām*'s primary scale'. He also points out the fact that most *maqāmāt* 'have one or more accidentals that are an important feature of the *maqām*'s overall character, occurring not haphazardly but rather in specific melodic contexts' (Marcus 2007: 27). For instance, in *maqām rāst* he attributes primary importance to the accidental d-half-sharp^1 that has two main functions: firstly, to serve as a lower neighbouring note to the note e-half-flat^1 and, secondly, to replace the d-natural^1 temporally when this features as a lower auxiliary in between two e-half-flats^1. As an accidental secondary in importance in

historical evolution that included, amongst other things, an increasing shift towards smaller intervals and more subtle microtonal shadings.

maqām rāst he identifies the a-flat^1 serving both as an upper neighbouring note to g^1 as well as providing a signal to an upcoming cadence on the tonic.

From the melodic point of view, Marcus (2007: 29) notes that another characteristic of *maqām rāst* is the generally stepwise movement of melodic phrases with inserted melodic leaps between the c^1 and e-half-flat^1 with the omission of d^1. This occurs mainly on phrases stressing the e-half-flat^1 and in phrases ascending to g^1. A leap similar to the one just described, though less common, is the one that occasionally occurs in ascending movement between e-half-flat^1 and g^1. In such cases the f^1 is temporally omitted.

In addition, Marcus (2007: 29) states that in *maqām rāst* one finds 'the use of multiple upper tetrachords'. For instance, when the b-half-flat^1 is replaced by b-flat^1 a *nahāwand* tetrachord on g^1 (g^1–a^1–b-flat^1–c^2) occurs. This is sometimes replaced by the sounding of the *hijaz* tetrachord that also builds on g^1 (g^1–a-flat^1–b^1–c^2). When referring to the use of upper tetrachords in *maqām rāst*, El Sibaei (2001: 55) notes the occasional use in *ma'lūf rāst* songs of the *bayyāti* tetrachord on g^1, with a^1 replaced by a-half-flat^1 and b-half-flat^1 by b-flat^1, that is g^1 (g^1–a-half-flat^1–b-flat^1–c^2). In addition, he also observes the occasional use of the lower pentachord *nikriz* on c^1 with f^1 replaced by f-sharp^1 and e-half-flat^1 substituted by e-flat^1 as follows: c^1 (c^1–d^1–e-flat^1–f-sharp^1–g^1). These pitch changes generate in the music a kind of 'passing modulation'. In this regard Marcus (1992: 175) notes that 'the importance of modulation [in Arab music] is ... recognized in statements which present modulation as one of the primary ways for a musician or composer to exhibit his intellectual and technical mastery of the art'. In relation to this, Shiloah (1981: 40) asserts that 'a skilled musician distinguishes himself by excelling in the modulatory progressions that allow him to move away from and back to the main *maqām*'. Modulatory phases in Libyan *ma'lūf* songs may be considered by some Arab music scholars as 'passing modulations', which, according to Marcus (1992: 179–80), are known in Arab music as *ḥaraka* (literally, a brief movement). Marcus (1992: 179–80) adds that these brief modulatory phrases 'play an important role since it is often only in these ... that some of the rarest and least-used modes ever appear in practice'.

YM is one of a set of 14 songs belonging to *maqām rāst* and *īqā' muṣaddar.* The following is a list of those 14 songs with initials in brackets for convenient reference when necessary:

'adrī (A)
aṭallat al-ḥajar (AH)
'inna l-hawā (IH)
jazta 'alā al-awṭān (JA)
āhi 'ala mā fāt nār al-hashā waqūdi(AMHQ)
āhi 'ala mā fāta law kān yanfa' (AMKY)
bushrā haniyya (BH)
jā zamān al-inshirāḥ (JAA)
dhāk an-nahār (DN)
'ashiqtu sulṭān al-milāḥ (ASM)
qad hājat ashwāqī (QHA)
lī ḥabīb (LH)
na'isa al-ḥabīb (NH)
yā Muḥammad (YM)

Rāst ma'lūf songs in El Sibaei's collection begin on the tonic c^1, the dominant note g^1 or the upper tonic c^2. Examples 4.3a, b and c classify the above songs according to whether they begin in the low (four songs), middle (four songs) or high (six songs) register.[2] YM belongs to the group of songs starting in the high register. Analysing the most frequently used intervals in *ma'lūf rāst* songs more generally, one notes upward leaps unfolding (in order of frequency) in thirds, fourths, fifths, sixths and octaves, whilst in their downward direction melodic skips are predominantly in thirds and, occasionally, in fourths. Moreover, the strong bond that exists between the fifth degree of this *maqām* and the tonic is very evident in all the *ma'lūf rāst* songs in El Sibaei's collection, as the forthcoming examples reveal.

With the exception of three songs, songs in this *maqām*, as in YM, consist of two sections. The first section begins on the upper tonic of the *maqām* and gradually descends to the lower register. By contrast, the second section begins in the low register and progresses gradually up to the high register, with the entire melodic material unfolding within an octave. Overall, the melodic line of this song, even as noted by Marcus above, is mostly stepwise, although occasional leaps occur, especially between c^1 and f^1 in instances when the former and the latter occur adjacently at the closure of a phrase and the beginning of a new one respectively. Modelled on Plakhova's observation of the Beirut *muwashshaḥāt*, one may infer that the range between c^1 and a^1 is the most 'active zone' in this song. Moreover, cadential emphasis in YM is primarily weighted towards d^1 (six times) with other phrases cadencing to c^1 (five times), c^2 (twice) and g^1 (once).

Example 4.3a Low register beginnings

2 A somewhat similar paradigmatic analysis to introductory passages was also employed by Stock (1996b: 102–104) in his analysis of three *erhu* (a Chinese two-stringed bowed instrument) pieces. To facilitate analysis, song texts are being omitted from both this and similar musical examples.

Example 4.3b Middle register beginnings

Example 4.3c High register beginnings

In itself, the general stepwise melodic motion allows for a better comprehension of the text. Indeed, YM presents a good balance between syllabic and melismatic singing, with the latter mostly employed at cadence points, as the syllabic setting in the first section of the song reveals (see Example 4.4). The melodic setting of the text is occasionally aided either by the inclusion of vocables or by the reiteration of syllables. The third phrase in Example 4.4, for instance, unfolds on the syllable 'A', which is a reiteration of the first syllable in the word *aqaddiy*. The inclusion of this syllable brings both the first hemistich and its melodic content to full completion. However, the interpolation of meaningless syllables in this kind of singing might have other functions, which may also match those noted by Hughes when he referred to the use of nonsense syllables in some Asian and European musical traditions. When referring to this aspect, Hughes (1989: 3) remarks that in these traditions nonsense syllables are sometimes used sophistically as a form of notation representing pertinent musical information related to articulation, 'tone color, resonance and/or pitch'. A more focused analysis of this aspect in the *ma'lūf* repertoire, currently beyond the scope of the present discussion, may reveal uses similar to the ones pointed out by Hughes above.

Example 4.4 *Ma'lūf* song *yā muḥammad* as transcribed by El Sibaei

The letters given to each phrase in Example 4.4 are intended to reveal the reiteration of some of the phrases as they emerge throughout the song. At this stage, it is worth noting the fact that the phrase marks shown in Example 4.4 were added by me and decided on the basis of close listening to different recordings of this song. A close look at the phrases in Example 4.4 makes one realize that Phrase D is the most reiterated throughout the entire song. It gains importance not only because of its frequent occurrence but also for its function in recalling for the listener melodic material retrieved from Phrase B that occurs only once (excluding repeats). Apart from that, the melodic material in Phrase B constitutes the bulk melodic material of Phrase D, with the latter generating a kind of 'nostalgia' for melodic content (in this case that of Phrase B) that only exists in its transformed form. Moreover, melodic interconnection applies to other phrases as well. Melodic material from Phrase H, for instance, surfaces as a transformed version of the melodic material emerging in Phrase E. Such reworking employs a diminution, the inclusion of an inverted appoggiatura and a melodic insertion. Extracts from the two phrases are aligned in Example 4.5 for comparison. Notably, each version in Example 4.5 retains eight beats, with the insertion occurring due to the contraction caused by the diminution. Devoid of any appoggiaturas, the same extracts show a cadential descending sequence of seconds—medium–medium–major—leading to the final note; according to Touma (1996: 29) such a descending sequence of seconds is typical of *maqām rāst*.

Example 4.5 The reworking of a phrase in *yā muḥammad*

At a higher level one may also uncover melodic criss-crossing in *rāst* songs belonging to *īqā' muṣaddar*. A scrutiny of the 14 *rāst* songs in this group shows the way in which melodic material is common to all the songs in this category. Example 4.6 below shows an alignment of a cadential unit occurring in all the *rāst* songs. Its frequent reappearance in *rāst* songs belonging to all the *īqā'āt* in this category makes it central in *rāst* songs belonging to this tradition, as I shall show later on, and it is also utilized by other songs in other *maqāmāt*. Example 4.6 aligns the melodic components of this unit on the basis of how they unfold. The same example also reveals how this unit emerges in different songs belonging to *īqā' muṣaddar*, either precisely or in modified form. While the initial and ending notes of this unit are consistent, the intermediary melodic content is not always so. For instance, the mediating melodic material in song JA relies on several 'backtrackings'

Example 4.6 An alignment of a cadential unit

before it actually resolves on the final cadence note. In addition, in all the aligned passages the cadencing on c^1 is generated from a melodic motion proceeding from the note g^1 to the auxiliary note a^1 and back to g^1. The middle segment revolves round the renegotiation of notes g^1–f^1–e^1 until the pattern proceeds to the final cadential notes e^1–d^1–c^1, accentuating one of the main characteristic features of this *maqām*, as remarked on by Marcus (above). To some extent, this also reiterates Plakhova's (2006: 204) observation of the f^1–e^1–d^1–c^1 unit being 'appurtenant to the final *rāst*-cadences in the 12 *rāst*-muwashshaḥat' in the Beirut collection. Moreover, she also notes that this unit distinguishes itself by its sharp rhythmic contrast when compared to the preceding uniform motion, something that also occurs in this case, as is evident in Example 4.6. Moreover, the consistent auxiliary movement g^1–a^1–g^1 serves as a reference point, a kind of announcement that a cadence on c^1 is approaching. When referring to the importance of reference points in music, Sloboda (1985: 259) notes that 'without reference points, it would be impossible for people to make the necessary anticipatory and planned adjustments to bring their behaviour into co-ordination with others'. Applying this to the songs of our concern, one may propound the idea that these reference points are useful as points of coordination, especially in the context of *ma'lūf* group singing.

Other melodic interconnection is also sparsely found in different songs within the same *īqā'* group. This may be noticed, for example, in songs belonging to groups beginning in the same register, as shown in Example 4.2. Songs AMHQ and QHA in Example 4.7 belong to the group beginning in the middle register; the melodic material shared in this group is evident.

Example 4.7 Common melodic material occurring in two songs belonging to the group beginning in the middle register

Further melodic criss-crossing is also present in songs not belonging to the same group. For example, although songs A and AMKY belong to the groups beginning in the low and high register respectively, they employ some common melodic material, as revealed in Example 4.8 below. The same figure reveals melodic material emerging in its truncated form in song A when compared to its occurrence in song AMKY.

In addition, whilst certain songs do not reiterate the same melodic material, they may reiterate the gist of the same melodic movement. The monotonic character in YM noted above, is, for instance, present in other songs such as in JA (see Example 4.9 below). In the Libyan *ma'lūf* monotonic passages are employed to

Example 4.8 Truncation techniques employed in melodic criss-crossing

Example 4.9 Monotonic movements

facilitate fitting in words within a phrase and, consequently, maintaining a balance between the lengths of sections within a song. In both AMKY and A the monotonic movement of f^{1} is preceded by c^{1}, which rapport stresses the relationship between the first and fourth degree of the tetrachord on *rāst* c^{1}. Apart from that, the note f^{1} attains importance when it serves as a common note for two conjunct tetrachords, that is two tetrachords having the same note in common. Similar monotonic passages are also employed in Phrases A and H of YM above, and in *rāst* songs belonging to other *īqā'āt*, as I shall show later.

Mālūf rāst songs in this *īqā'* make use of tetrachords belonging to other *maqāmāt*, as rightly pointed out by El Sibaei. Song DN, for instance, employs quite profusely the tetrachord *bayyāti* on g^{1} with the inclusion of the a-half-flat^{1} and the substitution of the b-half-flat^{1} by b-flat^{1} leading on to c^{2} (see Example 4.10). This tetrachord is very evident in this song as it is employed three times. Apart from that, a melodic movement implying pentachord *nikriz* can be noted in song IH, mainly, with the presence of the f-sharp^{1} (see Example 4.11). In the same song, one also notes the leap from c^{1} to e-half-flat^{1} with the omission of the d^{1}; this occurs in a phrase stressing the e-half-flat^{1} within an ascending movement to g^{1}. This characteristic was also pointed out by Marcus (above) as one of the characteristic note movements in *maqām rāst*.

Example 4.10 The employment of tetrachord *bayyāti*

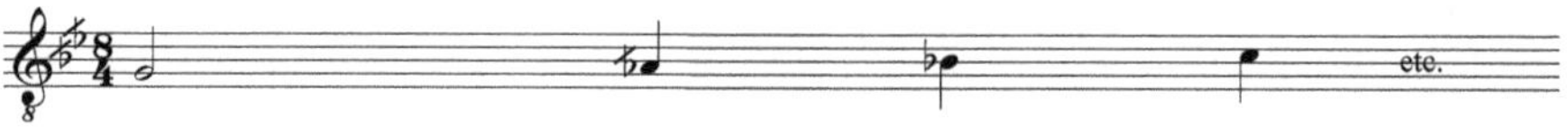

Example 4.11 Implied pentachord *nikriz*

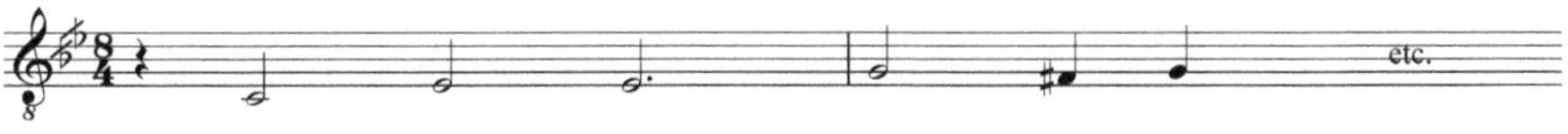

As in the case of *rāst* songs in *īqā‘ muṣaddar*, *rāst* songs in *barwal* share melodic material with songs belonging to the same *īqā‘*. The following list includes the titles of 11 *rāst* songs in *īqā‘ barwal*, with initials in brackets for quick reference.

al-khalā'a muqīma fī wādī fās (HMF)
ar-rakāyib sāru 'annā (RS)
darhā 'alā al-kāsāt (DK)
rashīq al-qadd (RQ)
sha'rik min janaḥ al-ghurāb (SJ)
fiq yā khammār (FYH)
qad khaṭaft naẓra (FHN)
miskīn man bil-hawā muqayyad (MMH)
hal tarā yā ḥubbī (HTH)
wa-ḥusnik ḥīna ishtahar (WHA)
yā 'ādhilī bi-llāh (YAA)

Like the *muṣaddar* songs discussed above, *rāst* songs in *īqā‘ barwal* may be classified according to whether their beginning is in the low, middle or high register. Example 4.11 shows that, with the exception of Song YAA in the middle register group, all the songs begin on c^1, c^2 or g^1. Apart from showing these three groups, Examples 4.12a, b and c below reveal the melodic affinity that exists between the initial melodic content of songs in each beginning group. Such affinity is so evident that certain beginnings are distinct from each other either by a slight change in their rhythmic content, as in Songs DK and RS in the low register, or else by the elaboration of plainer beginnings (compare, for instance, the first bar of HMF to the first bar of HTH, both in the low register group).

As in *muṣaddar* songs, melodic criss-crossing occurs at different levels, both between songs belonging to the same register group as well as between those in different groups. Songs RS and HMF (low register group), like songs RQ and FYH (low and middle register groups) share the reiteration of the same cadential unit (see Example 4.13 below). At this stage, it is worth noting that the cadential unit in RS and HMF is in itself a recall of the characteristic descending movement to c^1 noted in Example 4.6. This observation accentuates the point that certain melodic material is common to all rhythmic groups, as I shall show later on.

Songs with reiterated cadential units, although similar in pitch, may vary in their rhythmic content. Example 4.14 below aligns two different cadential units that, although stable melodically, vary rhythmically (compare, for instance, RQ to WHA and MMH to HTH, FHN and YAA).

The melodic criss-crossing so far explored widens further when one realizes that melodic material in one *īqā‘* appears in other *īqā‘* as well, either precisely or in modified form. The cadential unit plotted in Example 4.6, for instance, also shows up in songs belonging to *īqā‘ barwal*, even if at a lesser frequency. Aligning

Example 4.12a Low register beginnings in *rāst* songs (*barwal*)

Example 4.12b Middle register beginnings in *rāst* songs (*barwal*)

Example 4.12c High register beginnings in *rāst* songs (*barwal*)

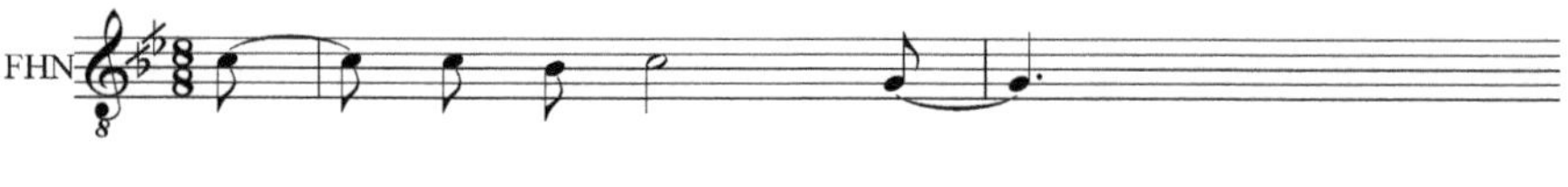

this cadential unit as it emerges in some *barwal* and *muṣaddar* songs reveals an interesting melodic correspondence. Example 4.15 shows this unit in songs NH in *muṣaddar* and MMH in *barwal*; melodically, the two passages employ the same content except for the inserted semiquaver note in MMH.

Example 4.13 The reiteration of cadential units

Example 4.14 Similar cadential units showing rhythmic variety

Example 4.15 A cadential unit common in both *barwal* and *muṣaddar* songs

The same cadential unit also occurs in *barwal* song SJ (see Example 4.16). The alignment in Example 4.16 of song SJ over *muṣaddar* songs YM and BH shows the employment of insertion and omission techniques; whereas in song SJ such a central cadential unit is extended by an insertion (framed), in BH the resolution of e^1 on the first d^1 (as in SJ and YM) is lacking due to the omission of the latter note.

Example 4.16 Insertion and omission techniques in the reworking of a cadential unit

Further scrutiny in this regard brings forth other instances of cadential criss-crossing. The first of the two cadential patterns in Example 4.13 occurring in songs RS and HMF (*īqā' barwal*), for example, is found in an augmented form in at least three *muṣaddar* songs: AMKY, JAA and QHA, as shown in Example 4.17. The same can be noted for the cadential pattern that occurs in songs RQ and FYH of the same example. This cadential pattern emerges in song NH (*īqā' muṣaddar*) with a slight rhythmic modification.

Example 4.17 Cadential units in *rāst* songs common in both *īqā' muṣaddar* and *barwal*

Apart from *muṣaddar* and *barwal* songs, El Sebaei's *rāst* collection includes songs in *murabba'* and '*allājī*, totalling five songs in all, as listed below:

Murabba'

qalbī yahwā m'ayshaq (QYM) *mā sabā 'aqlī* (MSA)
ya ṣaḥib al-bara'a (YSAB)

'Allājī

sallim 'alā dhāk al-ḥabīb (SADH) *yakhdum lī sa'dī* (YS)

Even if in small numbers, these songs may be categorized as belonging to the groups beginning in the low, middle or high register (see Example 4.18).

Example 4.18 Low, middle and high beginnings in *murabba'* and *'allājī* songs

Melodically, their beginnings are quite similar to the ones in *muṣaddar* and *barwal*. In addition, monotonic segments on f^1 preceded by c^1 noted in *muṣaddar* and *barwal* are persistently present here too, though slightly more so in *murabba'* than in '*allājī* songs. The cadential unit aligned in Example 4.6 above reoccurs in both groups as well; however, even here it follows a descending movement that leads from a^1 to c^1, with the same movement sometimes generated by the auxiliary movement g^1–a^1–g^1 as can be noted in Example 4.19 below.

Melodic interconnections between *rāst* songs and songs in the other *maqāmāt* exist at several levels as well. For instance, all *ma'lūf* songs in El Sibaei's collection, as in *rāst* songs, begin in either the low, middle or high register. Moreover, the beginning of some of the songs in other *maqāmāt* is similar to those highlighted above. For instance, there is affinity between the beginning of song *dam'ī jarā* (DJ) in *maqām hussayn* (*īqā' muṣaddar*) and the beginning of DK (partially reproduced in Example 4.12) in *maqām rāst* (see Example 4.20 for comparison of both beginnings).

Example 4.19 A persistently present cadential movement common to all *rāst* songs

Example 4.20 Similar beginnings in two different *maqāmāt*

Another frequently occurring musical element in this repertoire is the use of monotonic passages that sometimes even constitute entire sections. Such observation may be extended to songs in different *maqāmāt*. If, for instance, one compares a section from *rāst* song FYH in *īqā' barwal* to a section in song *ṣallū yā 'ibād* (SYA) in *maqām hussayn* (*īqā' barwal*) (see Example 4.21), the definite likeness between the two is evident. Such resemblance revolves round note f^1 as the long-standing monotonic note in both cases. While in *maqām rāst* note f^1 is the fourth degree, in *maqām hussayn* it becomes the third degree. Moreover, whilst the monotonic passage in FYH (*maqām rāst*) resolves on c^2 (the upper tonic of the same *maqām*), that in SYA (*maqām hussayn*) resolves on d^1 (the tonic of this *maqām*); it is as if a resolution to the tonic is necessary in each case to satisfy the sense of expectation generated by the same monotonic passage. In the *ma'lūf*, melodic material with some degree of affinity gains sense when understood not on its own terms—that is, simply as structure—but when understood in terms of the effect it is intended to evoke and how that effect relates to learned expectancy structures initially assimilated through repeated exposure to the same music and, lately, reinforced by techniques such as that of criss-crossing.

Example 4.21 Monotonic passages revolving around the same note

The compositional approach brought forward from the above examples suggests a process similar to what Treitler (1975) calls 'centonization', a term he employs to describe the formation of melodies from existing ones in Gregorian chant. Consistently featured melodic structures in the above examples may qualify as what Treitler calls 'melodic formulas', that is fixed melodic structures that the creator of songs would have exploited to create similarly designed, though different, melodic lines. The process that Treitler (1975: 11) describes in the following citation may shed further insights into similar processes that occurred or are possible in the making of new *ma'lūf* songs:

> In place of the paradigm in which one presumes an act of composition that produces a piece which, in the absence of writing, is submitted to memory and then repeatedly reproduced in performance, we might think of a repeated process of performance-composition—something between the reproduction of a fixed, memorized melody and the extempore invention of a new one. I would call it a *reconstruction*; the performer had to think how the piece was to go and then actively reconstruct it according to what he remembered. In order to do that he would have proceeded from fixed beginnings and sung toward fixed goals, following paths about which he needed only a general, configurational sense, being successively reinforced as he went along and recognized the places he had sung correctly. Different places in the melody would have been fixed in different degrees in his mind; there would have been some places where it would have been

> most helpful to him to have a note-for-note sense of exactly how it went and others where he could go by this way or that, making certain only that he passed through particular pitches or pitch-groups of importance and that eventually he arrived at the goal that he had before his mind's ear, so to speak. But there was always a tendency for paths to be worn smoother the more he sang the melody ... It may well be that [such melodic formulas] became stereotyped through precisely such a tradition as the one I have just set forth. The positions of the formulas within the melodies, that is, played as a crucial role in the process of the oral reconstruction of chants, one that brought about their classification as formulas.

To some extent, stereotyped melodies or melodic movements, including the monotonic ones noted in the above examples, are akin to the melodic formulas that Treitler attributes to Gregorian chants. However, as with Treitler, the central concept here is more what he calls the 'generative system' rather than the 'formula'. By a 'generative system' he means 'a set of conventions that ... a trained performer would have used to generate a particular chant afresh at each performance, or each time he wrote it down' (Jeffery 1992: 15). The making of a *ma'lūf* song may resemble the making of a chant as realized by Treitler, that is 'given a text, a knowledge of the principles [of generative system] should be sufficient for the making of ... a chant' (as quoted from Jeffery 1992). All this, together with the musical examples, reveals a compositional process based in a tradition of melodic *reconstruction*, to reiterate Treitler's term above. It is a compositional craft that brings together a set of conventions dictated by the same *ma'lūf* style with others prescribed by the *maqām* to which each song belongs. It is a tradition of melodic reconstruction that values the familiar, as this provides a sense of stylistic stability for the entire repertoire. This directs one to believe that the *ma'lūf* repertory was preserved not only in terms of text but also in terms of musical style, thanks to such a consistent approach to the making of new songs; it is as if reused and reworked melodies seemed to be the safest approach in the creation of the 'new'. Such musical style could only remain 'faithful' to the antiquity attributed to it by reusing and relying on pre-existing melodic material believed, by quite a good number of informants, to be the 'direct' lineage of the *turāth qadīm*.

Melodic Criss-crossing in Performance

Melodic criss-crossing, whilst a convenient technique for the making of new songs, requires the sheikh's mastery of the repertoire, particularly if such criss-crossing takes place in the course of performance or, as in modern *ma'lūf* ensembles, is employed in the course of transmission during a rehearsal session. In the case of the *ma'lūf*, melodic criss-crossing entails extensive knowledge of the melodic material contained both in songs belonging to that *maqām* and in songs in other *maqāmāt* found in the same repertoire. Such proficiency requires, amongst other skills, a keen discernment on the part of the sheikh to select what melodic material best fits his rendition when employing such criss-crossing and where, for instance, truncation and insertion techniques should be appropriately employed. Therefore, the emphasis placed by Araibi and other informants on the fact that the *ma'lūf* should be *maḥfūẓ* (memorized) refers not just to the memorization of the text and the melodies that go with it, but, in addition, to the insightful knowledge required to extract and blend the appropriate melodic content into newly shaped melodic lines; in other words, good knowledge of the 'generative system' that permits the composer of *ma'lūf* songs to generate the 'novel'.[3] For the purpose of analysing melodic criss-crossing in performance and its relationship with the creation of 'newly formed' melodic lines, I rely again on the cadential unit featured in song IH aligned in Example 4.5. The recorded example to which the following discussion refers is taken from the audio cassette collection of Araibi and his ensemble (referred to hereafter as FHA).

Example 4.22 below shows the cadential unit referred to above as transcribed by El Sibaei (S), whilst FHA^1 and FHA^2 are interpretations of the same unit by Hassan Araibi and his ensemble, with all three renditions employing the resolution of minim f^1 on crotchet e^1. The melodic content preceding that resolution varies to some degree, whilst the one that follows marks striking differences in the three renditions. Putting aside the variation that occurs in the opening part and concentrating on the melodic descent that follows, one gets the impression that the latter melodic material is either newly created or is a kind of variation on the descending melodic movement transcribed by El Sibaei. Nevertheless, further investigation reveals that both descending movements (framed) included in Araibi's interpretation were borrowed from other songs on basis of insightful knowledge of idiomatic melodic movements in *maqām rāst*. This puts at some distance the possibility of entirely new material being used here. Indeed, the descending cadential pattern in FHA^1 may be considered to be an augmented transformation of the melodic pattern that in El Sibaei's transcriptions occurs in songs RS and HMF, both belonging to *maqām rāst* and *īqā' barwal* (see Example 4.17). Also, both songs begin in the low register, as does song IH (see Example 4.12). The descending movement in FHA^2, on the other hand, is a reappearance of the cadential unit found in El Sibaei's transcriptions of *muṣaddar* songs JAA and DN (*maqām rāst*) (Example 4.6).

[3] When referring to similar mental processes in the creation of new musical material, Kleeman brings forth the importance of the information stored in the long-term memory of the performer: 'In his Long Term Memory, where information is stored more or less permanently, he has information about how the musical system of his culture operates. He knows the size of the intervals that constitute the scale(s); he has, in the small dimension, a sense of equal units of time and the ways in which these units are grouped and subdivided, and he has an intuitive grasp of the notes or combinations of notes that are more or less likely to follow others' (1985–1986:1).

Example 4.22 Melodic criss-crossing in performance

The interpretations highlighted above attest to Araibi's insightful knowledge of the *ma'lūf* repertory and his ability to criss-cross melodic material to generate variety from familiar melodic material within the same repertory. What he presents as 'new' may be considered as the displacement of the 'familiar'. Melodic criss-crossing, apart from maintaining the identity of a musical style through its implied 'economizing' on the melodic material employed, also offers to the listener the aesthetic pleasure of re-experiencing the familiar. In this regard, Thompson (2009: 104) notes that familiar music 'is, in effect, the result of a warm and fuzzy feeling that arises simply because we are able to predict events in that music'. When synthesizing predictability with the familiarity of a musical style, Wilson (1989: 105) remarks that 'the greater familiarity listeners have with a style, the more easily they can perceive patterns in a given piece in that style, and the sooner they can begin to become involved in the act of predicting'. The theory that arises from both performance interpretation and El Sebaei's transcriptions puts considerable weight on the highly valued aspect of prediction, as this would add pleasure to the listening experience in an attempt to reinforce order and stability. Nevertheless, such a process does not necessarily imply exact prediction of an upcoming event; rather, it involves listeners using past experiences to make sense out of seemingly new situations and structures. The making, singing and interpretation of *ma'lūf* evolves within a framework that brings together the principles of familiarity, prediction, order and stability on an equal level with the technical considerations that underpin the same framework.

Interpretative Aesthetic Parameters

This section focuses on processes mediating between stability and variation in *ma'luf* performances. The discussion includes an analysis of some of the phrases highlighted in song YM. For this purpose, I rely on two interpretations of this song. The first is that of a traditional ensemble called Firqat Hassan al-Kamiy (FHK) (Hassan al-Kamiy's Ensemble) performed on 25 July 2004 during the

Ma'lūf and *Muwashshaḥāt* Festival. The other performance is by a modern ensemble called Firqat ash-Sheikh Muhammad Ignas (FSMI) (Sheikh Muhammad Ignas' Ensemble) held on 26 July 2004 during the same festival. The present investigation begins by considering interpretations of Phrase D in YM. As already remarked, Phrase D holds a distinct place in this song, and an investigation of the way it transforms itself in performance might reveal constraints regulating its interpretation and, therefore, its possible transformations.

As noted in Chapter 3, modern *ma'lūf* ensembles emphasize their choral nature rather than the alternation of verses between sheikh and choir, as in traditional practice; variation hardly occurs, with consistency gaining preference for better coordination. For instance, recordings of song YM by FSMI reveal that whenever Phrase D is repeated, it always occurs as in its initial rendition; no variation takes place throughout its several repetitions. FSMI's interpretation of this phrase shows constraints brought about by 'modern' practices that stress choral singing. Comparing the way Phrase D was interpreted by FSMI and its rendition in El Sibaei's transcription reveals small interpretative differences understood to occur in oral transmission (see Example 4.23).

Example 4.23 Small-scale interpretative alterations

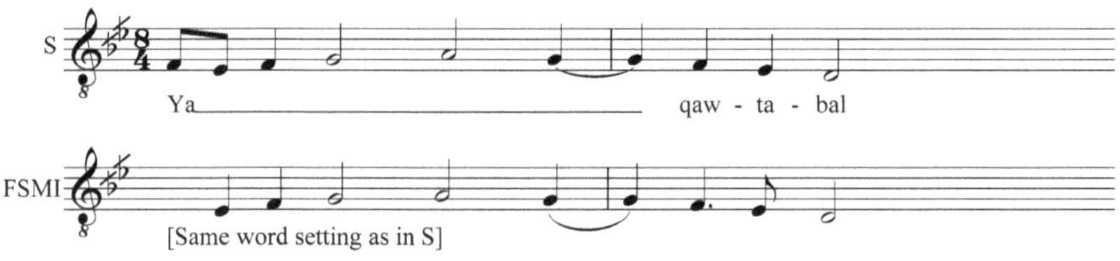

The reworking of the above phrase, however, attains a relatively higher degree of variability when interpreted by FHK (see Example 4.24 below). The sheikh 'takes liberty' in the way he interprets his solo verses, and this generates a whole range of variations throughout the entire song, as partially shown in Example 4.24. The alternating singing of the sheikh and choir in traditional practice allows the former to embellish his solo parts, and moulds them within certain aesthetic parameters. Therefore, the alignment in Example 4.24 shows stability in the ascending phase of the phrase and more flexibility in its descending segment, as if variation may only take place at a certain point in the phrase and not at another. This relates to Blum's assertion (1998: 32) that 'performers … learn not only when to act and what to do but also when not to act and what not to do'. Variation on what is expected to remain stable or, better, on what is traditionally kept stable could result in a faulty interpretation. Such constraints regulate the fine boundary between 'proficient' and 'defective' interpretations. In addition, one may also observe that once the beginning of a phrase is established by the singer and identified by the listener, then several other things may occur. At this stage it is possible to advance the idea that what may be stable in a phrase or musical unit is the phase at which variations may, or are expected to, occur.

Example 4.24 Stable and variant phases in a phrase

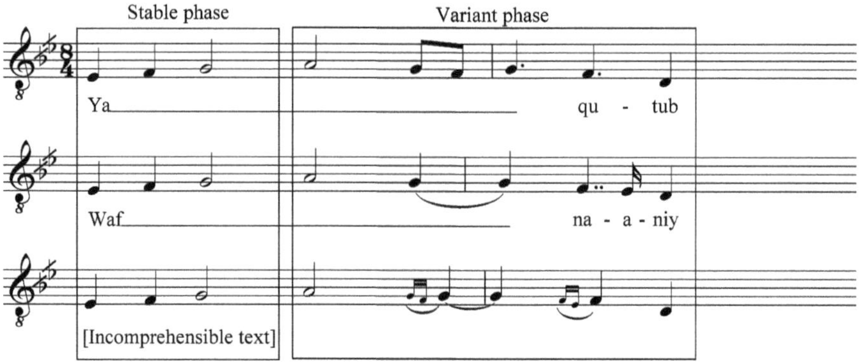

The positioning of a phrase in the music may regulate the degree of variation within that same phrase. Taking the opening phrase of YM, for instance, both recorded performances show strict adherence to the rendition transcribed by El Sibaei. At this early stage of the song, stability is essential for both performer and listeners in order for the former to give a solid start to the song and for the latter to identify the song and eventually the *nawba*. In a way this presents a macro situation similar to the one described in the case of Phrase D. Once the beginning is established and perceived, personal interpretative input, or what Snyder (2000: 89) calls the 'management of nuances', can continue flourishing according to aesthetic parameters attributed to phrases and units, as shown above. On the other hand, due to its positioning, the concluding phrase of the first section (see Example 4.25) employs a degree of variation in its interpretation emerging from the fact that now both performers and listeners are sufficiently acquainted with the song and, therefore, further adherence to strict reiteration is no longer necessary. Example 4.25 shows the different interpretations given to the last phrase of the first section in YM by the above two ensembles the first time it was sung by them; these can be compared to the above rendition as transcribed by El Sibaei.

Example 4.25 Three interpretations of a phrase from YM

The interpretation of the sheikh in FHK is relatively more committing than that of the other two. This could have evolved not only from the sheikh's solo 'liberty' but also from the high expressivity with which he interpreted the same phrase, as I could surmise from listening to the recording. The same recording reveals the point that melodic lines approaching sectional closures are relatively more embellished by the sheikh. All this suggests that expression, and the variation or elaboration that sometimes stem from it, are strongly regulated by information inherent in the musical structure itself. Relating all this to the process of criss-crossing as employed in this repertoire, one may put forward the assertion that such a process does not occur within a vacuum but its occurrence unfolds within a context of interpretative considerations that shape it intrinsically. By extension, such a complex scenario may be further widened if it takes into account extra-musical factors that in themselves may sustain, generate, restrain and regulate aspects such as stability and variation. These may include body movements, as in dancing, and other kinaesthetic expressions such as hand movements.

Chieronomy and Interpretation

In a descriptive account of a rehearsal session by FHA mentioned in Chapter 3, I referred to Hassan Araibi being seated behind a desk, positioned centrally in the rehearsal room, marking the rhythm of the music with his palm and fist on the desk in front of him. The use of hand movements, or chieronomy, in *ma'lūf* singing is not only employed for the marking of the rhythm but has other functions as well. For instance, in *ma'lūf az-zāwiya* the circular movement of the forefinger up in the air indicates that the same verse would be repeated. Also, in a *ma'lūf* parade, when the *nawba* approaches its winding-up and the last verse is reiterated several times, the sheikh and the *kinjī* turn around facing the *bandīr* players, and with their hands mark the last rendition of the final verse so that everyone concludes together. In a similar context, hand movements are used to complement the text, such as when participating singers put the palm of their right hand on their heart as a sign of reverence at the mention of particular venerable words such as the name of the Prophet Muhammad. Hand movements are also used in *ma'lūf* to assure the right setting of words with the melody, as I will argue in Chapter 5. In such a case, the hands indicate the proper division of the syllables with the music and any accents that are necessary for a skilful interpretation. In the context of modern *ma'lūf* performances, the sheikh makes use of chieronomic movements only to signal the beginning of the *nawba*, as the rest is entirely dependent on pre-agreed practices and instruction. The formality bound to the modern practice of *ma'lūf* excludes the kind of spontaneous chieronomy employed in the traditional context.

Another important area for the use of hand movements in *zāwiya* performances is to avoid any possible faults in the choral replies of the *raddāda*. During a performance at the *zāwiya as-saghīra* of *nawba qad hājat ashwāqī* (2 May 2004), one of the *raddāda* knelt upright, directing the choral replies by emphasizing the melodic contour of the singing, his hands moving up and down as in conducting. Chieronomy in music, as Yamaguti (1986: 31) observes, may be considered as a non-sonic representation of the music structure:

> we can … see non-sonic objects representing a music structure and, moreover, a culture at large. One such example is body movements accompanying, or at least associated with sound production—most notably, so called chieronomy or hand movements, as in teaching or conducting. Here, colotomic regularity of articulation or wave-like curved contours of melodies, for instance, may be observed; and in this case, even if inaudible (as in silent movies), they tell us something about an essential part of the music structure.

Whilst informants present at the session interpreted this in terms of spontaneous leadership, further considerations led me to realize that the man was actually filtering out personal nuances from the singing of the sheikh and the heterophony produced by the *ghayṭa* player so that the *raddāda* would easily be able to reproduce an unembellished version of the same verse. Through chieronomy, the member leading the *raddāda* was distinguishing 'personal' from 'collective' renditions of the sung verses. Example 4.26 shows a verse sung by the sheikh who was leading the session and the collective response by the *raddāda*. The same example shows how the line interpreted by the sheikh is relatively more embellished than that of the *raddāda*, with the latter maintaining the stable elements of the same verse. Such a case reveals how melodic stability may be better maintained in collective rather than in personal renditions.

Example 4.26 Two renditions of the same verse

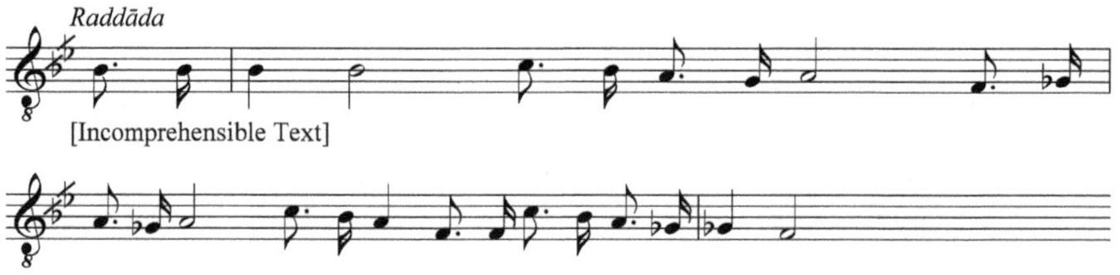

As the *nawba* progressed to a faster tempo, especially towards the end, the singing of the sheikh became less embellished and structurally more similar to the replies of the *raddāda*. While in slow tempo personal 'nuances' seemed possible, these seemed less likely to occur at a fast tempo. The same participant was forced to quit from leading the singing of the *raddāda* as it seemed that there was no longer the need to 'filter' the sheikh's calls. This leads one to hypothesize the fact that in oral music traditions another factor that may aid in the melodic stability of certain songs is the fast tempo in which these songs unfold, as it minimizes the variations originating from personal nuances so likely to occur in slow tempos. In light of this, one wonders whether *ma'lūf* songs in fast tempo, such as those belonging to *īqā' barwal*, are more resistant to change due to the lesser possibility of variations, and whether in such a case criss-crossing techniques would be harder or easier to deal with.

Conclusion

The present chapter called attention to the compositional technique of melodic criss-crossing as employed in Libyan *ma'lūf* songs and how this technique dovetails with aspects of performance such as interpretation and chieronomy. The criss-crossing approach turned out to be a convenient way of creating 'new' melodic content within this repertoire whilst, at the same time, providing stability in terms of musical style. Such criss-crossing has sometimes served to establish melodic formulas that are free of any categorization and, therefore, can be found in any *maqām* and *īqā'*. Such reworking and criss-crossing integrates with other techniques such as rhythmic modification, melodic insertion and omission, diminution and augmentation, and the imitation of a melodic gist. Moreover, the employment of criss-crossing techniques in performance attests to the solid knowledge and the 'generative grammar' of the repertoire possessed by the makers and performers of these songs. Such 'generative grammar' blends together the formalized melodic movements of a *maqām* with a tradition of music-making that, apart from valuing the familiar, also recognizes a framework of structural stability and order, both if new melodic material emerges before or in the course of performance. In addition, the interpretation of *ma'lūf* songs links to other aspects such as chieronomy and tempo that in the above discussion have surfaced as potential determinants in the regulation of variability and, by extension, in the generation of melodic criss-crossing.

The craft of music composition that transpires here, from El Sibaei's transcriptions as well as from the scrutiny of performances, highlights a kind of selection process wrapped in various cognitive constraints that in turn constitute an innate grammar for this repertoire. It is the kind of grammar that emphasizes what is melodically and rhythmically essential in a song, with discreet and relatively minimal employment of melodic embellishments that might not only spoil the comprehension of text but also restrain the application of techniques such as those of melodic criss-crossing and others related to it. An observation by Ramadan

(1976: 169) connects nicely with this essential structuring perspective and points out similar features found in Libyan Muslim architecture:

> Whereas the majority of the monuments of Islam display a veritable explosion of ornamented detail, Libyan Muslim architecture manifests a conspicuous lack of external ornamentation, emphasizing form and making the soundness of the structural mass an expressive, abstract support of the work itself.

Moving outwards from the musical structure of the *ma'lūf*, to possible parallels with Libyan Muslim architecture (which is distinct from Fascist architecture), to a general description of the Libyans as expressed by Muhamed Sacirbey in an online issue of *The European Courier* (24 February 2011) in an article entitled 'This was never Gaddafi's Libya', one can understand the general characteristic of a nation humble in nature and uncomfortable with the political direction imposed on it in the post-1969 Gaddafi era:

> Gaddafi was never a very good, not even a close approximation of the character and personality of Libyans. They are neither boastful nor turbulent, but rather accustomed to the humility and assiduous character of a nation accustomed to working and living close to nature. Maybe some of this or much may have changed due to easy oil wealth and an indolent 'revolution' over the last almost half century. However, whatever reserve the citizens of Libya held within from the period before Qaddafi is now pouring out with energy and determination upon the streets of its relatively young cities and towns.[sic.]

At this stage, one wonders whether the uprising against Gaddafi's rule, initiated on 15 February 2011, and the civil war between anti-Gaddafi rebels and pro-Gaddafi forces that eventually led to the overthrow of the regime, was linked not only to the longing for democracy but also to a state of life compatible with the social and cultural identity of the Libyans—an identity that cherishes what is also valued in the musical structure of the *turāth qadīm*, that is, a cohesive structure, that whilst lacking emphasis on melodic lavishness, allows for the flourishing of novel musical ideas and stylistically appropriate ways of matching words to music.

Chapter 5
The Libyan *Ma'lūf* in the Realm of Arab Music Aesthetics

Contemporary literature concerned with Arab music reveals a strong interest in the capacity of music to affect emotion and with the terms Arabs use in accounting for this. Such terminology is mainly concerned with the experience of listening and the musical affect generated from it. In the context of Sufism, the interest in the overwhelming power of music and its mystic dimension is evident both in treatises and in aphorisms dating back to the ninth century.[1] In more recent times this aspect of Arab music has been illustrated with vivid fieldwork experiences that include observations and ethnographic commentary of live performances (see, for instance, Marcus 2007), and interviews with renowned Middle Eastern performers, music scholars and the public at large (see, for example, Racy 1998, Danielson and Fisher 2002, Shannon 2006 and Stokes 2010). The consistent emphasis of my interviewees on the fact that the Libyan *ma'lūf* should be viewed not as particularly 'Libyan music' but, more widely, as pan-Arab music makes it inevitable for one to investigate this music tradition and its meanings in the wider dimension of concepts and issues that characterize debates on Arab music aesthetics, especially those related to *affect*, here understood as the music's expressive capacity.

The primary aim of the present chapter is to evaluate the aesthetic potential of the restyled *nawba* and the degree of affect that it generates and, consequently, how such experience differs from that in the *ma'lūf az-zāwiya*. The discussion will shed light, for instance, on how certain aesthetic values and parameters attributed to the *ma'lūf az-zāwiya* are transferred onto the *ma'lūf al-idhā'a* or, conversely, suppressed from being transmitted onto it. Although the present discussion will accentuate the *ma'lūf al-idhā'a*, an evaluation of what characterizes the listening and affective experience in the *ma'lūf az-zāwiya* is inevitable. In addition, the forthcoming discussion will also shed light on the aesthetic potential of the *ma'lūf al-idhā'a* to affect audiences and the degree to which this happens when compared with the emotional potential of other classical genres of Arab music alongside which the restyled *nawba* is normally performed. The present discussion will also highlight aspects of performance practices in the Libyan *ma'lūf* related to affect and the way these are visibly or sonically transformed in the course of performance. The synchronized collective swinging of *zāwiya* members during a *mawlid* parade (described in Chapter 2), for instance, is only one example of such transformation. On a slightly wider note, one may add that in Arab music, as might occur in other music traditions, affect can also

---

1 See Shiloah 1997 for a seminal discussion.

leave its imprint on the music itself. Arab musicians, for instance, may express affect by beating their drums in cross-rhythm to the consistent rhythmic cycle produced by the other percussionists, or by highly 'embellishing' the melodic content of an *istiftāh*, as sometimes occurs in the music tradition of our concern.

In order to answer the questions posed above and other related ones, the present chapter will commence by focusing on the concept of *samā'* and how this is related to the listening and affective experience as emerging in the *ma'lūf az-zāwiya*. The concept of *samā'* is described in the Sufi tradition as the integration of musical audition into the practice of meditation. The observations brought forward in this section will then provide the basis for some of my informants' claim that the *ma'lūf al-idhā'a* lacks the particular emotional capacity intimately experienced in the *ma'lūf az-zāwiya*. This will then be followed by a discussion of another important and related concept in Arab music, which is that of *ṭarab* or that ecstatic state reached in Arab art music. Such discussion will be illustrated with an ethnographic commentary derived from the 2004 *Ma'lūf* and *Muwashshaḥāt* Festival, which commentary will bring forth a real example of *ṭarab* as generated in an Arab musical genre similar in terms of presentation to the *ma'lūf al-idhā'a*. The section that follows will then discuss how the modern pre-composed *nawba* exists on a continuum running between *ṭarab* and sentimentality and how the above informants' claims fit into this intriguing scenario.

Samā' and the *Ma'lūf az-Zāwiya*

It has already been noted in Chapter 2 that the *nawba* is the ultimate phase of a three-part Muslim service held in the *zāwiya*, a service known as *ḥaḍra*. The *nawba* comes after the recitation of prayers from the Qur'ān and the *dhikr* ceremony. In the same chapter we saw that during a *ḥaḍra*, the atmosphere becomes overpowering to the extent that some members become overwhelmed, especially during *dhikr*. This strong emotionality starts building up from the beginning of the service, reaching an observable phase during *dhikr* and continues throughout the *ma'lūf*. Such overwhelming affect may lead certain members to mystical movements, such as the acute swaying of the upper part of the body in a trance-like state. At this stage the catharsis that participants go through during such ritual cannot pass unnoticed, as it has a bearing on the *ma'lūf* singing that comes afterwards and the emotionality that participants put into it. Shannon (2006: 124) lists some of the cathartic effects of the *dhikr* as had been explained to him by his informants in Syria and which may be applicable to the present discussion:

> Aside from its artistic aspects, an important function of the dhikr for some participants is what is known as *fishsh al-qalb*, the cathartic release of tensions from the heart (*qalb*) 'like air from a balloon', as one friend put it—'fishsh' being this sound. Another explained that performing the dhikr releases emotional tension and energy that otherwise might be released in violent ways ... The

> progression from slower to faster tempos and from lower to higher pitches in conjunction with repeated bodily movements has the effect of generating and releasing psychic and physical tension, according to many participants. Some further argued that dhikr is a good form of exercise, beneficial practically as well as spiritually.

Although during my own fieldwork I never witnessed instances in which bodily movements resumed during the *ma'lūf* phase of a *ḥaḍra* (because the affected person was eventually calmed down by the sheikh of the *zāwiya* towards the ending of *dhikr*), videotapes provided to me by some informants reveal examples where such movements continue even during the performance of *ma'lūf*. Whether such movements are present or not, the singing of *ma'lūf* in the *zāwiya* and *zāwiya*-related *ma'lūf* performances, such as in *mawlid* parades, comprises a very deep sense of reverence and strong emotionality normally expressed in group swaying, elaborate cross-rhythmic beating on the *bandīr*, loud shrills on the *ghayṭa*, hand gestures and deeply pronounced text. All these expressions manifest profound emotions strongly related, according to some informants, with mystical audition of *samā'*. Lewisohn (1997: 4) describes the Sufi *samā'* as follows:

> *Samā'*, which literally means 'audition', connotes in the Sufi tradition a hearing with the 'ear of the heart', an attitude of reverently listening to music and/or the singing of mystical poetry with the intent of increasing awareness and understanding of the divine object described; it is a type of meditation focusing on musical melody, by use of instruments, mystical songs or combining both.

At this stage, it is worth noting the fact that the term *ḥaḍra* as understood in North Africa 'is intimately linked to the concept of *samā'*', a process that according to classical Sufism intensifies 'the adepts' love of God and sensation of ecstasy' (Shiloah 2000: 70).

In his search for the basic theological and mystical concepts of *samā'*, Lewisohn relies, amongst others, on writings by the Persian writers Abū Hamid al-Ghazālī and Ahmad b. Muhammad al-Tusī. Ghazālī's work dates back to circa 1096–1111, and that of Tusī to 1248 (Lewisohn 1997: 4). Both authors highlight the fact that the three cardinal preconditions for the Muslim's mystic sensitivity to music are the 'right time', the 'right place' and the 'right company'. Although the two authors were mainly concerned with *samā'* in the context of Persian Sufism seven to ten centuries ago, their comments dovetail nicely with my own onsite observations of Libyan *ma'lūf az-zāwiya* performances and comments made by my informants.

Lewisohn (1997: 8–9) quotes Tusī as saying that the 'proper time [for *samā'*] is when their [i.e the Sufis'] hearts enjoy purity so that they desire to concentrate their aspirations in seeking their Beloved's goodwill'. At this point, Lewisohn remarks (1997: 9) that Tusī was mainly referring to the 'proper conditions which will enable him [i.e. the Sufi] to enter correctly into a genuine musical reverie, a time of the heart or soul rather than a specific temporal reality of the body'. In the context of a *ma'lūf az-zāwiya* session, the appropriate conditions to which Tusī refers could be found in and enhanced by the meaning attributed to that event incorporating *ma'lūf*. As already noted in Chapter 2, events like the *mawlid* as well as funeral and wedding rites employing *ma'lūf* are all endowed with particular signification; it is precisely the rich meaningfulness attributed to these events that shapes the right condition for *samā'*. Lewisohn (1997: 9) also quotes Ghazālī as asserting that '*samā'* should not be conducted during any times when one's heart is engaged [with worldly concerns], nor when it is time for ritual prayer [*namāz*] nor when eating or when one is distracted'. In the *ma'lūf az-zāwiya*, the 'right time' is both a temporal 'moment' as well as a metaphysical condition that refers to the heart's detachment from worldly preoccupations. Ghazālī's observation attains more importance when one considers the fact that, typically, *ma'lūf* sessions in *zāwiya* are held late in the evening when participants are free from the day's preoccupations and distractions. Such observation ties up with the assertion a taxi driver made to me, that for him the best time to listen to *ma'lūf* on his car stereo is on Thursday evening when dawn anticipates Friday, the day of rest for the Muslims and, therefore, when he starts feeling the sensation of rest.

The *zāwiya* is the 'right place' for traditional *ma'lūf* sessions. An occasional visitor such as myself attending *zāwiya* sessions is quickly made to feel welcome, let alone a *zāwiya* member, as I remarked in Chapter 2. The place itself also evokes nostalgic feelings that tie up *ma'lūf* sessions with memories of the past: oral history concerning deceased sheikhs, for instance, is recounted in the *zāwiya*. Copies of the Qur'ān and old manuscripts shelved on wooden bookcases around the walls of the *zāwiya* add to the aura of the place as an ideal venue for *samā'*. The 'right place' for *samā'* has other metaphysical connotations in the Sufi tradition. According to this metaphysical interpretation, such a location is illuminated by the enlightened hearts and souls of the gathered Sufis—in itself a collective spiritual disposition that transforms the 'place' into a sacred venue.

The final precondition for *samā'* is the 'right company'. *Samā'* is typically experienced in gatherings sharing the same religious values and sentiments. Throughout my fieldwork I sensed a strong feeling of brotherhood among members and, consequently, that had an impact on the singing of *ma'lūf*. Such brotherhood permitted novice *ma'lūf* singers, for instance, gradually to explore and develop in the art of *ma'lūf* and the Sufi values embroiled in the same art—a condition that contrasted sharply with the recruitment of a new member in a 'modern' *ma'lūf* ensemble, which engagement is loaded with a range of technical expectations and rigorous training to meet professional requisites. Such fraternal spirit was also enhanced by the collective singing of the *raddāda* replying to the solo calls of the sheikh. During *mawlid* parades the choral responses of the *raddāda* take place facing the sheikh and the *ghayṭa* player, with members resting their arms on each other's shoulders and swinging in synchrony to the music—all this being interpreted as a strong manifestation of fraternity and the solidarity that group identity implies.

If appropriate time, place and company are essential preconditions for the occurrence of *samā'*, particular moments of *samā'* are initiated and nurtured by

Figure 5.1 Hand movements in a *ma'lūf az-zāwiya* parade (Mawlid, 1 May 2004)

the listeners' sensitivity to the poetic text. Such textual sensibility is able to turn a poetic text into a profound impression on the soul. Some of my informants relied on metaphors to explain this. Muhammad Elimam (referred to in Chapter 4) explained to me how the text of *ma'lūf* penetrates the heart and leaves a *jerh* (wound) on the soul. Also, Sheikh Abu Sama (mentioned in Chapter 3) remarked that when he looks around during a *ma'lūf* session in the *zāwiya* and outside and sees *zāwiya* members 'swim in *ma'lūf* lyrics' ('*yū'mu fi kalamāt al-ma'lūf*'), in other words enraptured by the beauty of the text, he is inspired to select the most appropriate verses to sustain this mood further throughout performance. Melodic aspects, and the match of melody to text, also contribute to experiencing *samā'*. Hand gestures employed in *ma'lūf az-zāwiya* singing aid in accentuating particular words carrying high significance and the inflexions employed throughout its pronouncement (see Figure 5.1). Such gestures are only employed in *ma'lūf az-zāwiya*, as such spontaneity is at best out of place in *ma'lūf al-idhā'a* performances, if not actually implying the degrading of the ensemble to sheer amateurism.

The relationship between melodic high-points and hand gestures is just one instance of how the musical component contributes to the generation of a deep sense of reverence in *ma'lūf az-zāwiya* performances. For instance, the sound of the *ghayṭa* instils in Sheikh Abu Sama a sense of *salṭana*, a condition described by Racy (2003: 120) as inspiring 'affective music making ... the "magic" that momentarily lifts the artist to a higher ecstatic plateau and empowers him or her to engender *ṭarab* most effectively'. Moreover, the same sound imparts connotations and sentiments retrievable only through the scrutiny of actions, discourse and attitudes towards music. For instance, during *mawlid* parades, as noted in Chapter 2, women's excitement for *ma'lūf* and the festive spirit it brings are expressed through ululations that the same women shrill out either when standing to the side of the street or on balconies. Excitement during *mawlid* parades augments as the *barwal* section sets off. This engenders faster synchronized swinging by the participating men and more frequent ululation by the women. When performances are held in the *zāwiya* where women are not allowed, the context is devoid of women's ululations, but a proficient *ghayṭa* player will occasionally embellish his playing of the *barwal* section with long trills in the high register imitative of women's ululations as heard in street parades. This normally occurs towards the end of a *nawba* when quick reiterations of the same verse sung by the *raddāda* bring the *nawba* to an end. The characteristic sound of the *ghayṭa* trill in *ma'lūf az-zāwiya* performances may be viewed semiotically as a musical synecdoche, that is a referential sound structure to the characteristic trill of the *ghayṭa* as profusely employed in Libyan folk music. Tagg (1999: 26–7) defines a musical synecdoche as:

> any set of musical structures inside a given musical style that refer to other (different, 'foreign', 'alien') musical style by citing one or two elements supposed to be typical of that 'other' style when heard in the context of the style into which those 'foreign' elements are imported. By citing part of the other style, the citation then alludes not only to that other style in its entirety but also potentially refers to the complete genre of which that other musical style is a subset.

To some extent, Tagg's assertion merges well with what the sheikh of a *zāwiya* once remarked to me when I enquired whether his *zāwiya* would be holding any *ma'lūf* sessions during the *mawlid* period. 'We do not hold *ma'lūf* sessions in this *zāwiya*. We only perform *ma'lūf* outside *zāwiya* on *mawlid* day', he replied, adding that the '*ma'lūf* is folkloric [*fulklūr*] not religious'. Whether his thought evolved from the associative sound of the *ghayṭa* or from its inclusion in performing practices considered as excessively mundane in orthodox Islam is unclear. What seems certain, though, is the fact that in the context of Libyan music, and according to some informants' implicit statements, the sound of the *ghayta* brings to mind associations with folk music as employed in male wedding celebrations and folk festival events and, therefore, is considered as inappropriate in *zāwiya*.

Understanding and Experiencing *Ṭarab*

Wade (2004: 9) observes that 'for many people, the highest value of music is placed on affect'. Aesthetic preferences for particular music are sometimes determined by how much affect that music is able to evoke. While this has a great deal to do with the nature of the musical content comprised within the same music, ethnomusicology shows that affect is not solely a resultant of musical content but a composite of several interrelated processes, such as: the nature and intensity of communication between performer/s and audience during a performance; the popularity of the performer with the audience; his or her mood at the time of performance; and whether the audience is familiar with the style of music performed, as well as the kind of emotional synergy that evolves when humanly transformed feelings in music are decoded by all participants and commonly shared sentimental traits are recognized by them as pivotal for communal solidarity.

In a major 2003 publication Racy (2003: 5) states that 'in Arab culture, the merger between music and emotional transformation is epitomized by the Arabic concept of *ṭarab*, which may not have an exact equivalent in Western languages'. He proceeds by giving an account of three closely related denotations that this term holds. One refers to the artistic making of music, expressed in the occasionally used expression of *fann al-ṭarab* (the art of *ṭarab*) (Racy 2003: 6). This implies a solid knowledge of the Arab *maqāmāt* and *īqā'āt* as well as classical Arab musical forms. Such 'artistic' making of music is mainly found in urban areas and produced by extensive ensembles known as *firqāt*, which, as already noted in Chapter 3, are an offshoot of *takht* ensembles.

The other denotation of *ṭarab* refers to the 'extraordinary emotional state evoked by the music' (Racy 2003: 6). The evocation of *ṭarab* can be generated by a proficient singer known as *mutrib*,[2] by an instrumentalist or by an entire ensemble. When referring to the prominence of the voice over instruments in the engendering of *ṭarab*, Rouget (1985: 283) asserts that:

> it is the expressivity of the singing that is the operative factor [behind the state of trance], working through the combined action of the beauty of the voice and the emotional power of the words. The instruments have little, or even nothing, to do with it. ... Trance, as a manifestation of musical emotion, is so closely associated with singing that the musical instrument is sometimes regarded as unfavourable to the inducement of *ṭarab*.

While Rouget is right in pointing out the prominent role of the voice in the generation of *ṭarab* and the high value it holds in Arab music, both Racy's above-mentioned book and the ethnographic account presented below show that a proficient instrumental accompaniment is sometimes indispensable for a singer in the evocation of *ṭarab*. In fact, *ṭarab* can be generated through, and in the course of, instrumental improvisations.

The third denotation of *ṭarab* is its use as 'ecstasy', or that transformative state generated by the music (Racy 2003: 6). While the second denotation refers to the process that leads on to 'ecstasy', the third denotation refers specifically to the state of 'ecstasy'. Such an emotional state holds certain characteristics that can be

---

2 Note the consonantal root *ṭ–r–b* derived from *ṭarab*.

observed during performance. For instance, individuals under the effect of *ṭarab* may appear captivated by the listening experience and withdrawn from ordinary consciousness. Other observable characteristics prompted by the music include singing and clapping along with the music, the pronouncement of typical verbal exclamations (such as 'ah' or 'Allāh'), the stretching out of arms and sometimes even crying (Racy 2003: 198). From my attendance at festivals of Arab classical music in Tripoli, the most pronounced expression of *ṭarab* was manifested through the above verbal exclamations, clapping, whistling, words of praise directed towards the performer and ululations enunciated by women who, at festivals, sat in the back rows behind the seats occupied by men.

As we have just seen, the *ṭarab* performer must be endowed with *rūh* or the 'locally based ability to feel *ṭarab* music or to perform it affectively' (Racy 2003: 228). This implies a deep-rooted sense of 'Eastern-ness' or 'Arab-ness' (Racy 2003: 126) that together with the performer's genuine artistry is then transmitted through the performer's sense of 'feeling' (*ḥiss*); that is, the performer's ability to create music that is emotionally expressive. In the course of research I realized that the word *ḥiss* and its derivative words are loosely used as convenient replies for questions that are otherwise hard to answer or for which a straightforward answer is almost unconceivable. Such observation brings forth a particular situation I found myself in when I was in Testour with Araibi's ensemble. I was advised by a member of the Ensemble not to trust a particular stranger whom I had encountered a few moments before. When I asked why, the answer was: 'I felt so.' This and other incidents in which the expression 'I felt so' was loosely used made me realize how in Libyan society the sense of 'feel' predominates in everyday life situations, sometimes even over the intellect. This is akin to the way music is sometimes conceived, mainly as an activity that draws heavily on feelings, as Araibi asserted in one of our interviews:

> As artists (*funūn*) we talk to people emotionally through music. We never deal with people through the minds. At the same time, our feelings and emotions are those of normal people and, therefore, our feelings are not unfamiliar to them. ... Music is felt by heart not by mind.

In my first meeting with Araibi I was struck by his insistence that the Western musician is like an engineer who brings intellect before feelings into his art. For Araibi, in contrast, it is this sense of feeling that facilitates the memorization of so many tunes and texts in Arab music. 'Once the tune is played, the text starts flowing in', he told me.

The creative ecstatic state typically experienced by *ṭarab* performers is also linked to the state of *salṭana*—a state that elevates the performer from one who can provide *ṭarab* to one who can make his audience feel *ṭarab* (Racy 2003: 228). *Salṭana* is about the performer's sense of 'mastery' over a *maqām*, whereas *ṭarab* is about the listener's experience of it. The state of *salṭana* is generated and sustained on the part of the performer by continuous feedback from the audience (Racy

2003: 131). In reaching this aim, the performer establishes a good and effective rapport with the audience (Racy 2003: 35)—a rapport that takes into consideration the tastes and the expectations of his audience. Related to this, Shannon (2003: 78–9) reports a Syrian informant arguing that 'a musically exemplary performance might not necessarily guarantee that the participants would experience *tarab*. It is the *relationship* (*tawâsul*) between the artist and the listeners that is important, even more so than the music itself—and more important than the mere semblance of an appropriate atmosphere' (emphasis added). Also, in her major publication on Umm Kulthūm, Danielson (1997: 137) notes that Kamāl al-Najmī, in a review of Umm Kulthūm's concert in 1966, remarked that her concerts became extensively longer due to the growing number of audience requests for repetitions of lines and entire sections. The items she included in her programme and how she used to express them depended on her monitoring of the feedback from her audience.[3] It is a kind of relationship that 'at once reflects and produces the musical, social, and emotional states that allow artists and audiences to experience the feelings they gloss as *tarab*' (Shannon 2003:79, emphasis added).

Audience members taken up by the music and the evoked *ṭarab* are known as *sammī'a*, or 'diehard listeners' (Racy 2003: 40). These are members of an audience who react immediately by clapping or pronouncing words of exclamation at particular musical moments or passages within the music. Many *sammī'a* 'are totally familiar with the main performance genres, and take full notice of the technical manoeuvres that musicians make, although much of their knowledge is intuitive rather than theoretical' (Racy 2003: 41). What the *sammī'a* feel during the music and the way they transform what they feel into behaviour is then transfused among other members of the audience, a process identified by Meyer (1956: 21) as 'emotional designation' or 'designative behaviour'. According to Meyer, in this mode of behaviour the individual responds to an affective or stimulating experience by seeking 'to make others aware of his experience through a series of non-verbal behavioural signs' (Meyer 1956: 21).

The other aspect that evokes *ṭarab* is the music itself, which, in the context of *ṭarab* music, refers to a particular musical idiom or style with strong professional overtones. Racy (2003: 75) refers to 'the general fabric of *ṭarab* music and … the basic processes that enable the music to 'speak', or impress emotionally'. For instance, Racy describes *ṭarab* music as: highly lyrical; making effective use of *ṭarab* instruments; shifting from solo to group singing and/or playing; employing skilful accompaniment; and containing improvisation through which the performer manipulates a variety of musical components to affect the audience. All the three denotations of *ṭarab* just mentioned were present in a striking performance I attended during the 2004 Tripoli Festival of *Ma'lūf* and *Muwashshaḥāt*. Although

[3] A more recent example of an Arab singer who considers *ṭarab* as heavily relying on an effective rapport of performer and audience is the Syrian singer Sabāh Fakhrī. In an interview with Racy (1998: 103), Fakhrī asserts that the rapport between performer and audience develops gradually first by locating and establishing affinity with the *sammī'a*.

the festival is dedicated to performances of *ma'lūf* and *muwashshaḥāt*, other forms of Arab classical music, such as *waṣlāt* (traditional medleys with songs sharing the same melodic mode) and *qaṣā'id*, are also included. The session on which the following ethnographic depictions rely was held on 28 July 2005. The performance featured Sheikh Albahlul Saied Abourgab and his ensemble Firqat Bustān al-Madīḥīn (The Garden of Praises Ensemble).

As from summer of 2002, the splendid gardens of al-Markaza al-Qawmiya al-Markiziya in central Tripoli became the venue for this festival, the aim of which is to generate greater interest in *ma'lūf* and *muwashshaḥāt*. The festival includes both competitive and participatory sessions, with *zāwiya* ensembles participating in the former whilst the latter sessions are taken up by modern ensembles. A jury panel composed of renowned Libyan sheikhs of *ma'lūf* is entrusted with the task of judging *zāwiya* ensembles (see Figure 5.2). The *zāwiya* ensemble that wins the festival is presented with trophies and certificates by the organizing committee chaired, at that time, by Hassan Araibi. Moreover, the festival serves to make known the lives of renowned deceased sheikhs and to make public personal nostalgic accounts related to these sheikhs.

Figure. 5.2 The jury panel of the 2004 festival

Each festival is dedicated to a particular sheikh *ma'lūf* who has contributed strongly in the dissemination of the tradition. Posters announcing the festival, featuring a prominent picture of the sheikh to whom the festival is dedicated, are placed at traffic intersections all around Tripoli (see Figure 5.3 below). Throughout the period of the festival a portrait of the sheikh dominates one side of the huge stage on which performances take place. A large part of the prepared scripts of the festival compères comprises information regarding the life of the sheikh. Relatives of the sheikh to whom that year's festival is dedicated attend and take prominent seats. They are interviewed and asked to share with the audience their memories of the sheikh, his sayings about the *ma'lūf* and personal initiatives in the dissemination of the tradition. Most interviews highlight strongly the sheikh's commitment to the teaching of *ma'lūf*, his manner of leading *ma'lūf* performances and, seminal to all this, his exemplary and observant life as a Muslim.

Each traditional ensemble bears the name of a particular sheikh, who might have been either the *sheikh ma'lūf* of that *zāwiya*, the *ma'lūf* master of the sheikh currently leading the ensemble, or due to the fact that a son or other relative of the sheikh after whom the ensemble is named is a member of the ensemble. All three possibilities embody a powerful element of nostalgia, enhanced by the framed picture of the sheikh normally placed by the sheikh's relatives on stage in front of the ensemble (see Figure 5.4 below). According to a participant in one of these participating Sufi ensembles, factors such as the framed picture of the sheikh and the sense of belonging and brotherhood help the group to experience some of the conditions for *samā'* on stage, even if not at the same degree of intensity as those felt in *zāwiya*. Nevertheless, as an ensemble assembles on stage, the presenter gives a biographical outline of the sheikh and recounts anecdotes about him. In the course of performance modes of interpretation, vocal timbres and the way the leading *sheikh ma'lūf* selects the songs for the *nawba* reveal with whom that particular sheikh had trained in the art of *ma'lūf*. Music evokes images of the past through sound, and the *ma'lūf* is no exception in that.

The evenings of the festival commence with a traditional ensemble that begins its performance with instrumental music (normally in the rhythm *samā'ī* or *masmūdī kabīr*), followed by a *qaṣīda* or *muwashshaḥāt*. Then, for the performance of the *nawba*, the ensemble changes positioning, with the *bandīr* players, headed by the *ghayṭa*, sheikh and *kīnji*, grouped on one side of the stage and the *raddāda* sitting on the other. At this stage, it is worth noting the fact that *ma'lūf az-zāwiya* set-ups as they unfold on stage during the above festival are different from the performing *zāwiya* set-ups as described in Chapter 2. Apart from space constraints, this change is caused by considerations such as the placement of microphones and the avoidance of amplification feedback.

The publicly pronounced nostalgia, framed portraits on stage and vocal melismas evoking singing styles of particular well-known sheikhs transpire in dissonance with the sophisticated sound systems, hi-tech TV cameras chasing the best shots and sound engineers striving for the best sound quality. Then, the moments of nostalgia are somewhat curtailed by the sound of violins, cello and double bass tuning up for

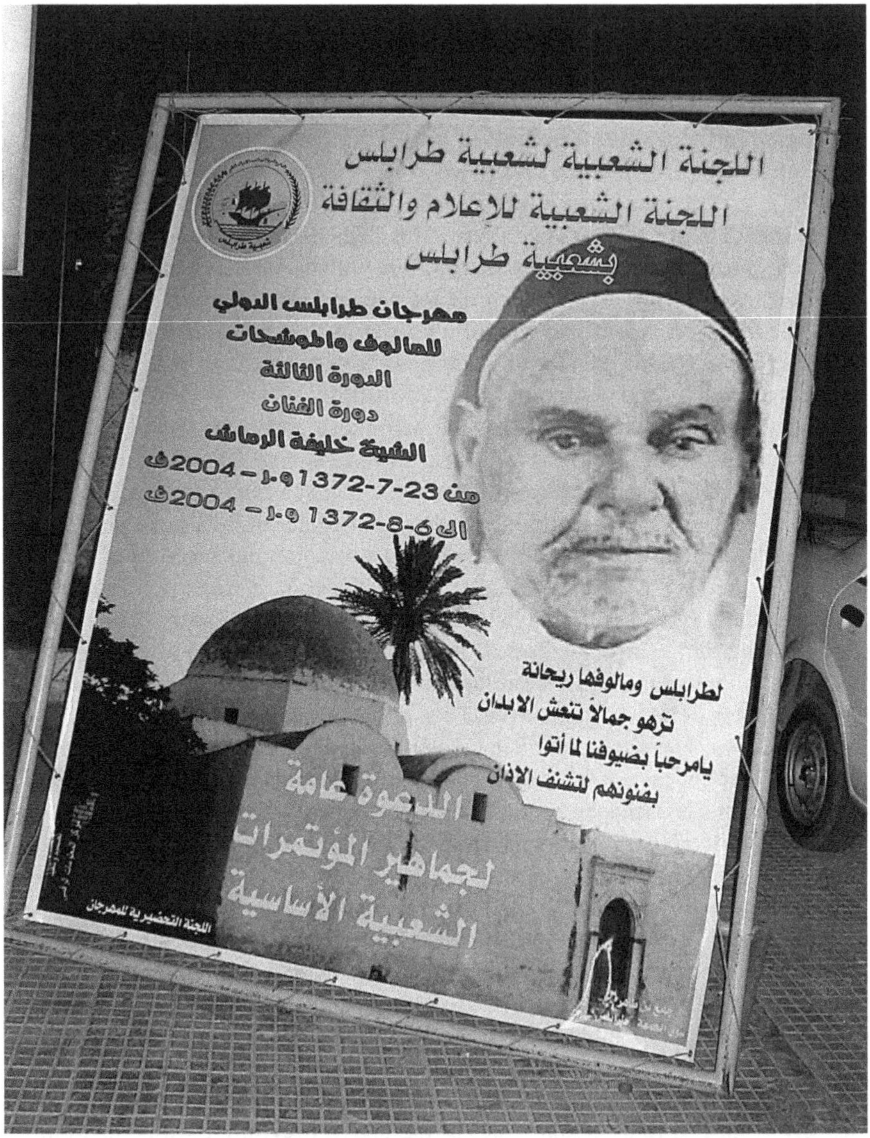

Figure 5.3 Poster announcing the 2004 festival in honour of sheikh Khaliyfa 'r-Rammāsh

Figure 5.4 Framed picture of a sheikh in front of a *zāwiya* ensemble

the next session of the evening. The entire performing scenario is transformed when a modern ensemble takes the stage; the framed picture of the sheikh is removed and the microphones shifted to provide for a different ensemble set-up and, consequently, a diverse sound aesthetic. Sheikh Albahlul's ensemble starts taking its place on stage as soon as the *zāwiya* members make their way down.

Whilst on stage, Sheikh Albahlul and the conductor assure themselves of the proper placement of the microphones for both the choir and the instrumentalists. For Sheikh Albahlul and his ensemble, as well as for other ensembles taking part in the festival, the sound system is an indispensable mediator in the projection of their music and, therefore, it demands serious attention. A proper placement supports the 'musical vision of size, power, coordination, planning and discipline' (Stokes 2009: 63), attributes most associated with ensembles like that of Albahlul. As the ensemble appears on stage it is greeted with clapping, whistling and words of encouragement. The instrumentalists sit behind stands with music while the choir, together with the sheikh in the middle, sit on a high platform placed behind the instrumentalists. Albahlul's ensemble comprises a male choir and a professional instrumental section composed of musicians well known in the recording environment of Tripoli. The ensemble reflects a nice blend of professional and amateur musical talents, and I had had the chance of visiting them in rehearsal that same morning (see Figure 5.5 below). Although Sheikh Albahlul is the sheikh of the ensemble and so is

Figure 5.5 Sheikh Albahlul (standing) rehearsing the singers

entrusted with almost all the vocal solos, the ensemble is led by a conductor who stands in front of the string section, as if to mark the fact that he is mainly there for the instrumentalists rather than for the vocalists, who remain the jurisdiction of the sheikh. The instrumental section of the ensemble includes a cello, six violins, an electronic *'ūd*, *qānūn* and a synthesizer. The percussion section is composed of a *darabukka*, *tār* and *bandīr*. The *bandīr* player sits behind the other percussionists with the sole role of reinforcing the *dumm* stroke of the *darabukka* so essential for the clear marking of the *īqā'*. Sheikh Albahlul is known for his compositions of *waṣlāt* in the *Ārusīyya* Sufi tradition. Since in Libya, as noted in Chapter 2, the *ma'lūf* is not practised by *Ārusīyya* Sufis, the repertory of Sheikh Albahlul's ensemble is devoid of *ma'lūf*. The sheikh's ability to put together *qaṣā'id* and *madīḥ* verses and melodies in the form of a *waṣla* is well recognized in the musical circles of Tripoli.

The performance starts with an instrumental piece in *īqā' samā'ī* (10/8), followed by three *waṣlāt* composed by Sheikh Albahlul. The second *waṣla* generates strong emotions from the audience as it all evolves from a syllabic motif introduced by Sheikh Albahlul on top of a drone note on the cello and synthesizer and a soft heterophonic accompaniment provided by the *qānūn*. The choir then transforms the motif into an antiphonal ostinato with Sheikh Albahlul 'improvising' melismatically on the syllable 'ah'. Sheikh Albahlul's voice sounds like a sigh, highly embellished and covering a wide range. All this evolves against an instrumental backdrop and an overall texture that becomes thicker through the successive entrances of other instruments. Such solo vocal enunciation stimulates members of the audience to pronounce loudly their admiration for Sheikh Albahlul. At one point, the sheikh explores another region of the *maqām* and the choir replies accordingly. This momentary shift brings a strong commotion among the audience until the sheikh returns to the initial region of the *maqām*. This *waṣla* is characterized by ululations, clapping and sometimes even singing along from the audience. Audience members sitting next to me described Sheikh Albahlul's voice as possessing *ṭarab*. His voice is full, with an exceptional melodic range, entirely in control, sensitive to the replies of the choir and the accompaniment of the instrumentalists. Asking a friend of mine, who was sitting next to me, how this state of *ṭarab* had been triggered, he pointed out that it was all the result of the natural voice register of the sheikh, his improvised vocal stretching, the individual–togetherness kind of singing, the unobtrusive instrumental accompaniment and vocal embellishments, as well as the sheikh's solid knowledge of the *maqām*. 'Above all', he continued, 'Sheikh Albahlul is very sensitive to the audience's expectation.'

The third *waṣla* follows the sequence of the previous one. It starts with a short instrumental prelude on the *qānūn* and a soft ostinato on the strings and synthesizer. After a short silent pause, Sheikh Albahlul, accompanied by the soft playing of the *qānūn*, synthesizer and strings, initiates a vocal improvisation. Then, the voice of the sheikh shifts up to the high register with members of the audience pronouncing verbal exclamations in response. Sheikh Albahlul shows an incredible sensitivity in the way he treats his *qaflāt* (plural of *qafla*), that is the cadential patterns that bring his vocal phrases to an end. As is typical in Arab music, his *qaflāt* are followed by a short silent pause intended to engender expectation. As Racy (2003: 104) rightly observes, such cadential patterns constitute powerful ecstatic devices. 'Ornamentation', too, involves a keen sense of judicious application as well as careful timing mainly aimed at generating a delay in the arrival at an expected target note. Sheikh Albahlul's sensitive rendition is also characterized by textual sparsity and elasticity, both contributing greatly to the nurturing of a nice balance between the semantic aspect of the lyrics and the emotional stimulation generated from it. The vocal range explored by Sheikh Albahlul and the controlled accompaniment on the *qānūn* intensify this. In addition, one can also mention the occasional, sustained fill-ins on the strings and the sporadic moving bass passages on the synthesizer that contrast effectively with the shrill sound of the *qānūn* as well as with the soft, embellished melody in the high register of the synthesizer. The whole improvisation is constructed on a series of tensions and releases over a delicate instrumental backdrop that evolves in accordance with skilful and affective accompaniment. The rest of the *waṣla* contains contrasting alternations between the choir and soloist, leading to a faster tempo that, as in the previous *waṣla*, brings the music to a delirious ending.

A fundamental aspect revealed by the above accounts concerns the range of processes implied in *ṭarab* music and the different roles taken up by both performers and audience members. It is as if the audience present for Sheikh Albahlul's performance was hearing more than just 'the music'. *Ṭarab* involves an intense exploration of the 'personality', to borrow Sloboda's term (1985: 3), behind the music performed—an intense journey undertaken by both listeners and performers.[4]

The Restyled Libyan *Nawba*: between *Ṭarab* and Sentimentality

An evaluation of the aesthetic issues that relate to the Libyan *nawba* as restyled by Araibi can unfold on a continuum running between *ṭarab* and sentimentality. Whilst a potted explanation of what upgrades a performance to *ṭarab* has already been given in the previous section, sentimentality in music may be understood in terms of the explanation provided by Stokes (2009: 65), that is that music 'produced by a division of labour in which audiences have no voice, give and take between musicians is not possible and the singer assumes an authoritarian and undemocratic role'. Moreover, Stokes (2009: 65) also points out that sentimentality is to be understood 'not simply in terms of the presence or absence of a certain kind of emotionality, but in terms of specific social relations and processes of musical production'. Sentimentality, both as viewed here and globally, is manoeuvred by what Balakrishnan refers to as the 'market state' (Stokes 2010: 30). In that sense, sentimentality, even as it transpires in musical situations such as this one, is in the hands of 'market interests' with the economic base dictating the institutional intriguing taking place at the superstructure. The recording industry together with official cultural policies and the cultural institutions that implement the same policies are at the forefront in the intricate process that regulates the continuum between *ṭarab* and sentimentality. Whilst particular elements qualify the modern Libyan *nawba* as *ṭarab* music, other features related to both its making and modes of production and transmission push it towards the sentimental end of the continuum. *Ṭarab* qualities in the modern *nawba* include the individuality inherent within the heterogeneous timbre of the *takht* ensemble; the particular role assigned to *ṭarab* instruments and the heterophony produced; the unfolding of a *nawba* within a strictly organized metre and motion; and the treatment of particular notes as central and, therefore, serving both for tonal reference as well as units that direct melodic creativity. At the same time, other aspects implied in the restyled *nawba* and that relate to particular social relations and processes

[4] In this regard, Gregory and Robinson (1997) (after Cone 1974) propose the idea of the 'musical persona', claiming that 'sometimes we may simply imaginatively understand and sympathize with the feelings of some musical persona—either the composer's persona or that of some "character" in the music—but without having to imagine feeling these very feelings ourselves'. When Levinson (1997: 228) refers to the imaginative processing of musical listening, he reiterates the idea of the persona that owns the emotions contained in the music. He suggests that when we focus intensively and sympathetically on a piece of music in a style relatively familiar to us and recognizing the emotions expressed in the music, we may come to identify and empathize with the music or, better, 'with the person whom we imagine owns the emotions or emotional gestures we hear in the music'.

of musical production incline this music towards sentimentality, especially if the evaluation takes Sheikh Albahlul's performance as a frame of reference.

As I already indicated, a feature of *ṭarab* music encountered in Araibi's *nawba*, and to which Racy (2003: 76) also makes reference, is the aesthetic beauty derived from the consistent sounding of instruments with multiple timbral features. When referring to timbral preferences, Wade (2004: 49) makes a distinction between 'heterogeneous' and 'homogeneous' ensemble sounds. She defines the former as sound combining 'instruments with different timbres' and the latter as a type of sonority that coalesces 'instruments with similar timbres' (Wade 2004: 160). Wade (2004: 49) also notes that a heterogeneous ensemble sound reflects 'a love for timbral richness'. Applying this explanation to the present case, one may relate ensembles like that of Araibi to heterogeneous sound groups in which the sounding of individual instrumental timbres is highly valued. This links nicely with the fact that in a *firqa*, individual instruments can be sonically identified due to their unique timbre, as well as due to their specific roles within the ensemble. Consequently, this may result in heterophony that implies substantial technical ability, as individuality is easily recognized and brought forth for the listener's attention and admiration.

The consistent timbral and textural character of the ensemble gains further expressive potential from instruments considered by Arab music aesthetics as *ṭarab* instruments, the most prominent of these being the violin. Racy (2003: 77) notes that its 'bowing gives it the possibility to produce long notes, while its fretless neck as well as its conventional Arab tuning enables the player to produce tonal nuances with great agility'. The violin is also highly valued for its emotional expressivity and a timbre resembling the human voice (Racy 2003: 77). The five principal roles of the violin in the modern Libyan *nawba* are those of participating in the instrumental preludes that initiate the modern *nawba*; providing a drone for instrumental *taqāsīm* (plural of *taqsīm*) occasionally inserted in the same instrumental preludes or, though very rarely, in between the *muṣaddar* and *barwal* sections; accompanying the vocal lines of the *nawba*, mainly monophonically (with some sparse heterophony); winding up a section or an entire *nawba* by playing a codetta; and supplying what in Arab music are known as *lawāzim*, that is short instrumental interludes or 'fillers' between vocal and/or instrumental phrases.

In the restyled Libyan *nawba*, *lawāzim* on violins are employed for seven main purposes. First, they may be employed to generate dialogues between instruments within the same ensemble, as noted, for instance, in Example 3.1b in Chapter 3. In this particular example, the *lāzima* (singular of *lawāzim*) on the violins takes the form of a consequent for an antecedent phrase supplied by the *qānūn*. The second type of *lāzima* consists of accented offbeat notes of short duration that reiterate particular notes in the vocal line (see Example 5.1 below). Such *lāzima* normally occurs at the closure of a verse just before the reiteration of motifs from the same verse. Example 5.1 shows the third type of *lāzima*, intended to add more interest to the music, initially by adding tension through the sounding of notes in the high register followed by a release through a downward cadential movement that winds up the singing of the same verse.

Example 5.1 A short *lāzima*

The fourth kind of *lawāzim*, as featured in Example 5.2, are somewhat longer and are intended to ornament a long held note sung by the choir.

Example 5.2 Ornamental *lawāzim*

The fifth type of *lawāzim* act as fully-fledged interludes to fill in gaps between vocal phrases (see Example 5.3). In this case, the *lawāzim* also reiterate and, at the same time, anticipate some of the melodic content of a verse. Moreover, such *lawāzim* allow for slots of repose between one vocal phrase and another.

Example 5.3 A *lāzima* as a fully-fledged interlude

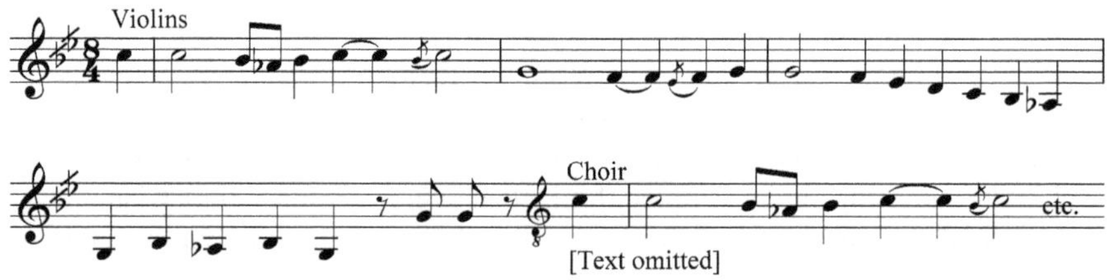

The sixth group of *lawāzim* employed by the violins function as episodic markers or lead-ins that point 'the musical narrative in the direction of something new' (Tagg 1999: 28). Example 5.4 shows a propulsive repetition that serves as an episodic marker for the *duhūl an-nawba* (i.e. the entrance to the *nawba*) or, put differently, acting as a bridge that links the instrumental prelude to the *muṣaddar* section.

Example 5.4 A *lāzima* as an episodic marker

The last kind of *lawāzim* place musical emphasis on the main beat, as can be seen in the last three bars of Example 5.5 in which the *lāzima* of four semiquavers on the strings resolves on and accentuates the first beat of each subsequent bar. This last type of *lāzima* occurs during a *taqsīm*.

Example 5.5 A *lāzima* placing musical emphasis on the main beat of the bar

As already noted, these *taqāsīm* (plural of *taqsīm*) are occasionally employed in the instrumental preludes to the *nawba*, as in Example 5.6 below, as well as in between sections.

All the types of *lawāzim* featured above provide the violin with possibilities to stand out from the rest of the ensemble and, therefore, to reinforce its individuality.

The second *ṭarab* instrument highly engaged in the accompanying role of modern ensembles is the *'ūd*. Normally, the *'ūd* is played by the sheikh of the ensemble and, as mentioned in the previous chapter, it symbolizes the leading role of the sheikh in the ensemble. When the performance follows no pre-agreed programme, the sheikh plays on the *'ūd* some indicative notes from the succeeding item to mark the upcoming work. The *'ūd* is sometimes entrusted with a *taqsīm* inserted in the instrumental prelude of a *nawba*. Example 5.6 shows an example of such a *taqsīm* taken from the instrumental prelude to *nawba jamru l-ḥawā*. As the same example shows, the violins and cello support the *taqsīm* by holding a long drone note. After a short rest, the violins play a *lāzima* with the *'ūd* echoing heterophonically.

The other two *ṭarab* instruments found in the modern *ma'lūf* ensemble are the *nāy* and *qānūn*. The main role of the *nāy* and *qānūn* is that of providing monophonic and heterophonic accompaniment for the singing. In addition, their individuality is sometimes emphasized in the instrumental prelude of the *nawba*, either by involving them in 'dialogues' with other instruments, by supplying a

Example 5.6 A *taqsīm* on the *'ūd* with a *lāzima* on the violins

Drone continues throughout until otherwise indicated. The note E is doubled an octave lower by the cello.

lāzima in unison (see Example 5.7) or, occasionally, by rounding off a phrase or an entire section by extending the same phrase (see Example 5.8). The transcription in Example 5.8 aligns the notes played by the *nāy* underneath those of the violins in an attempt to show the echoing techniques employed by the former.

Example 5.7 A *lāzima* (framed) played in unison by *qānūn* and *nāy* with the violins playing the rest of the example

Example 5.8 The *nāy* winding up an instrumental prelude

Another element in *ṭarab* music is the *īqā'*, as rightly noted by Racy (2003: 113):

> meter appears to generate ecstasy in a variety of ways. As repeated self-contained structures, rhythmic patterns generate an orderly temporal flow. Furthermore, through their distinctive internal designs, they evoke certain affects.

As already mentioned, the two main *īqā'āt* of the Libyan *nawba* are the *muṣaddar* and *barwal*. While the *darabukka* plays throughout, the *ṭār* is the *ṭarab* instrument that in the modern Libyan *nawba* customarily joins in at the *duhūl an-nawba*. A modern *ma'lūf* ensemble may include from four to six *ṭīrān* players, who normally stand at the back or at the side of the ensemble, synchronizing their upward and downward hand movements, as in the traditional *bandīr* playing of the *ma'lūf az-zāwiya*. Their role is that of complementing the orderly temporal flow of the rhythm as established by the *darabukka* and *daff*. The individuality of the *ṭār* is frequently highlighted when *ṭār* players, synchronically, accentuate the *dumm* stroke of the *darabukka* and fill in the rest of the rhythmic pattern with uplifted trills. Apart from that, and in order to add more variety to the rhythmic flow, a *ṭār* player may strike his instrument improvisatorially with plenty of offbeat strokes that evolve cross-rhythmically with the established rhythmic pattern as maintained by the other *tār* and percussion players. Such 'playing around the beat', as Racy (2003: 117) refers to it, must occur without any excessiveness that would obscure a smooth temporal flow. Due to their improvisatory nature, such strokes may be considered an expression of affect on the part of an individual *tār* player. In addition, such manoeuvres on the *tār* enhance the distinctiveness of its timbre.

Another aspect mentioned by Racy in the evocation of *ṭarab* is heterophony. Racy identifies two closely related types of heterophony, mainly the overlapping and simultaneous types. Regarding each type, Racy (2003: 80) notes the following:

> [Overlapping heterophony] occurs when a leading musical part, typically a vocal improvisation, is accompanied, for example, by an instrument such as the *qānūn*. In this case, the accompaniment 'echoes' the leading part at a slightly delayed pace, or in a rather 'out of sync' fashion. [Simultaneous heterophony] applies mostly when ensemble members produce slightly varied renditions of the same musical material at the same time. This happens when *takht* instruments perform the same basic composition together, but with each one rendering it differently through subtle variations, omissions, ornamental nuances, syncopations, anticipations, and so on.

It has been pointed out to me by some members of Araibi's ensemble that the prominent instrument in a *ma'lūf* ensemble for the generation of heterophony is the *qānūn*. Simultaneous heterophony, for instance, is most typically produced by the *qānūn* for musical passages played more skeletally by the *'ūd*. Such heterophony includes 'ornaments' that in Arab music are considered as 'the artist's form of personal expression, with which the artist discloses his distinctive *self*' (El-Mallah 1997: 48–9, emphasis in original). Overlapping heterophony is also employed, sometimes in an obligatory fashion due to its fixed place in professionally recorded *nawbāt*, such as in the widely diffused cassette collection of *ma'lūf* produced by Araibi and his ensemble. Recorded music, even in Arabic music, may fix in the listener's expectation an urge for heterophonic passages. This point can be further explained by considering a live performance by Araibi's ensmeble given in 2004. On that occasion the ensemble was commemorating its fortieth anniversary. The performance consisted of three-and-a-half hours of continuous music, coming to an end in the early hours of the following morning. Both the *nāy* and *qānūn* players were absent from the ensemble, and were not substituted. A member of the ensemble remarked to me that their substitution was unfeasible due to the high level of teamwork needed—something that could only be achieved through time and regular rehearsal. As an alternative, Yūsuf, Araibi's son, sat playing the violin just behind his father, in line with the choir and at some distance from the violin section. By that means, he could provide the necessary 'obligatory' overlapping heterophony produced in the recorded collection by the *nāy* and *qānūn*, which was deeply fixed in the listeners' expectation and memory. His positioning at the front and at a distance from the rest of the violins allowed his heterophony to sound distinct and relatively penetrating and, to some extent, served as a nice substitute for the heterophony that listeners are habituated to hear, even if less embellished when compared to the more highly ornamented type produced in the recorded version.

Considering the other end of the continuum and focusing one's attention on sentimentality, as understood above, one may bring forward the fact that in *ma'lūf al-idhā'a* performances 'audiences have no voice' and 'give and take between musicians is not possible'. Even if the modern *nawba* contains several elements of *ṭarab* music, as argued above, aspects such as the ones just mentioned drag it towards sentimentality rather than to the state of *ṭarab* as depicted in Sheikh Albahlul's performance. For instance, in the modern *nawba* the singing is predominantly choral and, therefore, the role of the sheikh is mainly that of leading what has been rehearsed several times beforehand. The inclusion of solo calls by the sheikh in the modern *nawba* is an exception rather than the rule, and when these do occur they emerge as agreed during rehearsal. It is worth noting here the fact that an element highly important for the stimulation of more emotionality, in both the *ma'lūf az-zāwiya* and *ṭarab* music, is the alternating singing of the soloist vis-à-vis the group. In order to make up for the absence in the modern *nawba* of the 'persona' that is traditionally evoked by the solo voice of the sheikh, some modern ensembles supplement the choral singing with singing at a parallel octave higher. For such an effect, female voices, or a blend of mature and younger voices, are sometimes employed. While parallel-octave singing is continuous in the former ensemble, it is sparsely used in all-male choirs. In the case of the latter formation, younger voices are occasionally engaged in short passages, either to provide a reply, to reiterate certain verses or to round up the cadential ending of a verse. This adds interest to the predominantly choral singing of the *nawba*, mainly by enriching the singing, accentuating the unique role of the voice within the ensemble whilst at the same time reminding listeners of the call-and-response structure of the *ma'lūf az-zāwiya* and the individual–togetherness element of *ṭarab* music.

In contrast to what takes place in *ṭarab* situations, one notes in modern *nawba* performances the absence of intense 'scanning' of the audience by the leading performer of the ensemble. We saw above how the emotional rapture of participants in a traditional *ma'lūf* session inspired Sheikh Abu Sama to come up with the most suitable verses for his *nawba* as enriched by the concept of *samā'*. The kind of 'audience-scanning' I observed during performances of the modern Libyan *nawba* was more concerned with on-the-spot programme decisions rather than with the performer's assessment of affect in the course of performance. It was common for Araibi, for instance, to start his performance by addressing the audience, as if good rapport needed the assistance of the spoken word rather than just that of the musical sound; further addresses occurred after every item. Occasionally, people would reply with clapping and words of approval, and members of the audience would request particular items. When requests were not called out, Araibi 'scanned' the audience to 'read' what the overall feeling was so that his next choice would provide the audience with what they wanted to hear. This brings forward the distinction between the kind of 'scanning' that is only intended to meet effective and proper unfolding of the programme and the more intense type that considers how best to trigger and nurture *ṭarab*. Due to the great reliance on choral singing and strict precomposition, the possibility for the leading sheikh to scan through audience affect in the course of an ongoing piece is practically nonexistent.

Returning to the instrumental preludes composed by Araibi and the critique concerning the allegedly unrelated content of these with the remaining *nawba* (see Chapter 3), it is now possible to hypothesize that these preludes open up possibilities for and accentuate features reminiscent of *ṭarab* music, such as in the inclusion of instrumental improvisations, improvised *qaflāt* and the insertion of *īqā'āt* other than the *muṣaddar* and *barwal*. Araibi, and the composers who followed his compositional style, attempt to maintain in the innovated *nawba* the highly valued elements of *ṭarab* music within a musical structure strongly inclined towards standardization and pseudo-individualization, two processes recognized by critical theory as dominant in the culture industry.

Conclusion

The allure of the *ma'lūf az-zāwiya* for some of my informants rests on the fact that the *zāwiya* context provides to the Sufi a composite of suitable conditions for *samā'*, the paramount of which is the strong fraternal spirit sustained by the sacredness of not just the place but of each participating Sufi. The link of *samā'* with *ma'lūf az-zāwiya* performances upgrades the entire musical activity to more than 'sheer' listening or musical participation. *Ma'lūf* sessions in the *zāwiya* cultivate the love for the *turāth* within a context enriched by the concept of *samā'*—an ambience that goes beyond all professional restraints and demands. Artistic growth in the *turāth* as it develops in the *zāwiya* is strongly pivoted on the love of the Sufi for this art, a kind of 'reverence' that shapes the entire process of assimilation in terms of both content and attitude towards it. In contrast, contexts like festivals and recording studios, in which *ma'lūf al-idhā'a* is typically performed, are devoid of the intense socio-religious communality experienced in the *zāwiya* and, therefore, this constrains the psycho-spiritual process so important to *samā'* and all possible interrelatedness that might exist with the *ma'lūf al-idhā'a*. Ensembles like Araibi's strive for higher levels of professionalism, dictated in most cases by commitments entailing financial implications and interests of the market. Establishing preconditions, such as the 'right time' for *samā'*, have become absolutely insignificant in a strongly consumer-orientated mode of music production in which preconditions are in the hands of market forces rather than regulated by the music makers themselves and the communal spirit that unites them.

It is worth mentioning here that music and affect are interrelated in terms of the pleasure experienced by listeners in decoding the affective world lying behind the music and in recognizing the fact that the same sensation is not extraneous to them but exists in the music as much as it is present in their consciousness.[5] For *ma'lūf az-zāwiya* followers such well-recognized affect as is kindled in *zāwiya* is nurtured by *samā'* and is precisely that which facilitates the decoding process that leads to so much emotionality and the transformation of that into eventual group swaying, cross-rhythmic drumming and hand movements. Looking at these ideas again from the perspective of contemporary *ma'lūf* performances, one notes that for *ma'lūf az-zāwiya* participants and followers such decoding becomes somewhat 'strenuous' and in a way 'incongruent' with the decoding process most experienced in *zāwiya.* Musical decoding and the way it unfolds during a performance is of vital importance in terms of scrutiny as it may shed light on elements that bind the participant to the performance. To a certain extent, musical decoding is in itself another mode of participation, in particular, if one applies Finnegan's (2003: 189) assertion that 'people participate in music in multifarious ways in the different roles they take, the occasion, or their own personal histories'. It is within this complex web of decoding, and affective impulses and responses to it, that further musical affect is generated and forged. Considering the remaking of the *nawba* as a creative act that in itself manifests a cultural process would lead us to the evaluation of a musical genre recycling its structure whilst ransacking it for links with *ṭarab* music and cleverly alluding to it. All this occurs within the framework of a postmodern popular culture 'identifiable by its self-conscious awareness of its status as a cultural product' (Strinati 2004: 225) and characterized, amongst others, by the delicate blend of recycling and innovation.

[5] In this regard, one notes some diametrically opposed views on music and affect. Fisk (1997: 182), for example, argues that while he does not believe 'that music represents real-life emotions or tells a story simulating real-life actions', he is of the opinion that 'musical feelings and actions are ... feelings and actions that we have allowed music to appropriate, transforming them into music; they are not something outside music that it represents but rather something inside us that we vouchsafe to it. ... In becoming music, these feelings and actions never become articulated in just the ways they would in situations outside of music. But we can conjecture what they might otherwise have been or, for ourselves, what they could become. For the faculties on which musical emotions and actions draw must be the same faculties, at least to a degree, that we employ to feel emotions and configure actions generally, and that we develop, for the most part, outside of music.' On the other hand, when referring to what occurs within us at the hearing of expressive music, Walton (1988: 359) suggests that we hear music and conceive it as an imaginary experience of our own emotional and psychological states. For instance, we understand melancholic music because we have at some time in life experienced melancholy. And we long for a particular motif or theme within the music that the composer or performer, with great skillfulness, conceals from us from time to time due to the fact that the sense of longing exists in the music as much as it exists in us. In time we learn to associate particular music with particular affects and emotional states.

Epilogue

As revealed throughout this work, the Libyan *ma'lūf* holds its distinct mode of thinking and discourse with all sorts of debates shaping and influencing what occurs in all its aspects. What the *ma'lūf* means in contemporary Libyan society is very much determined by the way the Libyans think and talk about it, with all this intrinsically moulded by factors that from the outside may appear as irrelevant to the tradition, though in real terms they are not so.

Issues that in some way or another relate to *ma'lūf*, such as the recognition of professional musicians, patronage, innovation, the debate between the sacred and the secular, modernity, authenticity, traditionalism and ideology, are all linked to personal and social circumstances and, therefore, to the innermost sensibilities of people and the way they respond to the world around them. The new political system in Libya that will come in effect through democratic elections will definitely further increase the rate of social and economic change that the Libyans will face in the coming years; this will leave an impact on the life of the *ma'lūf*. To some extent, an increased rate of socio-economic change had gained some momentum in 2003 when the United Nations lifted 11 years of sanctions against the country and the eventual opening up to the West. Muhammad's rapport with the *ma'lūf* may serve as an example of the changing dynamics of individual interactions with this musical tradition resulting from a more demanding economic and political scenario experienced at that time.

Back in 2004, during one of my visits, I met Muhammad, a family man in his forties and manager of a travel agency that was venturing into the prospects of a promising tourist industry. Muhammad's work required of him long working hours that hardly spared him time to cherish participation in *ma'lūf az-zāwiya* sessions as he used to do in his youth; that time had become almost nostalgic for him. The financial pressures exerted upon him as the sole breadwinner for his family and the challenges he had to face in order to succeed in his job have distanced him from an art he used to adore not only for its beauty of text and melodies but also for the opportunity it provided him to experience the sense of Muslim fraternity as a *zāwiya* member:

> That could only be felt through regular attendance to *ma'lūf az-zāwiya* sessions and interaction with sheikhs whose passion is that of sharing *ma'lūf* verses from whom they might have learned no one knows. With much regret the *ma'lūf* has become for me like a hobby for which I can only spare very little time. One must devote time for it in order to get fully acquainted with it because it's an infinite art—something that I can't afford to do regularly any longer. You know, if I won't pay my telephone bills they would suspend my telephone line after a three-day overdue with extra charges to reconnect. The same happens for the

> other bills I have to pay. Life is changing here for everyone and, whether you like it or not, money has become an absolute priority. The very few occasional times I go to *zāwiya* I feel all these pressures and mundane preoccupations behind me, thanks to the sense of fraternity I experience there that disconnects me, even if momentarily, from the world outside.

In view of the fact that Gaddafi had always looked upon Sufi lodges as haunts for Islamic fundamentalism, some extra information from Muhammad on this aspect could perhaps explain the tension that has existed between *zāwiya* brotherhoods and the Gaddafi administration and, eventually, between the world 'inside' *zāwiya* and that 'outside'. It took a while for Muhammad to express what had been at the very tip of his tongue to share with me, though in consistent discreetness:

> In *zāwiya* we experience a unique sensation not so easy to experience here [referring to Libya] as things stand at the moment, even if this is a Muslim country. And the *ma'lūf* as practised in its *zāwiya* form during *mawlid* and other public events provides us with the chance to share with others the value of brotherhood so essential in Muslim life.

Muhammad's comments can be understood in light of the fact that, since the 1969 revolution, Libya has experienced a growing sense of individualism most evident amongst the educated young. Many of these educated and increasingly independent young people nowadays prefer to set up their own households at marriage rather than to live with their parents, that is independent households have replaced the more traditional pattern. Consequently, such independence has brought more financial burdens and responsibilities, with very restricted time available for unprofitable activities, as hinted by Muhammad above. In this sense, an investigation into a music tradition such as the Libyan *ma'lūf* divulges information as much about the people that in some way connect to it as about the tradition itself, and about all that which makes them, not only citizens of a country or a region but also as citizens of a world whose frontiers are increasingly becoming political and geographical rather than cultural and social.

Consistently changing national, regional and international economic orders, and their impact on individuals and families, are certainly determining what occurs on the bonding terrain between a music tradition and its makers, producers and consumers. It is a territory in which theoretical paradigms related to issues such as 'modernity', 'authenticity' and 'hybridity' are continuously challenged by concepts of globalization and the new global order emerging from them—all linked to global monetary manoeuvring. The Libyan *ma'lūf*, both in *zāwiya* and outside, will continue evolving within a kaleidoscope of meanings and their re-evaluation, with all this being reshaped by new political scenarios at local, regional and global levels.

One wonders how the tradition of our concern will respond to a diverse political ideology and the different socio-political order that will arise from it. This may all develop into a future that will see a Libya much more open to the world, one in which musicians, for instance, whilst continuing to work in the context of a 'traditional ambivalence' (Bohlman 2002: 63) like their North African and eastern Mediterranean counterparts, attain the skills needed of them to confront the challenges of a new world order with the backing of an effective political system. This could be a system in which patronage will no longer depend on framed pictures of revolutionaries on stage during state-sponsored public *ma'lūf* performances, or concealed pressures to perform at state receptions even if such involvement seems to be rather unfitting. The political system envisaged here will make traditional practices more accessible to the public worldwide, mainly through a more effective use of IT and the media and a stronger tourist industry, as well as new ventures into the recording industry and all the business generated by this. To these, one may also add more creative initiatives emphasizing musical hybridity of the *ma'lūf* with contemporary and popular musical genres, all this becoming 'the new authenticity'—in itself a deviation from the conventional debate so far persisting in Libya about what constitutes 'authenticity'. In this challenging set-up, intra- and intercultural processes of musical translation would become the norm rather than the exception. In such a new socio-political background, stories of sheikhs transmitting *ma'lūf* in *zāwiya* and safeguarding *al-turāth* from deviating excessively from the 'authentic' tradition, or debates concerning the diverse emotionality of listeners to the *ma'lūf az-zāwiya* and the *ma'lūf al-idha'a* will be attired with added shades of interpretation as proposed by possible new performing practices and consequent nostalgias, and the further pondering that these might trigger. All this will be shaped by a new way of thinking, a new way of how the Libyans will perceive the world around them, see their place within it and react to it. In such a new political order, preservation as a concept may attain an added shade of understanding within a national cultural strategy and policy that will allow the world for a better and effective access not just to *ma'lūf*, but, more widely, to Libya's wealth of cultural heritage.

On my way back to Tripoli Airport during my second trip to Libya, Sadeeq, the driver, turned to me and asked, 'Shall we see you again in Libya for more work on the *ma'lūf*?' In his eyes I could read a sense of pride and the expectation of a positive reply, which, in fact, I gave both verbally and by the trips that followed in the months and years after. The Libya that I shall experience in my next trip will be different from the Libya I left behind in many respects. The borderlines in discourse between the 'musical' and the 'social', for instance, might merge more, observing no constraints whatsoever. That would open up a new perspective on a music tradition that has much more to say, not necessarily about itself, but about what occurs in the hidden corridors of human consciousness.

Glossary

adhān: call to prayer
bandīr: a single-headed drum
bās: a small hand-drum
daff: a tambourine with a diameter of approximately twelve inches
darabukka: a goblet drum
dhikr: a Sufi ritual in which certain religious verbal phrases are repeated
firqa: a large urban ensemble
ghayṭa: a double-reed wind instrument
ḥaḍra (plural, *ḥaḍrāt*): a Sufi religious service
ḥiss (also *iḥsās*): feeling, or to feel the music and performing it with feeling or ecstatically
idhā'a: broadcasting
īqā' (plural, *īqā'āt*): melodic mode
jins (plural, *ajnas*): the basic building block for the *maqām*, consisting of a group of three to five notes that form a trichord, tetrachord or pentachord
kamanja: Western violin
kinjī: an assistant to the *sheikh ma'lūf*.
lāzima (plural, *lawāzim*): a short instrumental filler or interlude
ma'lūf: the name used in Libya and Tunisia for the Andalusian *nawba* repertoire
madīḥ: a vocal form with religious content
maqām (plural, *maqāmāt*): melodic mode
mawlid: a religious festivity celebrating the Prophet's birth
mawwāl: a vocal improvisation that uses colloquial poetical text
mu'āraḍāt (singular, *mu'āraḍā*): pastiche verses
muwashshaḥ (plural, *muwashshaḥāt*): a pre-composed, metrical song
naqqārāt: a pair of small kettle drums
nawba: a suite comprising different vocal and instrumental parts; also a cylindrical drum used in *ma'lūf* parades
nāy: a vertical end-blown reed flute
qafla (plural, *qaflāt*): a final cadence usually followed by a pause
qānūn: a trapezoidal zither
qaṣīda (plural, *qaṣā'id*): a vocal genre based on classical Arabic poetry
qirā'a: Qur'ānic cantillation
raddāda: a male choir in a *ma'lūf* performance
rūḥ: to feel *ṭarab* music or performing it affectively
salṭana: a state of ecstasy experienced by performers in the course of performance
samā': in the context of Sufism, it refers to listening to spiritual music
takht: a small instrumental ensemble

taqsīm (plural, *taqāsīm*): instrumental improvisation
ṭār (plural, *tīrān*): a single-headed tambourine with a diameter of approximately eight inches
ṭarab: the ecstatic feeling generated by the music
turāth: heritage
ughniya (plural, *ughniyāt*): a song
'ūd: a pear-shaped lute with five or six strings
waṣla: a medley of vocal and instrumental pieces
zajal: poetic text in colloquial Arabic
zāwiya (plural, *zawāyā*): a Sufi lodge

Bibliography

Abdelkafi. 1994. *Weddings in Tripolitania*. Tripoli: Dar al-Fergiani.

Abudaber, Mahmud. n.d. 'An Interview with Ayman Al Atar' in *AymanAlatar.com* (online): http://www.aymanalatar.com/Interview%20with%20Ayman%20Al%20Atar.htm (accessed 1 July 2010).

Ahmida, Ali Abdullatif. 1994. *The Making of Modern Libya: State Formation, Colonization, and Resistance, 1830–1932*. Albany, NY: State University of New York Press.

Albergoni, Gianni and Jaques Vignet-Zunz. 1982. 'Aspects of Modernization among the Bedouin of Barqah', in E.G.H Joffé and K.S. McLachlan (eds.), *Social and Economic Development of Libya*, Wisbech: MENAS Press, 189–93.

Almbladh, Karin. 2006. 'An Andalusian muwashshaḥ and its mu'āradāt: Nasīmu l-raudi fāḥ', in E. Emery (ed.), *Muwashshah: Proceedings of the Conference on Arabic and Hebrew Strophic Poetry and its Romance Parallels, School of Oriental and African Studies (SOAS), London, 8–10 October 2004*, London: RN Books, 13–22.

Alvarez, Lourdes M. 1998. 'Zajal, Medieval', in J. Scott Meisami and P. Starkey (eds.), *Encyclopedia of Arabic Literature*. New York: Routledge, 2: 818–19.

———. 2006. 'Reading the Mystical Signs in the Songs of Abū Al-Hasan Al-Shushtarī', in E. Emery (ed.), *Muwashshah: Proceedings of the Conference on Arabic and Hebrew Strophic Poetry and its Romance Parallels, School of Oriental and African Studies (SOAS), London, 8–10 October 2004*, London: RN Books, 23–32.

Anon. 2010a. *JobinLibya.com* (online): http://www.jobinlibya.com/english/article_education-in-libya (accessed 24 July 2010).

———. 2010b. *Temehu* (online): http://www.temehu.com/tours/festival-music.htm (accessed 20 July 2010).

———. 2010c. *Cheb Jilani* (online): http://www.faridatrache.com/Maghreb/Cheb-Jilani.php (accessed 3 July 2010).

Ashiurakis, Ahmed Mohamed. 1993. *Your Guide to Libya: Past and Present*. Tripoli: Paper and Printing Sector Arab Revolution Presses.

Beaudry, Nicole. 1997. 'The Challenges of Human Relations in Ethnographic Inquiry: Examples from Arctic and Subarctic Fieldwork', in G.F. Barz and T.J. Cooley (eds), *Shadows in the Field*, New York: Oxford University Press, 63–83.

Benbaabali, Saadane. 2006. 'Love and Drunkenness in the Muwashshah as Sung in the Maghreb', in E. Emery (ed.), *Muwashshah: Proceedings of the Conference on Arabic and Hebrew Strophic Poetry and its Romance Parallels, School of*

Oriental and African Studies (SOAS), London, 8–10 October 2004, London: RN Books, 37–53.

Bertarelli, L.V. 1937. *Libia*. Milano: Consociazione Turistica Italiana.

Blacking, John. 1995. *Music, Culture and Experience: Selected Papers of John Blacking*. R. Byron (ed.), Chicago: University of Chicago Press.

Bleuchot, Hervé. 1982. 'The Green Book: Its Context and Meaning', in J.A. Allan (ed.), *Libya Since Independence: Economic and Political Development*, London: Croom Helm, 137–64.

Blum, Stephen. 1998. 'Recognizing Improvisation', in B. Nettl with M. Russell (eds), *In the Course of Performance: Studies in the World of Musical Improvisation*, Chicago: The University of Chicago Press, 27–45.

———. 2002. 'Hearing the Music of the Middle East', in Virginia Danielson, Scott Marcus and Dwight Reynolds (eds), *The Garland Encyclopedia of World Music*. New York: Garland Publishing, 6: 3–13.

Bohlman, Philip V. 2002. *World Music: A Very Short Introduction*. New York: Oxford University Press.

Brandily, Monique. 1982. 'Music and Social Change', in E.G.H Joffé and K.S. McLachlan (eds), *Social and Economic Development of Libya*, Wisbech: MENAS Press, 207–14.

Bronson, Bertrand H. 1951. 'Melodic Stability in Oral Transmission', *Journal of the International Folk Music Council*, 3: 50–55.

Cerbella, Gino and Ageli, Mustafa. 1949. *Le Feste Musulmane in Tripoli: Appunti Etnografici*. Tripoli: Tipografia Commerciale F.lli Barbiera.

Chittick, William C. 1995. 'Sufism', in John L. Esposito (ed.), *The Oxford Encyclopedia of the Modern Islamic World*. New York: Oxford University Press, 4: 102–109.

Ciantar, Philip. 1996. *Styles of Transcription in Ethnomusicology*. MA dissertation, University of Durham (UK).

———. 2002a. 'Libya and Its Andalusian Musical Heritage', *The Malta Independent on Sunday* (1 September).

———. 2002b. 'Hassan Araibi and the Libyan *Ma'lūf* Musical Tradition', *The Sunday Times of Malta* (6 October).

———. 2003. 'Continuity and Change in the Libyan *Ma'lūf* Musical Tradition', *Libyan Studies*, 34: 137–46.

———. 2006. 'Nostalgia, History and Sheikhs in the Libyan *Ma'lūf*: Listening Contexts in the Shadows of the Past', in E. Emery (ed.), *Muwashshaḥ: Proceedings of the Conference on Arabic and Hebrew Strophic Poetry and its Romance Parallels, School of Oriental and African Studies (SOAS), London, 8–10 October 2004*, London: RN Books, 55–70.

Collins, Carole. 1974. 'Imperialism and Revolution in Libya', *MERIP Reports*, 27: 3–22.

Cone, Edward T. 1974. *The Composer's Voice*. Berkeley and Los Angeles: University of California Press.

Danielson, Virginia. 1997. *The Voice of Egypt: Umm Kulthūm, Arabic Song, and Egyptian Society in the Twentieth Century*. Chicago: The University of Chicago Press.

Danielson, Virginia and Fisher, Alexander J. 2002. 'History of Scholarship: Narratives of Middle Eastern Music History', in Virginia Danielson, Scott Marcus and Dwight Reynolds (eds), *The Garland Encyclopedia of World Music*. New York: Routledge, 6: 15–27.

Davis, Ruth F. 1997a. 'Cultural Policy and the Tunisian Ma'lūf: Redefining a Tradition', *Ethnomusicology*, 41: 1–21.

———. 1997b. 'Traditional Arab Music Ensembles in Tunis: Modernizing Al-Turāth in the Shadows of Egypt', *Asian Music*, 28: 73–108.

———. 2002. 'Al-Andalus in Tunis: Sketches of the Ma'lūf in the 1990s', *Journal of Music and Anthropology in the Mediterranean* (online): http://www.umbc.edu/MA/index/number7/davis/dav_00.htm (accessed 20 October 2011).

———. 2004. *Ma'lūf: Reflections on the Arab Andalusian Music of Tunisia*. Lanham MD: Oxford: Scarecrow Press.

Douglas, Gavin. 2003. 'The Sokayeti Performing Arts Competition of Burma/Myanmar: Performing the Nation', *The World of Music*, 45: 35–54.

During, Jean. 1992. In L. Lewisohn (ed.), *The Legacy of Mediaeval Persian Sufism*, London: Khaniqahi Nimatullahi Publications, 277–87.

Elsner, Jürgen. 1997. 'Listening to Arabic Music', *The World of Music*, 39: 111–26.

———. 2002. 'Urban Music of Algeria', in Virginia Danielson, Scott Marcus and Dwight Reynolds (eds), *The Garland Encyclopedia of World Music*. New York: Routledge, 6: 465–80.

Emerson, Robert, Rachel I. Fretz and Linda L. Shaw. 1995. *Writing Ethnographic Fieldnotes*. Chicago and London: The University of Chicago Press.

Evans-Pritchard, E.E. 1949. *The Sanusi of Cyrenaica*. Oxford: Clarendon Press.

Farmer, Henry George. 1957. 'The Music of Islam', in E. Wellesz (ed.), *The New Oxford History of Music: Ancient and Oriental Music*. Oxford: Oxford University Press, 1: 421–64.

———. 1965. *The Sources of Arabian Music*. Leiden: E.J. Brill.

Al Faruqi, Lois Ibsen. 1974. *The Nature of the Musical Art of Islamic Culture: a Theoretical and Empirical Study of Arabian Music*. Ph.D. dissertation, Syracuse University, NY.

Fathaly, Omar I. and Palmer, Monte. 1980. *Political Development and Social Change in Libya*. Lanham, MD: Lexington Books.

Fergiani, Mohammed Bescir. 1983. *The Libyan Jamahiriya*. London: Darf Publishers Ltd.

Finnegan, Ruth. 2003. 'Music, Emotion and the Anthropology of Emotion', in Martin Clayton, Trevor Herbert and Richard Middleton (eds), *The Cultural Study of Music: A Critical Introduction*, New York and London: Routledge, 181–92.

Fisk, Charles. 1997. 'What Schubert's Last Sonata Might Hold', in J. Robinson (ed.), *Music and Meaning*, Ithaca: Cornell University Press, 179–200.

El-Giernazi, Fawzi. 1984. *The Tawarig People & Folk Dances of Southern Libya*. Ottowa: Jerusalem International Publishing House.

Gregory, Karl and Robinson, Jenefer. 1997. 'Shostakovich's Tenth Symphony and the Musical Expression of Cognitively Emotions', in J. Robinson (ed.), *Music and Meaning*, Ithaca: Cornell University Press, 154–78.

Guettat, Mahmoud. 1980. *La Musique Classique du Maghreb*. Paris: Sindbad.

———. 2001. 'The Andalusian Musical Heritage', in Virginia Danielson, Scott Marcus and Dwight Reynolds (eds), *The Garland Encyclopedia of World Music*. New York: Routledge, 6: 441–54.

Habib, Henri. 1979. *Libya: Past and Present*. Malta: Edam Publishing.

Harrison, Robert S. 1967. 'Migrants in the City of Tripoli, Libya', *Geographical Review*, 57: 397–423.

Hardy, Paula. 2002. *Libya*. Surrey: Zerzura Editions.

Jalajel, David. 2007. 'Enjambment in Arabic Poetry—A Practical Exploration for Poets', in *Ghazal Page* (online): http://www.ghazalpage.net/prose/notes/enjambment.html (accessed 28 July 2010).

Jeffery, Peter. 1992. *Re-Envisioning Past Musical Cultures: Ethnomusicology in the Study of Gregorian Chant*. Chicago: The University of Chicago Press.

Joffe, George. 1988. 'Islamic Opposition in Libya', *Third World Quarterly*, 10: 615–31.

Jones, Lura JaFran. 2001. 'North Africa: Overview', in Virginia Danielson, Scott Marcus and Dwight Reynolds (eds), *The Garland Encyclopedia of World Music*. New York: Routledge, 6: 429–39.

Kleeman, Janice E. 1985–1986. 'The Parameters of Musical Transmission', *The Journal of Musicology*, 4: 1–22.

Langlois, Tony. 2009. 'Music and Politics in North Africa', in L. Nooshin (ed.), *Music and the Play of Power in the Middle East, North Africa and Central Asia*, Surrey: Ashgate, 207–27.

Lee, Tong Soon. 1999. 'Technology and the Production of Islamic Space: The Call to Prayer in Singapore', *Ethnomusicology*, 43: 86–100.

Leon Jackson, Rovi. 2010. 'Hamid El Sharī', in *iTunes Preview* (online): http://itunes.apple.com/se/artist/hamid-el-shari/id14717961 (accessed 15 July 2010).

Levinson, Jerrold. 1997. 'Music and Negative Emotion', in J. Robinson (ed.), *Music and Meaning*, Ithaca: Cornell University Press, 215–41.

Lewisohn, Leonard. 1997. 'The Sacred Music of Islam: Samāʿ in the Persian Sufi Tradition', *British Journal of Ethnomusicology*, 6: 1–33.

Lodge, David and Bill Badley. 2000. 'Popular/Street Music: Cairo Hit Factory', in S. Broughton, M. Ellingham and R. Trillo (eds), *World Music: The Rough Guide*. London: Rough Guides, 1: 338–46.

El-Mahdi, Salah. 1978. 'A Few Notes on the History of Arabian Music', *The World of Music*, 20: 5–13.

El-Mallah, Issam. 1997. *Arab Music and Musical Notation*. Tutzing: Hans Schneider Verlag.

Marcus, Scott L. 1992. 'Modulation in Arab Music: Documenting Oral Concepts, Performance Rules and Startegies', *Ethnomusicology*, 36: 171–95.
———. 2007. *Music in Egypt: Experiencing Music, Experiencing Culture*. New York; Oxford: Oxford University Press.
Martinez, Luis. 2007. *The Libyan Paradox*. London: Hurst & Company.
Mason, John P. 1975. 'Sex and Symbol in the Treatment of Women: the Wedding Rite in a Libyan Oasis Community', *American Ethnologist*, 2: 649–61.
Merriam, Alan P. 1964. *The Anthropology of Music*. Evanston, IL: Northwestern University Press.
Meyer, Leonard B. 1956. *Emotion and Meaning in Music*. Chicago: The University of Chicago Press.
Nattiez, Jean-Jacques. 1990. *Music and Discourse: Toward a Semiology of Music*, trans. Carolyn Abbate. Princeton: Princeton University Press.
Nettl, Bruno. 1996. 'Relating the Present to the Past: Thoughts on the Study of Musical Change and Culture Change in Ethnomusicology', *Journal of Music and Anthropology in the Mediterranean* (online): http://www.umbc.edu/MA/index/number1/nettl1/ne1.htm (accessed 20 October 2011).
———. 2005. *The Study of Ethnomusicology: Thirty-one Issues and Concepts*. Urbana: University of Illinois Press.
Ostler, Alan. 1912. *The Arabs in Tripoli*. London: John Murray.
Panetta, Ester. 1963. *L'Italia in Africa: Studi Italiani di Etnografia e di Folklore della Libia*. Roma: Istituo Poligrafico dello Stato.
Peters, E.L. 1982. 'Cultural and Social Diversity in Libya', in J.A. Allan (ed.), *Libya Since Independence: Economic and Political Development*, London: Croom Helm, 103–20.
Pfaff, Richard H. 1970. 'The Function of Arab Nationalism', *Comparative Politics*, 2: 147–67.
Plakhova, Anna. 2006. '*Maqām Rāst* in the Art of the *Muwashshaḥ*', in E. Emery (ed.), *Muwashshaḥ: Proceedings of the Conference on Arabic and Hebrew Strophic Poetry and its Romance Parallels, School of Oriental and African Studies (SOAS), London, 8–10 October 2004*, London: RN Books, 197–210.
Poché, Christian. 1995. *La Musique Arabo-Andalouse*. Arles: Actes Sud.
Al Qathafi, Muammar. 1999. *The Green Book*. 3rd Edition. Tripoli: World Center for the Study and Research of *The Green Book*.
Racy, Ali Jihad. 1978. 'Arabian Music and the Effects of Commercial Recording', *World of Music*, 20: 47–58.
———. 1981. 'Music in Contemporary Cairo: A Comparative Overview', *Asian Music*, 13: 4–26.
———. 1982. 'Musical Aesthetics in Present-Day Cairo', *Ethnomusicology*, 26: 391–406.
———. 1998. 'Improvisation, Ecstasy, and Performance Dynamics in Arabic Music', in B. Nettl with M. Russell (eds.), *In the Course of Performance: Studies in the World of Musical Improvisation*, Chicago: The University of Chicago Press, 95–112.

———. 2003. *Making Music in the Arab World: The Culture and Artistry of Tarab*. Cambridge: Cambridge University Press.

Rajūba, Abd al-Rizāq Muhammad. 1993. *Qatra min Bahar al-Ma'lūf* (A Drop from the Ma'lūf Sea). Tripoli: Ash-Sharka 'Āma Lil Warq wa at-Tabā'

Ramadan, A.M. 1976. *Reflections Upon Islamic Architecture in Libya*. Tripoli: The Arabic House for Book.

Reynolds, Dwight. 1995. *Music of Algeria: Selected Recordings* (online): http://www.saramusik.org/articles/reynolds.html (accessed 20 October 2011).

———. 2000. 'Music', in María Rosa Menocal, Raymond P. Scheindlin and Michael Sells (eds), *The Literature of Al-Andalus*, Cambridge: Cambridge University Press, 60–82.

Rouget, Gilbert. 1985. *Music and Trance: A Theory of the Relations Between Music and Possession*. Chicago: University of Chicago Press.

Sacirbey, Muhamed. 2011. 'This was Never Gaddafi's Libya', *The European Courier* (online): http://europeancourier.org/test/2011/02/24/this-was-never-gaddafis-libya/ (accessed 21 April 2011).

Schimmel, Annemarie. 2001. 'The Role of Music in Islamic Mysticism', in Anders Hammarlund, Tord Olsson and Elisabeth Ozdalga (eds), *Sufism, Music and Society in Turkey and the Middle East*, London and New York: RoutledgeCurzon, 9–17.

Scheindlin, R.P. 1998. 'al-Shushtarī', in J. Scott Meisami and P. Starkey (eds.), *Encyclopedia of Arabic Literature*. New York: Routledge, 2: 716–17.

Schuyler, Philip D. 1978. 'Moroccan Andalusian Music', *The World of Music*, 20: 33–43.

———. 1987. 'Maroc: Musique Classique Andalous-Maghrebine', *Ethnomusicology*, 31: 176–9.

Simms, Rob. 2004. *The Repertoire of Iraqi Maqam*. Lanham MD: Scarecrow Press.

El-Shawan, Salwa. 1984. 'Traditional Arab Music Ensembles in Egypt since 1967', *Ethnomusicology*, 28: 271–88.

———. 1985. 'Western Music and its Practitioners in Egypt (ca. 1825–1985): The Integration of a New Musical Tradition in a Changing Environment', *Asian Music*, 17: 143–53.

Shannon, Jonathan H. 2003. 'Emotion, Performance, and Temporality in Arab Music: Reflections on Tarab', *Cultural Anthropology*, 18: 72–98.

———. 2006. *Among the Jasmine Trees: Music and Modernity in Contemporary Syria*. Middletown, CT: Wesleyan University Press.

Shiloah, Amnon. 1979. 'The *'ūd* and the Origin of Music', in *Studia Orientalia, Memorae D. H. Baneth*, Paris, 395–407.

———. 1981. 'The Arabic Concept of Mode', *Journal of the American Musicological Society*, 34: 19–42.

———. 2000. 'Jewish and Muslim Traditions of Music Therapy', in P. Horden (ed.), *The History of Music Therapy since Antiquity*, Aldershot: Ashgate Publishing Ltd, 69–83.

El Sibaei, Abdalla M. 1981. *Traditional and Folk Music as a Vehicle for Music Education in the Libyan Society*. M.Mus dissertation. University of Michigan.

———. 2001. *Turāth an-Nawba Al-Andalusiyya Fīy Liybyā* (The Andalusian Nawba Heritage in Libya). Sabha: Al-Markaz Watiniy lil Māthurāt al-Shaʿbiya.

Sloboda, John A. 1985. *The Musical Mind: The Cognitive Psychology of Music*. New York: Oxford University Press.

Snyder, Bob. 2000. *Music and Memory: An Introduction*. Cambridge, MA: The MIT Press.

Standifer, James A. 1988. 'The Tuareg: Their Music and Dances', *The Black Perspective in Music*, 16: 45–62.

Stern, Samuel Miklos. 1974. *Hispano-Arabic Strophic Poetry: Studies by Samuel Miklos Stern*. Oxford: Oxford University Press.

Stock, Jonathan P.J. 1996a. *World Sound Matters: An Anthology of Music from Around the World* (Teacher's Manual). London: Schott.

———. 1996b. *Musical Creativity in Twentieth-Century China: Abing, His Music and Its Changing Meanings*. New York: University of Rochester Press.

Stokes, Martin

———. 2009. "Abd al-Halim's Microphone', in Lauden Nooshin (ed.), *Music and the Play of Power in the Middle East, North Africa and Central Asia*, Surrey: Ashgate, 55–73.

———. 2010. *The Republic of Love: Cultural Intimacy in Turkish Popular Music*. Chicago: The University of Chicago Press.

Strinati, Dominic. 2004. *An Introduction to Theories of Popular Culture*. London and New York: Routledge.

Tagg, Philip. 1999. *Introductory Notes to the Semiotics of Music* (online): http://tagg.org/html/semiotug.html (accessed 18 July 2012).

Tenzer, Michael. 2000. *Gamelan Gong Kebyar: The Art of Twentieth-Century Balinese Music*. Chicago: The University of Chicago Press.

Thompson, William Forde. 2009. *Music, Thought, and Feeling: Understanding the Psychology of Music*. New York, Oxford: Oxford University Press.

Touma, Habib Hassan. 1996. *The Music of the Arabs*. Portland, OR: Amadeus Press.

Treitler, Leo. 1975. '"Centonate" Chant: *Ubles Flickwerk* or *E pluribus unus*?', *Journal of the American Musicological Society*, 28: 1–23.

Turino, Thomas. 1991. 'The History of a Peruvian Panpipe Style and the Politics of Interpretation', in Stephen Blum, Philip V. Bohlman and Daniel M. Neuman (eds.), *Ethnomusicology and Modern Music History*, Urbana: University of Illinois Press, 121–38.

———. 2008. *Music as Social Life: The Politics of Participation*. Chicago: University of Chicago Press.

Vandewalle, Dirk. 1986. 'Libya's Revolution Revisited', *MERIP Middle East Report*, 143: 30–43.

Van Maanen, John. 1988. *Tales of the Field: On Writing Ethnography*. Chicago: The University of Chicago Press.

Wade, Bonnie C. 2004. *Thinking Musically: Experiencing Music, Expressing Culture*. New York: Oxford University Press.
Walton, Kendall. 1988. 'What Is Abstract about the Art of Music?', *Journal of Aesthetics and Art Criticism*, 46: 351–64.
Wang, Ying-fen. 1992. 'The "Mosaic Structure" of Nanguan Songs: An Application of Semiotic Analysis', *Yearbook for Traditional Music*, 24: 24–51.
Wax, Murray L. 1980. 'Paradox of "Consent" to the Practice of Fieldwork', *Social Problems*, 27: 272–83.
Wilson, Dana. 1989. 'The Role of Patterning in Music', *Leonardo*, 22: 101–106.
Wright, John. 2005. *Travellers in Libya*. London: Silphium Press.
Wright, Owen. 1993. 'Nawba', in C.E. Bosworth, E. van Donzel, W.P. Heinrichs, Ch. Pellat (eds), *The Encyclopaedia of Islam*. Leiden, New York: E.J. Brill, 7: 1042–3.
Yamaguti, Osamu. 1986. 'Music and Its Transformations', in T. Yoshiko and Y. Osamu (eds), *The Oral and the Literate in Music*, Tokyo: Academia Music, 29-37.
Zwartjes, Otto. 2006. 'The Muwashshah and the kharja: an Introduction', in E. Emery (ed.), *Muwashshah!: Proceedings of the Conference on Arabic and Hebrew Strophic Poetry and its Romance Parallels, School of Oriental and African Studies (SOAS), London, 8–10 October 2004*, London: RN Books, 1–11.

Index

Page numbers in italic denote figures, examples or photographs. For an explanation of index entries in italics, please refer to the Glossary on pages 167–168.

Abu Rayana, Sheikh Muhammad, 52, 54
adhān, 13
Afandi, Sheikh Gheddur, 53
Africa, North
  Maghreb, 31–3
  nawba, 31–6
  Sufism, 32–3
Albahlul, Sheikh, 149, 150, *150*, 151
Algeria, 71
  jawq ensembles, 71
  nawba, 35, 36, 55
'allājī' songs, 125
Alvarez, Lourdes M., 49, 54
Andalusian
  ensembles, 69–71
  nawba, 33, 69, 73
  architecture, 12
  heritage, 36
  refugees, 12, 32, 50, 92
  repertoire, 33
Arab music, 29, 30, *30*, 34, 81, 91, 111, 151
  Arab Music Ensemble, 69
  heterophony, 158
  instruments, 153
  modulation, 113
  National Centre for the Research and Study of Arab Music, 82, 84
  radio broadcasts, 13
  recording industry, 19
  rhythmic modes, 35
  students of, 22
  vs. Western music, 69
  see also darabukka; īqā'; maqām; tarab
Arab nationalism, 78
Arabic, 13
  poetry, 33, 51, 61
  pop music, 13
  qaṣīda, 34
  verse, 33–4
Araibi, Hassan, 1, 65, 73, *74*, 77–81, *85*, 130, 144, 158, 159
  biography, 74–6
  contribution to musical tradition, 73–4
  criticism of, 79–80
  ensembles, 48, 54, 66, 68, 79, 86–91, *89*, 93–8, *97*, 178
  meetings with, 85–6
  restyle of *nawba*, 67, 99–106, 159
architecture, 12
Ārusīyya ensembles, *44*, 45
al Attar, Ayman, 20
audience, 76, 159
  rapport with, 143, 145, 150–51
  sammī'a, 145

bandīr, 16, 18, 40, *42*, *43*, 61, 76, 101, 150
bands, marching, 24, *25*
barwal nawba, 55, 59–61, *60*, *103*, 103–4, 121–2, *123*, 135, 142
  cadential patterns, 123–4, *124 ex. 4.17*, 125
bayyāti, 113, 120, *120*
Blacking, John, 78
broadcasting, 19, 65, 80
  Libyan Broadcasting Centre, 68, 76
burial ceremonies, 47–8, 54

cadential units, 59, 100, *100*, 102, 104, 117, *118*, 121–6, *123*, *124*, 125, *126*, 129
calls and responses, 59, 61, 104, *105*, 159
catharsis (in *hadra*), 138–9
cello, 19, 37, 66, 72, 76, 86, 147, 150, 155
ceremonies, 17, *17*

burials, 47–8, 54
  and folk music, 16
  ma'lūf az-zāwiya, 37
  mawlid, 37–45, *39*, 46–7, 142
  weddings, 47–8
chieronomy, 133–4, 135, *141*
choirs
  see vocalists
Córdoba (Spain), 31
criss-crossing, melodic, 107–9, 111–12, 116–20, *119*, *120*, 121–35, 130, *130*
culture
  Libyan, 3
  Western, 8–9
Cyrenaica (Libya), 4–5, 6

dār al-funūn, 12
darabukka, 35, 46, 59, 101, 150, 157
Davis, Ruth, 32, 72
desert communities, 18
dhikr, 38–9, *39*, 45, 89, 138–9
discourse, musical, 29–31, *30*
double base, 37, 66, 72, 86, 97, 147

education
  General Organisation for the Theatre, Music and Folk Arts, 9
  music education in Libya, 11, 22–4
  music schools, 22–4
  post-revolution policies, 11
Egypt, 81
  Al-jīl (generation music), 20
  Egyptian music, 17, 50, 68–9
  firqa (ensemble), 72
  pop music, 20
  takht ensemble, 69–70
ensembles, 81–3, 87–8, 153
  Andalusian, 69–71
  Arab Music Ensemble, 69
  Ārusīyya ensembles, *44*, 45
  Egyptian, 72
  The Ensemble of *Ma'lūf, Muwashshaḥāt* and Arab Melodies, xv, 66
  firqat al-Mahrajān al-Ghinā'iyya (The Festival Singing Ensemble), 87
  firqat al-Mūsīqā al-'Arabiyya (Arab Music Ensemble), 69, 70
  firqat ash-Sheikh Muhammad Ignas (Sheikh Muhammad Ignas' Ensemble), 131–2
  firqat Hassan al-Kamiy (Hassan al-Kamiy's Ensemble), 130–33
  jawq ensembles, 71
  mixed, 80
  at the Music Research Institute, 86–91
  nawba ensembles, 35–6
  performances, 92–8, 133–4, 135
  Rashidiyya Institute, Tunis, 71
  recruitment, 91
  rehearsals, 67, 72, 87, 90–91, 93
  socialization, 83
  stage set-up, 94, 96, 147
  takht ensembles, 69–70
  and timbral features, 153
  see also ma'lūf ensembles

Fakhrī, Sabāh, 14
Fascists (Italian), 6–7
Al-Fātiḥ University, 9, 22, 23
The Festival Singing Ensemble, 87
festivals, 18, 20, 73
  Libyan Song Festival, 20
  Testour, Tunisia, 66, 73, 92–8, xv
  Tripoli Festival of *Ma'lūf* and *Muwashshaḥāt*, 55, 88, 130, 145–9, *146*, *148*, *149*
Fezzan (Libya), 4, 5, 16
folk music, 16, 19–20, 80, 81, 142
  recording industry, 19
  youth songs, 19
  zamzamāt singers, 16, 47
fulklūr, 142
funerals
  see burial ceremonies

Gaddafi, Colonel Muammar, 15, 24, 136, 164
  1969 revolution, 7–9
  The Green Book, 8
  Revolutionary Command Council, 7–8
Gaddafi era, 19, 73, 136
gender segregation, 15, 94
General Organisation for the Theatre, Music and Folk Arts, 9
al-Ghādiy, Sheikh Jamāl Muhammad, 52

al-Ghādiy, Sheikh Kamel Muhammad, 52, 62
al-Ghannay, Ali Mansūr, 51, 108
ghayṭa (shawm), 40, *41*, 45, 56–9, 141–2
  see also istikhbār
al-Ghazālī, Abū Hamid, 139, 140
The Green Book (Gaddafi), 8
Guettat, Mahmoud, 61

ḥaḍra, 37, 45–6, 138–9
hand movements
  see chieronomy
heterophony, 134, 152, 153, 158–9
ḥiss, 144

Idris l, King, 7, 77–8
instrumentalists
  see musicians
īqā', 30, 34–5, *35*, 107, 109, 150, 157, 160
  īqā' barwal, 121, *124*
  īqā' muṣaddar, 117, 121, *124*
'Īsāwiyya order (Sufi), 32–3, 49
Islam, 5, 9, 26–7
  Sufism, 32–3
  Sunni movement, 6
Islamic Arts and Crafts School, 24, *25*
Islamic Call Society, 1
istiftāḥ, 56, 57–9, *58*, 100
istikhbār, 56, 57, *57*
Italian occupation, 6–7, 24, 73

Jamahiriya, 8
Jilāni, Cheb, 20, *21*
Jones, Lura JaFran, 32

kinjī, *41*, 45
Kulthūm, Umm, 14, 145

Langlois, Tony, 30, 106
lawāzim, 153–5, *154*, *155*, *156*, *157*
Lewisohn, Leonard, 139–40
Libya
  1969 revolution, 7, 77–8
  Cyrenaica, 4–5, 6
  demographics, 3–4
  desert communities, 18
  educational policies, 11, 22–4
  Fezzan, 4, 5, 16
  folk music, 81
  geography, 3–4, *4*, 77
  King Idris l, 7, 77–8
  language, 5, 8
  post-revolution years, 7–8, 80
  pre-1969 revolution, 5–7
  prohibition of *mawlid* celebrations, 46–7
  sanctions (United Nations Security Council), 2
  see also Colonel Muammar Gaddafi; Tripoli
Libyan Broadcasting Centre, 68
Libyan Song Festival, 20

Maghreb
  migration to, 12, 31–3
  nawba tradition, 35, 55–6, 71, 92
  Sufism, 32–3
Ma'had Jamāl Ad-Dīn Al-Mīlādī music school, 22
Malta, 1
ma'lūf
  in Arab music, 29, 30
  'authentic' texts, 29, 50, 51–2, 63, 165
  in burial ceremonies, 47–8, 54
  chieronomy, 133–4, 135, *141*
  classification of, 109–10
  composing, 50–2, 99, 107–9, 127–8, 135
  in Libya, 36–7, 48–50, 142
  ma'lūf al-idhā'a, 13, 36–7, 65, 159, 160
  ma'lūf at-taqlīdī (*see ma'lūf az-zāwiya*)
  ma'lūf az-zāwiya, 36–7, 66–7, 97, 106, 133, 139–40, 141, *141*, 147, 160–61
  modernization of, 68–73, 76–8, 81–2, 104
  parades, 39–45, *44*, 46–7, 133, 139–40, *141*, 142
  preservation of, 48–9, 73, 79, 128
  teaching, 48, 52
  in weddings, 37, 47–8
  see also criss-crossing (melodic)
ma'lūf ensembles, 36, 48, 55, 68, 76, 131, 147
  The Ensemble of *Ma'lūf, Muwashshaḥāt* and Arab Melodies, 66
  set-up, *46*, 94, *96*, *97*, 147, 149, 153

in *tūsīla* (wedding parades), 47
ma'lūf festivals
Testour, Tunisia, 66, 73, 92–8
maqām (melodic mode), 22, 30, 34, 88, 112, 116, *126*
in Libyan *ma'lūf*, 56
maqām hussayn, 126
maqām jaharkah, 99, 100, 101, 102
maqām muhayyar, *56*, 99
maqām rāst, 111–13, *112*, 114, 117, *118*, 120, *122*, 126
Marcus, Scott L., 112–13
Martinez, Luis, 1, 7
mawlid celebrations, 37–45, *39*, 46–7, 142
meditation
samā', 139
melodic movements, 57, 102, 120, 128, 129, 135
memorization, 127, 129
vs. notation, 87, 88
al-Mīlādī, Sheikh Jamal ad-Din, 50–51
modernization, 66–73, 76–8, 81–2, 104
see also Araibi, Hassan
modulation, 113
monotonic passages, 119–20, *120*, 125, 126–7, *127*
Morocco
ensembles, 70–71
nawba, 34, 35
mu'āraḍā, 50–51
murabba' songs, 55, 125, *125*
murakkaz, 59, 103, *103*
muṣaddar nawba, 55–6, 59, 60, *101*, 104
music
in desert communities, 18
importance in Sufism, 33, 35–6
influence of migration, 32
military, 24
music education in Libya, 22
and politics, 81
pop, 13, 18–19, 20
radio in Libya, 13
sacred *vs.* secular music, 37–8
see also Arab music; folk music; recording industry
Music Research Institute (Tripoli), 84, 86
music schools
High Institute of Music, 22, 23
Ma'had Jamāl Ad-Dīn Al-Mīlādī music school, 22
Rashidiyya Institute, Tunis, 7, 36, 71–2, 75
music teachers, 24, 80
musical activity, 9, *10*
musical education, 11, 22–4, *23*
see also music schools
musical ensembles
see ensembles
musical festivals
see festivals
musical instruments, 22, 23, 24, 36, 157
accompaniment to *Muwashshaḥ* poetry, 33–4
burning of, 8–9, 20
in musical ensembles, 70–72, 76, 149–50
string arrangements, 19
Western instruments, 76
woodwind, 24
see bandīr; *darabukka*; double bass; cello; *ghayṭa*; *naqqārāt*; *nāy*; *qānūn*; *tār*; *'ūd*; violins
musicians, 17, *23*, *25*, *26*, 29–30, *42*, 72, 87–8, 93–4, 104, 113
as a career, 19, 24
in Egypt, 69–70
see also Araibi, Hassan; bands, marching; ensembles; recording industry
muwashshaḥ, 33–4

naqqārāt, 40, *41*, 91–2
nawba, 39–40, 45–6, 90, 138, 142, 147
in Algeria, 35, 36, 55
Andalusian, 33, 69
modern, 153, 159, 161
North African, 31–6
patterns in, 104
regional differences in, 34–5
restyle by Hassan Araibi, 99–106
in Spain, 31–2
structure of, 56–9, 60–61, 99–103
and Sufism, 32, 35–6, 37
in Tunisia, 34, 36
see also barwal nawba; īqā'; maqām; muṣaddar nawba; ṭarab

nāy, 14, 19, 22, 69, 72, 76, 86, 87, 91, 96, 101, 155, 157, 158
nawba ensembles, 35–6
nikriz, 113, 120, *121*
North Africa
  see Africa
nostalgia, 117, 147
notation
  vs. memory, 87

origin of *ma'lūf* in, 48–50
Ostler, Alan, 16
Ottoman Empire, 6

parades
  ma'lūf, 39–45, *44*, 46–7, 133, 139–40, *141*, 142
  tūsīla (wedding), 47
patterns, 29, 104, 130
  rhythmic, 158
performances, 92–8, 142, 147–50
  chieronomy, 133–4, 135
petroleum sector, 77
Pfaff, Richard, H., 78
Phoenicians, 5
phrases
  stable *vs.* variant, 131–2
Plakhova, Anna, 112, 119
poetry
  Arabic poetry, 33, 51, 61
  mu'āraḍā, 50–51
  and music, 61–2
  strophic poetry, 33
  Sufi, 33
  zajal, 33–4, 49–50
politics, 81
pop music
  Ayman al Attar, 20
  Cheb Jilāni, 20, *21*
  fusion with Libyan folk music, 19, 26
  Hamid al-Shaeri, 20
  Libyan Song Festival, 20
  Western, 13
prayers, call to, 13

Qādiriyya order (Sufi), 32–3, 38, 50
qānūn, 52–3, 76, 150, 151, 155, 158
qaṣīd, 20, 24, 39
qirā'a, 13
Qur'ān
  recitation of, 13, 38, 47, 75

Racy, Ali Jihad, 17, 70, 143–5, 151, 153, 158
raddāda, 40, 55, 59, 60, 134–5, 140
radio, 13, 19
  radio orchestra, 72
al-Rammash, Sheikh Khalifa Imhammed Farhat, 53–4
Rashidiyya Institute, Tunis, 36, 68, 71–2, 75
RCC (Revolutionary Command Council), 7–8
recording industry, 18–20, 36–7, 65, 66, *67*, 80–81, 90, 106, 152
  in Egypt, 20, 69
  in post-revolution Libya, 80–81
registers, *113*, *114*, 121, *122*, 125
religion
  Islam, 5, 6, 26–7
  religious rites, 33
  religious verse, 51
  Sanusi order, 6
  see also Sufism; Sunni movement
responses, *105*
  physical, 138–9, 142, 144, 145
  verbal, 151
  see also calls and responses
Revolutionary Command Council, 7–8
  see RCC

sacred *vs.* secular music, 37–8
salṭana, 141, 144–5
samā', 139–41, 159
  sammī'a, 145
Sama, Sheikh Abu, 89, 141
Sanusi order
  see Sufism
Al-Sanussi, Muhammad Idris
see Idris l, King
Sayala, Sheikh Ali Amin, 51
Second World War, 7
secular *vs.* sacred music, 37–8
sentimentality, 152, 159
al-Shaeri, Hamid, 20
Shannon, Jonathon H., 138–9, 145
El-Shawan, Salwa, 68–9, 70

Sheikh Abu Jirād Ensemble, 55
sheikhs, 45, 48, 51–3, 56–7, 59, 67, 79, 94, 133–4, 155
  sheikh az-zāwiya, 45
  sheikh ma'lūf, 40, *41*, 45–6, 53, 90, 147–9, *148*
  sheikh Qur'ān, 13
  teaching *ma'lūf*, 48, 52
  see also Araibi, Hassan; ma'lūf, composing
al- Shushtarī, 48–50, 54
El Sibaei, Abdalla, 9, 16, 50, 53, 75, 109, *110*, 113, 114, 129–32
singing, 70, 89, 91, 101, 131, 142, 151
  in modern *nawba*, 159
  see also istiftāḥ; raddāda
social conditions, 7–8, 25
social structures, 164
  gender segregation, 15, 94
Spain
  Christian reconquest, 31–2
  Córdoba, 31
  migration of Jews and Muslims from, 32
  Moorish invasion, 31
staff notation, 36
Stokes, Martin, 152
strophic poetry, 33
Sufism, 54
  Ārusīyya ensembles, *44*, 45
  development of, 32–3
  ḥaḍra, 37, 45–6
  ḥaḍra, 138–9
  mawlid celebrations, *37*, 37–45, *39*, 46–7, 142
  Mecca, 6
  and the *nawba*, 32, 35–6, 37
  orders, 32–3
  parades, 39–45, 47
  poetry, 33
  role of *ma'lūf az-zāwiya*, 37
  samā', 139–41
  Sanusi order, 6
  zāwiya (Sufi lodge), 6, 26, 37, 38, *39*, *40*, 45–6, 47
Sunni movement, 6

takht ensembles, 69–70
tār, 76, 157–8
ṭarab, 142–3, 144–5, 151–2
  instruments, 153, 158
  in restyled Libyan *nawba*, 152–3, 152–5, 157–60
Tarābulus al-Gharb
  see Tripoli
tawshīḥ
  see muwashshaḥ
teaching
  ma'lūf, 48, 52
technology
  influence on music, 13
tempo, 151
Tenzer, Michael, 108
Testour (Tunisia), 66, 73, 92–8
timbral features, 153
tourism, 17
Treitler, Leo, 127, 128
Triki, Muhammad, 71–2
Tripoli, 5, 6, 11–15, 16, *26*, 147
  burning of musical equipment, 8–9, 20
  as a centre for *ma'lūf*, 12
  Islamic Arts and Crafts School, 24, *25*
  Music Research Institute, 84, 86
  National Centre for the Research and Study of Arabic Music, 66
  post-revolution musical activity, 12–14
  pre-revolution musical activity, 9, *10*
  see also festivals
Tripolitania (West Libya), 4
Tuareg music, 16
Tunisia
  Andalusian refugees, 50
  ma'lūf in, 50, 71, 72
  nawba, 34, 36
  Rashīdiyya Institute, 36, 68, 71–2, 75
  Testour *ma'lūf* festival, 66, 73, 92–8
  The Tunisian Musical Heritage, 72
Tunisian Ministry of Culture, 72
The Tunisian Musical Heritage, 72
Turkey, 53
al-Tusī, Abmad b. Muhammad, 139

'ūd, 76, 89, 155
ughniya (song), 14
United Nations, 7
  sanctions, 2
universities

Al-Fātiḥ University, 9, 22, 23
Al-Markaz al-ʿĀlī lil-Mihan al-Mūsīqiyya w al-Masraḥīyya, 22, 23

violins, 22–3, *86*, 87, 91, 153, 154, 155, *156*, 157
vocalists, 88, *88*, 91
    see also singing
voice, 14

Wang, Ying-fen, 108
weddings, 47–8
    role of *ma'lūf*, 47–8
    tūsīla (parade), 47
West, the, 8
    cultural values, 8–9
    symbols of, 8–9
    Western music, 68–9
Wilson, 130
wind music, *26*
Wright, Owen, 50–51

yā muḥammad, 111–14, 117, *117*, 131, 132
    transcription, *116*
Yamaguti, Osamu, 134

zajal, 33–4, 49–50
zamzamāt singers, 16, *17*, 17–18, 47
zāwiya (Sufi lodge), 6, 26, 37, 38, *39*, *40*, 45–6, 142
    brotherhood, 164
    ensembles, 55, 146–7
    the grand *zāwiya*, 49
    performances, 133–4, 139
    samāʿ, 140, 160
    weddings, 47
Ziryāb, 31
Zwartjes, Otto, 33

Ingram Content Group UK Ltd.
Milton Keynes UK
UKHW020628300323
419387UK00004B/6

9 781409 444725